'. . . a gripping account of danger at sea, dramatic shipwrecks, courageous castaways, murder, much missing gold and terrible loss of life.'—*The Queensland Times*

Larrikins, Bush Tales and Other Great Australian Stories

'. . . another collection of yarns, tall tales, bush legends and colourful characters . . . from one of our master storytellers.'
—*The Queensland Times*

Great Anzac Stories

'. . . allows you to feel as if you are there in the trenches with them.'—*The Weekly Times*

'They are pithy short pieces, absolutely ideal for reading when you are pushed for time, but they are stories you will remember for much longer than you would expect.'—*The Ballarat Courier*

Great Australian Journeys

'Readers familiar with Graham Seal's work will know he finds and writes ripper, fair-dinkum, true blue Aussie yarns. His books are great reads and do a lot for ensuring cultural stories are not lost. His new book, *Great Australian Journeys*, is no exception.'—*The Weekly Times*

'An alternative history of outback Australia over the past 200 years.'—*Country Style*

'Epic tales of exploration, survival, tragedy, romance, mystery, discovery and loss come together in this intriguing collection of some of Australia's most dramatic journeys from the 19th and early 20th century.' —*Vacations and Travel*

GREAT
CONVICT
STORIES

Also by Graham Seal

Great Australian Stories
Great Anzac Stories
Larrikins, Bush Tales and Other Great Australian Stories
The Savage Shore
Great Australian Journeys
Great Bush Stories

GREAT
CONVICT
STORIES

Dramatic and moving tales from
Australia's brutal early years

GRAHAM SEAL

ALLEN&UNWIN
SYDNEY•MELBOURNE•AUCKLAND•LONDON

This edition published in 2019
First published in 2017

Allen & Unwin
83 Alexander Street
Crows Nest NSW 2065
Australia
Phone: (61 2) 8425 0100
Email: info@allenandunwin.com
Web: www.allenandunwin.com

 A catalogue record for this
book is available from the
National Library of Australia

ISBN 978 1 76052 748 8

Set in Sabon by Midland Typesetters, Australia
Maps and Cover design by Julia Eim
Cover images: chains, David Moore/Alamy Stock Photo; painting, T.G. Glover
'Sydney Harbour, N.S. Wales'; convict indent list © State of New South Wales
through the State Records Authority of NSW 2016
Printed and bound in Australia by Griffin Press

10 9 8 7 6 5

Contents

AUSTRALIA
CONVICT LOCATIONS

- King Island

Goose Island •

Bass Strait

• Swan Island

• Launceston
• Brickendon and Woolmers Estate

TASMANIA

• Ross Female Factory

Macquarie Harbour •
Sarah Island •

• Darlington Probation
Station

• Oatlands

• New Norfolk
• Derwent Valley

• Maria Island

• Hobart

• Coal Mines Historic Site

Port Arthur •   • Point Puer

• Moreton Bay

Champion Bay

Swan River •
Fremantle •
Bunbury • • Pinjarra

• Albany

Kangaroo Island •

NEW SOUTH WALES

• Castlemaine
Williamstown • • Port Phillip
Geelong •

TASMANIA

NEW SOUTH WALES

• Port Macquarie

• Mudgee
Bathurst •
Hill End •
Blue Mountains • • Newcastle
Parramatta • • Sydney

Picton •
• Sussex Inlet

Gundagai • • Berrima
Canberra • • Goulburn
• Duntroon House

Prologue
Lashland

I saw a man walk across the yard with the blood that had run from his lacerated flesh squashing out of his shoes at every step he took. A dog was licking the blood off the triangles, and the ants were carrying away great pieces of human flesh that the lash had scattered about the ground. The scourger's foot had worn a deep hole in the ground by the violence with which he whirled himself round on it to strike the quivering and wealed back, out of which stuck the sinews, white, ragged, and swollen.

The infliction was 100 lashes, at about half-minute time, so as to extend the punishment through nearly an hour. The day was hot enough to overcome a man merely standing that length of time in the sun, and this was going on in the full blaze of it. However, they had a pair of scourgers who gave each other spell and spell about, and they were bespattered with blood like a couple of butchers.

'Landing of Convicts at Botany Bay', from Captain Watkin Tench's A Narrative of the Expedition to Botany Bay, *1789.*

Introduction

'More pitiable objects were perhaps never seen.' So Surgeon John White described many of the nearly eight hundred convict men and women landed from the First Fleet transport ships after an eight-month voyage from England. About thirty died at sea and many were suffering from scurvy and dysentery. Along with marines, administrators, officials and their families, the convicts had been banished across the sea to found a new penal colony at the far end of the British empire.

Who were these mostly unwilling founders of modern Australia? What compelling stories would they and those who followed them have to tell?

Some were hardened criminals. Some were impoverished tradesmen and workers. A few were political prisoners. The 162,000 or more convicts transported to Australia between 1788 and 1868 were men and women from all walks of life and many different parts of the world. Their crimes were various and while some were harshly or even unjustly treated, by the standards of the time their punishments were mostly expected.

But whatever their sins and their origins, the large number of people who arrived here as 'transports' laid the basis of a new country and have had a continuing influence on the way Australians think about themselves. The convicts established the dislike of authority often associated with our national identity. Their real and imagined doings influenced the larrikin sense of humour we value and often practise. Their existence and the growing opposition to 'the system' also produced the attitude known as 'the convict stain', a prejudice that for decades obliged many to suppress their convict connections. Australians have only recently begun to confront what was once considered a blot on the national story. The impact of the family history movement, as well as the passing of time, have led to many taking pride in identifying an ancestor who came here in chains. But attitudes change slowly and the convict past still lies uneasily in our history.

Historians have studied and restudied the transported convicts, trying to establish their origins, beliefs and impact on the country's development. Some have seen them as habitual criminals; others as mostly working people. Some see them as the beginning of an invasion. Little has been agreed and what has been established is subject to change as new generations of researchers examine the penal past from different perspectives. But however the era is interpreted, its many, often contradictory, elements continue to fascinate writers, filmmakers and family historians. Along with Ned Kelly and the Anzac tradition, the history and mythology of convictism is compelling and controversial. Just as the iconic figures of the bushranger and the digger remain with us, so do the images of ragged wretches weighed down in iron chains.

The stories in this book are from the human experience of transportation. You will read chilling accounts of cruelty, murder, cannibalism and revenge. You will also read about many convicts, men and women, whose crimes were more than redeemed as they found success, prosperity and perhaps even happiness. Children as young as nine or ten may also have been transported to New South Wales and Van Diemen's Land, as Tasmania was then known. Even younger children came as the offspring of convict mothers. Often bastards and often soon orphaned, these children were legally free, but they shared many of the same hardships as the convicts. Even the free wives and children of convicts were subject to many of the endless rules that governed the harsh life of the prisoners.

The history of convict transportation includes graphic violence of all kinds, the horrors of the whip, the treadmill, solitary confinement and literally murderous labour. These terrors were all the more frightening for being part of an enclosed system which allowed prisoners limited rights of redress. The few avenues for complaint they did have were controlled by officials who could be more brutal than those under them. Frequently the overseers, floggers and even the executioners were convicts themselves.

As well as the injustices and corruption of the penal system, disease on lengthy sea voyages and in filthy conditions ashore was a constant threat. Mortality rates on transport ships depended largely on the attitude and actions of their masters. Death was a frequent passenger in the cramped and unventilated prisons below decks where convicts could be chained for long periods. Yet even contemporaries were appalled at the fatalities of the Second Fleet and on many later convict ships. After surviving the voyage, convicts would then have to endure the often harsh and unsanitary conditions of labouring for the government or working for a 'master' as an assigned servant.

This intensive system of punishment and pain lasted longer than modern Australia's first century. It spread through much of the country, either through direct transportation or the movement of convicts and ex-convicts to all the existing colonies. Even after transportation ended, those sentenced to Australian penal servitude still had to serve out their sentences, in more than a few cases, for life. The system took many years to fade completely away. British control of Fremantle Prison did not end until 1886. The last known living transported convict passed away in 1938, just before the start of the Second World War.

As more and more convicts were sent to Australia, free settlement also grew, eventually generating strong public resistance to transportation. Stories of grisly floggings, working in iron gangs, savage ill-treatment, sodomy and seemingly unending violence were widely published in colonial and British newspapers, fuelling the political debate over the benefits and evils of the system. The British government eventually bowed to this pressure and ceased transportation to New South Wales in 1850, though convicts were still sent to Van Diemen's Land until 1853. From 1850 to 1868, the Swan River colony of Western Australia also received male convicts from Britain.

Whatever the rights and wrongs of the convict era and whatever we have since made of it, there is no escape from the fact that the nation was founded by men, women and children who were exiled across the seas after being found guilty of committing crimes. A lot of these crimes we would now consider to be trivial offences or misdemeanours, such as stealing a handkerchief or pilfering food. But convicts were also transported for murder, rape and other violent acts. A limited but significant number were being punished for what we would call 'political' crimes. Many committed further offences and were transported for a second or even third time to Port Arthur or Norfolk Island.

Some of the many locations associated with convicts in New South Wales, Tasmania, Western Australia, Queensland, Norfolk Island and Victoria are listed at the back of this book. They give a sense of the extent of the convict contribution to the building of much of the country and its original infrastructure. The steady flow of books, television shows and movies about the penal system and its victims has also influenced how later generations have thought about the convict past. Often these works play into the folklore of convictism as well as its history. Appreciating both the myths and the realities is the key to understanding the founding and continuing significance of the convicts 'transported beyond the seas'.

A Note on Weights, Measures, Distances and Money Values

This book tries to put the reader back into touch with the sufferings, fears, hopes and horrors of convict life through the prisoners' own words and thoughts. Spelling and punctuation in original source documents have been modernised wherever necessary.

The following basic conversion scales give the modern decimal equivalents of imperial distances, weights and measures appearing in this book:

DISTANCE
1 inch = 2.54 centimetres
1 foot = 30.48 centimetres
1 yard = 91.44 centimetres

WEIGHT
1 ounce = 0.028 kilograms
1 pound (weight) = 0.45 kilograms
1 stone = 6.35 kilograms
1 ton (British/Imperial) = 1016 kilograms

MONEY
Converting historical money values into contemporary equivalents is, at best, a very approximate and often misleading calculation, due to inflation and the varying costs of living from time to time and in different places. Usually it is clear whether amounts given in pounds, shillings and pence are average, large or small. Where this is not evident, some guidance is given in the text.

'Convicts embarking for Botany Bay', Thomas Rowlandson, c.1790. Rowlandson was a prolific artist in Georgian England, with a keen interest in social commentary and politics.

1
Unpromising Beginnings

To become a new people at Botany Bay

Street ballad, London, c. 1786

Trouble on the Way

The trouble began even before the First Fleet arrived at Botany Bay. Governor Arthur Phillip commanded eleven ships and almost 1500 sailors, soldiers, administrators and convicts sailing towards what was for them an unknown land. Barely a month after departing England in May 1787, convicts aboard the transport ship *Scarborough* plotted a bloody mutiny. The ringleaders were 24-year-old Philip Farrell and 28-year-old Thomas Griffiths, both ex-sailors with seven-year sentences. Their plot was foiled from within, as would be so many other convict escape attempts. Farrell and Griffiths were transferred to another ship in the fleet, the *Sirius*, for punishment. Both men were flogged and transferred to yet another ship for the remainder of the voyage. Another fifteen or so would-be mutineers among the *Scarborough* convicts were chained to the deck in double irons.

And so the scene was set for one of history's greatest forced migrations and its accompanying violence and brutality. But the transportation of convicts to Australia was a vast and long-lasting episode of many human stories with many different beginnings and endings. The *Scarborough* would sail again to Australia with the Second Fleet and would again experience a convict mutiny. This time the plot was also foiled by a convict. His name was Samuel Burt and he boasted of his role in a letter home:

> The convicts began to whisper from one to the other their mutinous intentions; the plot being communicated to myself, I readily agreed to the scheme, assenting to every proposal of plunder and murder, until such time as I became completely master of the conspiracy, and the ringleaders of it. I then apprised the captain of the ship, and the military officers, of the danger they were likely to encounter; and so thoroughly did my information prepare them for the business, that with little or no trouble the ringleaders were secured, and the scheme entirely frustrated.

The mutineers gave up 'such confessions that human nature would almost shudder at the thoughts of' and 'it is supposed will be tried and executed immediately on their arrival in New South Wales', Burt wrote. His role in preventing what might have been another early atrocity of the transportation system was rewarded at Port Jackson with an easy job as a stores clerk. He was later given a pardon in recognition of his actions which, as David Collins the colony's deputy judge advocate recognised, had been 'at the risk of his own life'.

Yet there were several ironies here. Samuel Burt had once been so careless of his life that he tried to throw it away. While most convicts were transported for crimes against property and violence, Samuel Burt was transported for love. Spurned in his advances to a young lady he resolved to commit suicide. But his method was unusual.

Instead of poison, shooting or throwing himself from a cliff, Burt would get the law to do the job. He forged a bank note for 100 pounds, knowing that this meant a certain death sentence. Then he immediately wrote a note of confession and turned himself in. As planned, he was convicted of forgery and deception and sentenced to death, but was offered a commutation by a sympathetic court because of the emotional extremity of his case. He refused the offer several times—'I now feel myself forever cut off from the union of a person that was most dear to me, death to me will be preferable to life,' he stated at his sentencing.

While Burt languished in the foul miasmas of Newgate Prison awaiting his next and final appearance at the Old Bailey, the lady who had rejected him began to visit. After several meetings, perhaps impressed by his extreme devotion, she at last agreed to marry. Burt was naturally overjoyed and accepted the King's mercy. But before the marriage could take place, the woman was struck down by gaol fever she contracted from her visits to Burt. Devastated once more, he sailed with a life sentence in the Second Fleet where his betrayal of a convict mutiny at the risk of his own death gifted him a new lease of life in the penal colony of New South Wales.

The Hungry Land

When Captain Cook first landed at Botany Bay in April 1770, two Gweagal warriors threatened him and his men with fishing spears. The British fired three times on the warriors, wounding both. By contrast, the First Fleet's early encounters with the Indigenous inhabitants of Botany Bay in January 1788 were friendly. When Governor Phillip and some of his men first went ashore, the local people helpfully pointed out where to find fresh water.

But only a few days later, while the British were dining on a harbour beach, Phillip felt the need to draw a circle in the sand. He placed armed marines to guard the perimeter from the young warriors. When the fleet landed at Sydney Cove five days later, the Aborigines disappeared into the vast surrounding bush and were not sighted again until 4 February, when stones were thrown at boats fishing off Manly. By now, the

French under naval commander La Perouse had unexpectedly and inconveniently arrived in Botany Bay. They wasted no time in building a stockade and in less than a week they were engaged in armed conflict with the indigenous people.

Further afield, some convicts were quick to realise the market value of indigenous artefacts. They stole spears, shields and gum, selling these to sailors aboard the transport ships for a thriving London market in savage exotica. By the same token, Aborigines quickly perceived the usefulness of metal tools and began taking shovels and picks. They were fired on by the British.

Food was the cause of the first executions among the settlers. The early omens were bad. On 2 February five sheep kept beneath a tree were killed by lightning: 'The branches and trunk of the tree were shivered and rent in a very extraordinary manner.' Concerned about how long his limited supplies would last, Governor Phillip gave clear warnings that stealing food would lead to a death sentence. Barely a month after arriving at Sydney Cove, four convicts were caught stealing food from the precious stores. All were punished severely, one becoming the first British person executed in Australia.

By 10 March the French were sailing away to a shipwrecked fate and the British continued settling and exploring. As they encountered different Aboriginal groups they realised many were short of food. The first recorded British death at Aboriginal hands occurred on 21 May when William Ayres and Peter Burn, both convicts, were attacked at Woolloomooloo as they foraged for greens. Ayres staggered back to camp with a spear in his back and Burn was never seen again.

Two more convicts were killed on or around 30 May near Darling Harbour (*Gomora* in the indigenous Eora language), apparently in revenge for the earlier murder of an Aboriginal man. Heading a party seeking the killers, Phillip confronted a large group of armed but friendly Aborigines. They told Phillip where to find fresh water and warned the British not to eat a poisonous species of toadstool they had unwittingly picked up in the bush.

By June there were reports of Eora dying for lack of food and seemingly ill, possibly from smallpox contracted from the British. Fishing boats were more frequently attacked in attempts to obtain their hauls and in July there were reports of starving and sick Aboriginal people. A goat was stolen in August and spears thrown the following month at a boat crew who did not offer the Eora what they considered to be a sufficient share of the fish caught in their waters. Another convict was killed at Botany Bay in October, again harvesting greens for food. Later that month Phillip's determination not to fire on the Eora was broken when he commanded his men to retaliate against a spearing.

It was now clear that the land around Sydney Cove was unsuitable for sustaining the level of agriculture needed to feed the colony and the first farm was established at Rose Hill. It was fortified and guarded by armed marines. But the crops would take months to grow, if they did at all. In the meantime, food became scarce. There were constant raids on private gardens planted by many of the convicts as well as attempts on the government stores.

In early March 1789 convicts attempting to steal Eora spears were attacked. One was killed and many wounded. Phillip had the survivors flogged, to the horror of Arabanoo, an Eora man captured two months earlier. By mid-May, Arabanoo was dead, a victim of the smallpox epidemic that wiped out the Cadigal group of around fifty people, but for three survivors. By October most contacts were unfriendly and no Aboriginal people would come near the settlers.

The following month, the British kidnapped two Aboriginal men at Manly Cove. Phillip hoped to use them to open a friendly dialogue with the surviving disaffected people of the region. Wollarawarre Bennelong, a Wangal man, and Colebee, a Cadigal man, were both shackled like convicts. Less than three weeks later Colebee chewed through the rope securing his leg irons and returned to the bush. Bennelong, a survivor of smallpox, got along well with his captors. Still in chains, he shared Christmas dinner with the governor and officers, joining in the eating, drinking and singing, after which he simply fell asleep. In April 1790, Phillip trusted Bennelong enough to have his irons removed. The following month Bennelong threw off his European clothes and fled back to the bush. But he would return, donning European clothes again, a pattern that would persist as he performed the difficult role of a cultural go-between.

By this time, food for the settlement was close to running out. In March 1790 the *Sirius* was wrecked off Norfolk Island en route to China to obtain supplies, escalating a dangerous situation into a crisis. Harvests had failed and no supply ships had arrived. The assessment of remaining supplies showed that they would be unlikely to last out the year. Phillip reduced rations by two-thirds. Everyone, regardless of position, received a weekly allowance of 2 pounds of pork, 2½ pounds of flour and 2 pounds of rice. It was not until the Second Fleet arrived in June 1790 that there was enough food available to end the famine. But not the tensions.

The reluctance of the Eora to cede their land and the brutality of some convicts and marines were major causes of the conflicts in and around the early Sydney settlement. But lack of food and subsequent competition for available resources between the indigenous people and the newcomers aggravated the situation, despite attempts at reconciliation on both sides.

In September 1790, Bennelong invited Phillip to a feast of whale blubber. Another Aboriginal man speared the governor through the shoulder. It is thought that the assailant was protesting the establishment of the Rose Hill farm on his traditional territory. Good relations with Bennelong were restored, however, and in early October he brought the remainder of his people in to the British settlement.

Yet the troubles continued. In December a convict hunter was speared near the Cook's River, thought to be revenge for his known attacks on Aboriginal people. An expedition to bring in the perpetrators for punishment was unsuccessful.

Just after Christmas, Aboriginal people stole potatoes. They were pursued and fired on by Phillip's troops. A man named Bangui was killed. A few days later Phillip and Bennelong had a confrontation over stolen fish during which Bennelong demanded to know, 'Who killed Bangui?'. He vowed to revenge the man's death, stealing a hatchet as he departed.

By the start of 1791 it was clear, to some at least, that the local people would not simply give up their country. Deputy judge advocate David Collins wrote: 'While they entertained the idea of our having dispossessed them of their residences, they must always consider us as enemies; and upon that principle they made a point of attacking the white people whenever opportunity and safety concurred.'

The hungry years lasted until the end of 1792 when Governor Phillip returned to England taking Bennelong and Yemmerrawanne with him. But food supplies in the colony remained a concern for a long time. Convicts would bend much of their forced labour to ploughing, planting, sowing and harvesting. Many would be sentenced for stealing food and suffer 'the cat', the treadmill and heavy irons.

The Orgy That Wasn't

The women convicts of the First Fleet's *Lady Penrhyn* went ashore at Sydney Cove on 6 February 1788. Most had seven- or fourteen-year terms and there were a few 'lifers' among them. The surgeon aboard the former slave ship that had brought them to the ends of the earth, Arthur Bowes Smyth, wrote, 'The Men Convicts got to them very soon after they landed, & it is beyond my abilities to give a just discription [*sic*] of the Scene of Debauchery & Riot that ensued during the night'. According to subsequent writers, a wild orgy of rum, sex, storm and lightning followed, a fitting act for the foundation of a colony of convicts.

Popular as this story has become, in one version or another, historians have found little evidence of it ever happening. Bowes Smyth was nowhere near the scene of the alleged orgy, he was on the *Lady Penrhyn* quite a long way out in the harbour. None of the other keen diarists of the First Fleet, such as officers Watkin Tench or Ralph Clark, seem to have noticed the orgy either. They certainly did not mention it in their accounts, an unlikely omission, especially for Ralph Clark who believed women convicts were all 'damned whores'.

Why Bowes Smyth believed that 'Debauchery & Riot' occurred as soon as the women set foot in New South Wales is worth considering. He was certainly glad to see the women leave the ship: 'We had the long wish'd for pleasure of seeing the last of them,' he wrote. The *Lady Penrhyn*'s voyage from England had been tedious and troubled with illness, lack of food and indiscipline. Many of the women were prostitutes and suffered from venereal disease. Although attempts were made to keep men and women separate, cohabitation quickly became commonplace. In April 1787, a month or so before they set sail for Botany Bay, five women were chained up for having relations with crewmen. There is no record of the sailors being punished.

During the voyage seventy-year-old Elizabeth Beckford died of 'dropsy', or oedema, her bloated corpse buried at sea. She was not the last. Jane Parkinson died as they sailed from Cape Town to New Holland, as Australia was often known. Off Van Diemen's Land the lumbering transport was lashed by a storm so fierce that the women fell to their knees praying for deliverance. Short of food once again, the *Lady Penrhyn* finally made Botany Bay in late January 1788, only to discover that Arthur Phillip had decided the place was unsuitable for settlement. He had departed for Port Jackson.

By the time the *Lady Penrhyn* finally anchored in the great body of water that would become known as Sydney Harbour, the 101 women and more than 70 male crew and marines had been cooped up on the 30-metre by 8-metre vessel, in some cases for more than a year. The women were flogged, chained, punished with thumb screws and had their heads shaved bare. Bowes Smyth wrote in his journal:

> I believe I may venture to say there was never a more abandon'd
> set of wretches collected in one place . . . The greater part of them
> are so totally abandoned & callous'd to all sense of shame &
> even common decency that it frequently becomes indispensably
> necessary to inflict Corporal punishment upon them.

The doctor was clearly not well disposed towards his female charges. When he finally did 'see the last of them', he was likely to assume that they would behave in what he considered their typically debauched manner. Bowes Smyth was a product of his time and circumstances, as were all those who arrived on the first and subsequent fleets.

The double standard that masqueraded as respectability and punished only women for acts that involved a male partner continued in the colony. Four of the convict women of the *Lady Penrhyn* became the de facto partners of officers and the judge advocate. Esther Abrahams and Lieutenant George Johnston began what would become a lifelong relationship during the voyage. They did not marry for another quarter of a century.

Bowes Smyth also recorded an incident when one of the sailors was caught in the women's tents. His hands were tied and he was publically drummed out of camp to the tune of 'The Rogue's March', a ceremony used for dishonourable discharge from the army and usually followed by a flogging.

These more domestic relationships and official attempts to maintain propriety are not the stuff of myth. They lie forgotten in history while the more salacious story lives on. Historians have been trying to scotch the orgy myth ever since one of their own mistakenly set the yarn spinning in 1963. Manning Clark wrote of it, though soon withdrew the assertion after a more careful look at the available evidence. But it was too late. The lewd rumour neatly captured popular views of early colonial society and the image of degraded convicts that had grown up over the generations. The 'orgy that wasn't' gathered further currency from a procession of later writers and television shows repeating and embellishing the alleged scene. A yarn of ribald abandonment still resonates with a common view of the founding of Australia. No matter how often and convincingly historians demolish the myth, many Australians still prefer to believe it.

Encountering Others

The first weeks and month of settlement were filled with new encounters for the British and the Indigenous people around what had now become Port Jackson. Early interactions between convicts, Aborigines, free settlers and soldiers set the tone for much that was to come.

Richard Williams was the second mate aboard the First Fleet supply ship *Borrowdale*, arriving in Botany Bay on Sunday, 20 January 1788. In his journal he wrote of a group of twenty-five Aborigines he saw on the beach at Botany Bay. Over the following months, the mariner recorded many of the events of the earliest days.

He heard the first sermon to be preached in the new land on 3 February: 'from the 116 Psalm, verse 12. "What shall I render unto the Lord, for all his benefits towards me?"' Some newcomers had little opportunity to give thanks for whatever benefits the vicar had in mind. Williams writes that on 'Monday, Feb 18, one of the convicts was executed'.

On the morning of Friday 18 April, Williams went up the river in a small flotilla:

> At a quarter of a mile distant turned a point of land and surprised 4 canoes of the natives, they had a fire ashore, and were enjoying themselves, but on seeing us they immediately fled, leaving behind their canoes, containing fishing implements, a shield made from the bark of a tree, a Calabash shell with food, which was chiefly fish.

Williams and his companions gave chase and soon overtook one of the children who, not surprisingly, 'seemed much affrighted, cried greatly, and began to climb the rocks, &c to escape'. But the encounter ended well:

Three of the men savages, who were quite naked, returned and sat down with us by the fire for near an hour. The child was about two feet and half high of a chocolate colour, well proportioned, short, black curly hair, ornamented each side of his head with small fish bones, and behind two bunches of white and yellow feathers, from bird called a Cockatoo, cemented to small locks of hair with gum.

On Sunday 27 April, Williams joined a group of convicts fishing: 'We put into a bay about two miles and a half from where the ships lay, and spoke with some of the natives, [men] who had three children with them, one of which was an infant, whom I took in my arms.'

The journal-keeping sailor documented the troubles that afflicted the colony, such as on 'Friday, May 2, one of the convicts was hanged for robbing the ship Charlotte's tent ashore'. Later that month, on Friday 30 May, he recorded: '2 of the convicts were brought into the buildings, who were killed by the natives in the most barbarous manner, by being cut and pierced in various parts of the bodies; it was supposed to have been thro' revenge for taking away their canoes.' On Wednesday 25 June, Williams noted that 'two convicts were executed'.

Richard Williams set sail in *Borrowdale* in mid-July, together with three other returning transports. The ships all carried government despatches and private letters that would inform officials and loved ones at home of the great adventure that was the First Fleet and the 'new nation at Botany Bay'. Some of those left behind assembled on South Head to see the ships on their way, perhaps wondering what their fates would be.

Laying Down the Law

On a Thursday morning in early February 1788, Governor Phillip called his flock of convicts and their jailers together. Drums and fifes were played, the colours were flown and the marines shouldered their arms as they formed a circle round the male and female transports.

The convicts were ordered to sit and the gentlemen asked to come into the centre of the ring to join the governor, lieutenant-governor, surveyor general, clergyman and other officials. They all stood behind a makeshift table on which rested two red leather cases. The cases were unsealed and opened so that everyone present could witness the beginning of European law in New South Wales. The judge advocate picked up the papers and read out Phillip's commission. Then the governor began to speak. He was not happy.

According to surgeon Arthur Bowes Smyth who witnessed and wrote about the event:

> The Governor harangued the convicts, telling them that he had tried them hitherto to see how they were disposed. That he was now thoroughly convinced there were many amongst them incorrigible, and that he was persuaded nothing but severity would have any effect upon them, to induce them to behave properly in future. He also assured them that if they attempted to get into the women's tents of a night there were positive orders for firing upon them.

And furthermore, said Governor Phillip:

> Not more than 200 out of 600 were at work, that the industrious should not labour for the idle. If they did not work, they should not eat. In England, thieving poultry was not punished with death; but here where a loss of that kind could not be supplied, it was of the utmost consequence to the settlement, as well as every other species of stock, as they were preserved for breeding. Therefore stealing the most trifling article of stock or provisions should be punished with Death.

The governor was careful to point out here that while executing criminals would offend his 'feelings towards his fellow creatures', he would nevertheless ensure that justice was carried out. He would be true to his word. He was.

A few weeks later the first offender to be hanged in the colony dangled from a gum tree for stealing food.

Phillip's harangue went on to promise the convicts would not be overworked and outlined the pecking order that would determine who would be first to have a roof over their heads:

> Their labour would not be equal to that of a husbandman in England, who has a wife and family to provide for. They would never be worked beyond their abilities, but every individual should contribute his share to render himself and Community at large happy and comfortable as soon as the nature of the settlement will admit of. That they should be employed erecting houses for the different officers, next for the marines, and lastly for themselves.

When the speech was over, the formalities ended as they began and the ragged band of unwilling settlers was dismissed, while:

> The Governor retired to a cold collation under a large tent erected for that purpose to which the general officers only were invited and not the least attention whatever was paid to any other person who came out from England. The Masters of the different ships paid him the compliment of attending on shore during the reading of the Commission, which they were not under any obligation to do, notwithstanding which there was no more notice taken of them or even to provide the slightest accommodation for them than the convicts themselves.

The excluded convicts, sailors and soldiers did have some consolation, though. The mutton slaughtered the previous day for the governor's cold meat lunch was full of maggots.

A Practical Problem

The execution of Thomas Barrett on 27 February 1788 revealed a flaw in the preparations for the settlement of New South Wales. There was no hangman.

With three other convicts, Barrett had plundered the government food store of butter, peas and pork. A hurriedly convened court of officers declared them guilty and three of the four were sentenced to hang just before sunset. The fourth and youngest of the men, probably John Ryan, was lucky—he was sentenced to 300 lashes.

Around 6 p.m., the condemned men were brought in heavy irons to the large gum tree between the male and female convict camps that was to be their gallows. All the other convicts were assembled to witness the fate of those who broke Governor Phillip's law, menaced by a large group of armed marines. Arthur Bowes Smyth, the surgeon, recorded what happened next in his journal:

> When they arrived near the tree Major Ross read a respite of 24 hours for Lovall & Hall, but Barrett who was a most vile Character was turn'd off abt. . . . 6 o'Clock p.m. he expressed not the least signs of fear till he mounted the ladder & then he turn'd very pale & seem'd very much shock'd.
>
> It was some time before the man (a Convict who had undertaken the Office of hangman,) cd. be prevail'd upon to execute his office nor wd. he at last have comply'd if he had not been severely threaten'd by the Provost Marshal, Mr. Brewer & Major Ross threaten'd to give orders to the Marines to shoot him.

The Reverend Mr Johnson prayed fervently with the condemned before Barrett was allowed a final request:

> Just before Barrett was turned off he confess'd the justice of his sentence & that he had lead a very wicked life, he requested leave to speak to one of the Convict Men (a very bad kind of Man) on Seddiway, wh. was granted him, & he also expressed a wish to speak to one of the women convicts, but was refused, he then exhorted all of them to take warng. by his unhappy fate & so la[u]nched into Eternity; the Body hung an hour & was then buried in a grave dug very near the Gallows.

It seems that Barrett took a long time to die. His reluctant executioner may have been John Ryan, reprieved from his savage flogging in return for hanging his long-time friend. Lovall and Hall were pardoned but 'banished to some uninhabited place', probably Pinchgut Island (Fort Denison in Sydney Harbour).

Phillip's example to the convicts had little effect. Only two days later another four convicts were quickly condemned for stealing food and sentenced to hang that evening. Once again, the practical problem of who would do the job presented itself. Phillip must by now have realised that hanging was going to be a frequent event in the colony. A permanent executioner was needed.

As the four men waited beneath the hanging tree with nooses around their necks, Phillip reprieved one with a flogging. Another, James Freeman, was then made an offer difficult to refuse. Freeman would be given a conditional pardon if he would agree to become the colony's public executioner. As the chief medical officer of the First Fleet, John White, wrote: 'After some little pause, he reluctantly accepted.'

The food stealers were luckier than the first group. The judge advocate reprieved the remaining men. However, the colony's new hangman had little time to learn his trade before being required to 'turn off' another unfortunate, the twenty-year-old John Bennett, on 2 May.

In November 1789 Ann Davis became the first woman executed in the colony. She was convicted of stealing clothes and other goods from a convict house. A week later, Freeman was given 100 lashes for drunkenness.

Another nineteen executions of convicts and civilians, as well as marines, are recorded in the colony between 1788 and 1792, all presumably carried out by Freeman. After serving in the position until the end of his original seven-year sentence for highway robbery, Freeman worked as a farm labourer around the Hawkesbury River settlements of Richmond and Windsor. He was not successful in gaining a land grant and died a pauper in 1830. The ex-hangman was buried in an unmarked grave in a distant corner of St Matthew's Anglican Church, Windsor. His pardon was the first to be given in New South Wales.

Thomas Barrett also left a legacy. A skilled engraver and forger, he was commissioned by Surgeon-General John White to craft a medal commemorating the arrival of the transport ship *Charlotte* at Botany Bay. Today, 'The Charlotte Medal' (also known as the 'Botany Bay Medallion') is in the collection of the National Museum of Australia. It is considered to be the country's earliest colonial work of art.

The Lure of Gold

One of the beliefs that circulated among convicts was that there must be gold in the ground of this new world. Many searched for a strike and in August 1788 a man named Daley finally reported success. He had a 'specimen' or sample to prove it but kept the location of his find to himself. He would only reveal the secret if he were freed and sent home to England, together with a certain convict woman, and given a sum of money for his trouble.

Daley claimed to have sold some of the gold to 'a gentleman' aboard the *Golden Grove*. When a muster of everyone in the colony was called, Daley was unable to identify his client but still insisted that he had discovered gold. He offered to take a party into the bush and reveal the exact location of his find. Major Ross, acting as governor at the time, sent an officer and twenty men to escort Daley to the spot. After about ten miles of hard going through the bush, Daley was given permission 'to go aside', presumably for a toilet break, but did not return. Instead, he made his way back to the settlement alone and told Ross that the mine was so large that it would take many men to work and guard it.

Ross immediately raised another detachment to go in search of the first group. Before they could leave, the missing party came out of the bush with the real story. Daley was clapped in irons and sent for a brutal flogging. After each 100 lashes he was asked whether the goldmine was real. He insisted that it was 'until he had received three hundred, when he confessed the whole to be a falsehood'. The specimen Daley provided was really made of shavings from a gold coin and possibly bronze mixed together with clay and fired hard.

Not long after this incident, Daley was found guilty of burglary and hanged. But among the convicts it was whispered that he had found gold but was prepared to take his floggings rather than reveal the real location of his find. This belief was bolstered by the fact that small quantities of the precious metal were bought and sold in the earliest days of the colony, possibly sourced from convict bolters who found ways across the Blue Mountains long before the official crossing in 1813. The lure of gold and other mineral wealth was established this early in modern Australian history, the first example of a strong tradition of fabulously rich deposits and reefs.

This Solitary Waste of the Creation

Less than a year after the First Fleet deposited its cargo of felons at Port Jackson, an unidentified convict woman wrote home. She was not happy but hoped for better times:

> I take the first opportunity that has been given us to acquaint you with our disconsolate situation in this solitary waste of the creation. Our passage, you may have heard by the first ships, was tolerably favourable; but the inconveniences since suffered for want of shelter, bedding, &c., are not to be imagined by any stranger. However, we have now two streets, if four rows of the most miserable huts you can possibly conceive of deserve that name. Windows they have none, as from the Governor's house, &c., now nearly finished, no glass could be spared; so that lattices of twigs are made by our people to supply their places.

Plans were in hand for a church to be built as soon as the bricks could be made. It would be erected 'at the extremity of the lines, where since our arrival the dead are buried'.

A churchyard was an early necessity in the colony: 'Notwithstanding all our presents, the savages still continue to do us all the injury they can, which makes the soldiers' duty very hard, and much dissatisfaction among the officers. I know not how many of our people have been killed.'

The female convicts were having an especially hard time:

> As for the distresses of the women, they are past description, as they are deprived of tea and other things they were indulged in in the voyage by the seamen, and as they are all totally unprovided with clothes, those who have young children are quite wretched. Besides this, though a number of marriages have taken place, several women, who became pregnant on the voyage, and are since left by their partners, who have returned to England, are not likely even here to form any fresh connections.

But there were some compensations:

> We are comforted with the hopes of a supply of tea from China, and flattered with getting riches when the settlement is complete, and the hemp which the place produces is brought to perfection. Our kingaroo [sic] rats are like mutton, but much leaner; and there is a kind of chickweed so much in taste like our spinach that no difference can be discerned. Something like ground ivy is used for tea; but a scarcity of salt and sugar makes our best meals insipid.

The letter concluded with a reference to Norfolk Island, where the *Golden Grove* took a party of marines, free settlers and thirty-two male and female convicts in October 1788, joining the group already there:

> The separation of several of us to an uninhabited island was like a second transportation. In short, every one is so taken up with their own misfortunes that they have no pity to bestow upon others. All our letters are examined by an officer, but a friend takes this for me privately. The ships sail tomorrow.

The vessels carrying this letter and many others were the First Fleet store ships the *Fishburn* and *Golden Grove*. They sailed for England in November. It would be many long months before the writer of this discouraging note and the straggling settlement of naval officers, free settlers and convicts to which she had been condemned would hopefully be relieved by the arrival of the Second Fleet.

Free by Servitude

Joseph Smith was only fourteen when he arrived in the struggling settlement at Sydney Cove aboard the Second Fleet ship *Neptune*. It was during Arthur Phillip's time and he had seven years to serve before retaining his liberty—if he lived that long.

The young Joseph soon discovered that everything was in short supply, or in no supply at all: 'There were only eighteen houses in the colony then . . . myself and eighteen others laid in a hollow tree for seventeen weeks.' Food was especially scarce:

> There was plenty of hardship then: I have often taken grass, pounded it, and made soup from a native dog. I would eat anything then. For seventeen weeks I had only five ounces of flour a day. We never got a full ration except when the ship was in harbor. The motto was 'Kill them, or work them, their provision will be in store'. Many a time have I been yoked like a bullock with ten or thirty others to drag along timber. Bout eight hundred died in six months at a place called Toogabbie [Toongabbie], or Constitution Hill.

He claimed that men would kill for a month's food and that:

> I would have committed three murders for a week's provisions! I was chained seven weeks on my back for being out getting greens, wild herbs. The Rev Marsden would come it tightly [in nightly? Transcript unclear] to force some confession. Men were obliged to tell lies to prevent their bowels being cut out by the lash. The laws were bad then. If an officer wanted a man's wife he would send the husband to Norfolk Island.

The work was beyond hard:

Old Jones killed three men in a fortnight at the saw by overwork. We used to be taken in large parties to raise a tree; when the body of the tree was raised, Old Jones would call some men away—then more; the men were bent double—they could not bear it—they fell—the tree on one or two, killed on the spot. 'Take him away; put him in the ground.' There was no more about it.

Joseph Smith's memories of the hard early years were still strong even fifty-six years after his landing. He recalled a large mass grave into which bodies were hurled each day without ceremony: 'The native dogs used to come down at night and fight and howl in packs, gnawing the poor dead bodies.'

He said he knew 'a man so weak, he was thrown into the grave, when he said "Don't cover me up, I'm not dead; for God's sake don't cover me up!" The overseer answered, "Damn your eyes, you'll die tonight, and we shall have the trouble to come back again."' Joseph testified that the man was still alive and living at Richmond.

He told plenty of flogging tales as well:

The governor would order the lash at the rate of five hundred, six hundred or eight hundred; and if the men could have stood it they would have had more. I knew a man hung there and then for stealing a few biscuits, and another for stealing a duck frock. A man was condemned—not time—take him to the tree, and hang him. The overseers were allowed to flog the men in the fields. Often have the men been taken from the gang, had fifty, and sent back to work.

Surviving all these hardships, Joseph Smith was released at the end of his sentence and went to work for himself, now 'free by servitude' as the records put it. He stowed away to Norfolk Island where he worked in the governor's garden and was well treated. He was then employed by the Wentworth family and often carried the infant William Wentworth, later to be an eminent politician, in his arms.

Now, in 1845, Joseph Smith was a wealthy man with 1000 pounds in cash, four farms with 500 head of cattle, and his own house with many acres of land and more cattle. Most of his wealth was already shared with two of his lucky children, though he seems to have had many more. And he was happy: 'We are never without a chest of tea in the house; we use two in the year. I have paid 40 pounds for a chest of tea in this colony. Tea is a great comfort.'

This convict-cum-pioneer lived another eleven years after telling his colourful story. He married several times and fathered at least five children. He is buried at St Albans on the Hawkesbury River with his final partner, ex-convict Margaret Raycroft (Raycraft). Pioneers all.

A Meek and Tender Wife

'My father is quite innocent,' said the eighteen-year-old girl at the Old Bailey on 1 July 1812. Her name was Susannah Lalliment (also Lilbemont) and she was accused with her father of stealing a ten-pound note from her employer in Whitefriars. The proceedings wound on with damning evidence building to the verdict. The jury declared Susannah's father not guilty but she was found guilty and sentenced to death.

It must have been obvious to the judge, jury and lawyers in the court that Susannah was covering up for her father, who was not required to plead. Fortunately, she was recommended to mercy because of her age. But Susannah's troubles were only just beginning.

The War of 1812 between Britain and America allowed for 'privateering', a form of legalised piracy in which ships were given sanction to attack and capture each other's vessels, rob them and often sell them on. In November 1812, the transport *Emu* bound for New South Wales was captured by the heavily armed American ship, the *Holkar*. The Americans found more than forty female convicts, some with children, aboard. In January, the women and children were landed at the Cape Verde Islands and the Americans sailed away with their prize. Among the castaways was Susannah Lalliment.

The women spent almost a year on the island of St Vincent. Although looked after by local Catholic nuns, the group was in desperate straits by the time they were picked up by the British *Isabella* and returned to England. They were then transported again aboard the *Broxbornebury*.

The voyage of the *Broxbornebury* was stormy, both in terms of weather and human relations. The captain was a harsh disciplinarian, flogging at least one sailor and attempting to imprison one of the convict women in the pillory. The woman resisted so violently that the surgeon feared for her life and with difficulty convinced the captain to relent. Two other women and two of the children died.

When the ship arrived at Sydney Cove in July 1814, she was quarantined for months. Many of the crew deserted as soon as they got the chance, including the armourer, Aaron Walters. Although not a convict, he went into hiding and escaped recapture. Susannah was assigned as maid to a doctor in Parramatta. The next year, Aaron and Susannah were married. Like many other early settlers, the couple set up at St Albans on the Hawkesbury River, attracted by the good farming land and the convenience of the Great North Road connecting Sydney and the Hunter Valley. They prospered and had many children, their descendants now plentiful.

Susannah would never see her father again. She died in July 1840 and was buried near St Albans, perhaps with her last-born. Aaron had her headstone engraved:

SACRED TO THE MEMORY OF SUSANNA WALTERS
Who DEPARTED THIS LIFE ON THE 3RD of JULY 1840
Aged 47 years
Also In Memory of HARRIET WALTERS Aged 6 months
Beneath this silent grave doth lie

a meek and tender wife
It was God that called her from on high
to inhabit eternal life
Before the vital spark had fled
one favour did she crave
When she was layed among the dead
This spot might be her grave.

Aaron lived another twenty-six years and was buried in the same ground. His headstone reads:

SACRED TO THE MEMORY OF AARON WALTERS
Who DEPARTED This LIFE THE 2ND JULY 1866
AGED 82 YEARS
In sure and steadfast hope to rise
And claim his mansion in the skies
A Christian here his flesh laid down
The cross exchanging for a crown.

The Last First Fleeters

The main contender for the title of longest surviving First Fleet convict is Elizabeth 'Betty' King, married at that time to a soldier named Thomas Thackery. She had been convicted of thieving five handkerchiefs worth one shilling at Manchester in 1786 and received a sentence of seven years transportation. In her early twenties, Betty departed the Plymouth hulks (notorious prison ships) on the *Friendship* but was transferred to *Charlotte*, aboard which she arrived, having often been placed in chains on the voyage out. Officer Ralph Clark was glad to see the back of her and the other troublemakers when they left his ship for the *Charlotte*: '30 sheep came on board this day and wair put in the Place where the women convicts Were—I think we will find much more Agreable Ship mates than they were.'

Betty was among the largest group of convict women landed for the first time on 6 February 1788. To the cheers of the already landed convicts and guards, she distinguished herself by being the first to jump ashore and dash up the beach near what is now The Rocks. So goes one of the stories. While she was not the first British convict or free woman to step ashore in New South Wales—smaller groups of soldiers' wives and convict women had already been landed—Betty made the biggest and most enduring impact. She was generally known as the first white woman ashore for the rest of her long life.

Celebrity did not save Betty from twenty-five lashes. She went to Norfolk Island in 1790 where she was flogged the following year for leaving her settlement without permission. On Norfolk, Betty lived with a James Dodding for some years, and was able to purchase a 10-acre block of land in 1800 from a marine named Samuel King. Moving to Van Diemen's Land in 1807, Betty and James separated and she married the same Samuel King in 1810. They settled in the Derwent Valley north of Hobart where they farmed at 'Kings Rocks'. The ex-convict and the ex-marine prospered. By 1815 they owned 48 acres of land between them, Samuel 28 acres and Betty 20 acres. Samuel died in 1849 and Betty passed away in August 1856 at the age of eighty-nine. The two are buried together in the Methodist Chapel at Back River.

This story has a neatly folkloric ending. As well as possibly being the first convict woman ashore, Elizabeth (Thackery) King is believed to have been the last female survivor of the First Fleet.

Michael Norton is thought to be the longest-lived of the free First Fleeters. He was perhaps in his early nineties in the mid-1860s, though believed he was a decade older. Norton was not a convict but was born aboard the ship taking his cavalryman father to serve in India. The family returned to England after a few years and, barely more than a boy, Norton was drafted into a group of marines on the way to Botany Bay with Arthur Phillip. It seems that he drilled with the marines but never enlisted, serving as an assistant cook.

Norton worked for three years as a servant to Major Johnston then went sawing logs and labouring along the Hawkesbury

River. He remained here, virtually isolated for seventy years, around Colo where he had been known as 'Old Mick' by locals who called him that when they were young. Mick reasoned that he must have already been elderly fifty years before. He never married and was still in good health. He was reckoned to be pretty acute for his advanced age, though had trouble with numbers. In 1863 Old Mick made the big journey to Sydney, interested to see sights of which he had only been told, mainly a railway train and steamships.

We hear no more of this man. He presumably returned to the Colo bush and died there soon after with a solid claim to being the last First Fleeter, bound or free.

'Battle of Vinegar Hill', convict uprising at Castle Hill, Sydney. Inscription below image says, 'Major Johnston with Quartermaster Laycock and twenty five privates of ye New South Wales Corps defeats two hundred and sixty six armed rebels, 5th March 1804.'

2
Perilous Voyages

The waves were high upon the sea, the wind blew up in gales
I'd rather have drowned in misery than come to New South Wales

'Jim Jones at Botany Bay'

A Sight Truly Shocking

Oh! if you had but seen the shocking sight of the poor creatures
that came out in the three ships it would make your heart bleed;
they were almost dead, very few could stand, and they were
obliged to fling them as you would goods, and hoist them out of
the ships, they were so feeble; and they died ten or twelve of a day
when they first landed.

It was not only this unidentified convict woman who was
appalled at the state of those who arrived aboard the Second
Fleet in 1790. The Reverend Richard Johnson, chaplain to
the settlement at Sydney Cove, was not prepared for what he
saw—and smelled. Johnson went aboard the convict ships in
the fleet to inspect the newcomers:

Was first on board the Surprise. Went down amongst the convicts,
where I beheld a sight truly shocking to the feelings of humanity,

a great number of them laying, some half and others nearly quite naked, without either bed or bedding, unable to turn or help themselves. Spoke to them as I passed along, but the smell was so offensive that I could scarcely bear it.

Johnson visited the *Scarborough* next but the captain talked him out of going below. The condition of the convicts aboard the *Neptune* was so bad that he did not even try to go below decks. But the end of the voyage was not the end of the dying: 'Some of these unhappy people died after the ships came into the harbour, before they could be taken on shore—part of these had been thrown into the harbour, and their dead bodies cast upon the shore, and were seen laying naked upon the rocks.'

Johnson went straight to the governor with his sorry tale. He later described the scene in a letter:

In consequence of which immediate orders were sent on board that those who died on board should be carried to the opposite north shore and be buried. The landing of these people was truly affecting and shocking; great numbers were not able to walk, nor to move hand or foot; such were slung over the ship side in the same manner as they would sling a cask, a box, or anything of that nature. Upon their being brought up to the open air some fainted, some died upon deck, and others in the boat before they reached the shore. When come on shore, many were not able to walk, to stand, or to stir themselves in the least, hence some were led by others. Some creeped upon their hands and knees, and some were carried upon the backs of others.

Fortunately, a tent hospital arrived as part of the Second Fleet's much-needed cargo. About a hundred tents were pitched with great haste, and in each of these tents there were about four sick people: 'Here they lay in a most deplorable situation. At first they had nothing to lay upon but the damp ground, many scarcely a rag to cover them. Grass was got for them to lay upon, and a blanket given amongst four of them.' Around five hundred convicts were in need of medical attention:

> The misery I saw amongst them is inexpressible; many were not able to turn, or even to stir themselves, and in this situation were covered over almost with their own nastiness, their heads, bodies, cloths, blanket, all full of filth and lice. Scurvy was not the only nor the worst disease that prevailed amongst them (one man I visited this morning, I think I may safely say, had 10,000 lice upon his body and bed; some were exercised with violent fevers, and others with a no less violent purging and flux.

It turned out that most of the convicts had been shackled together below decks for days at a time, up to their waists in bilge water, and 'many died with the chains upon them'. Most were not released until a few days before they reached harbour. The reverend did what he could, though his compassion was soon tempered by observation and experience of 'the villany [*sic*] of these wretched people'.

> Some would complain that they had no jackets, shirts, or trowsers, and begged that I would intercede for them. Some by this means have had two, three, four—nay, one man not less than six different slops given him, which he would take an opportunity to sell to some others, and then make the same complaints and entreaties. When any of them were near dying and had something given to them as bread of lillipie (flour and water boiled together), or any other necessaries, the person next to him or others would catch the bread, &c., out of his hand, and, with an oath, say that he was going to die, and therefore that it would be of no service to him. No sooner would the breath be out of any of their bodies than others would watch them and strip them entirely naked.

It was a case of survival of the fittest:

> Instead of alleviating the distresses of each other, the weakest were sure to go to the wall. In the night-time, which at this time

is very cold, and especially this would be felt in the tents, where they had nothing but grass to lay on and a blanket amongst four of them, he that was strongest of the four would take the whole blanket to himself and leave the rest quite naked.

At the time he wrote this letter, around July 1790, Johnson had buried eighty-four convicts, one child and one soldier. By August the death toll was more than a hundred, with 'numbers yet sick, some likely to die, and others never to appearance will be fit for any employment'. He was still struggling to cope:

Never did I see such a scene of Misery in my days, in every sense truly wretched, naked, filthy, dirty, louzy, & many of them unable to stand, to creep, or even to stir hand or foot. Have been a great deal amongst them, till I have come home quite ill.

The reverend continued to do his duty, despite being unable to convince the governor to build a church and being assigned no convict to help him cultivate his garden or shoot his meat. His frequent representations and complaints led Major Grose, while acting as governor, to call him 'a discontented and troublesome character'.

By the middle of 1794 Johnson was still unhappy with his lot but able to report:

The Colony at this time seems to be in a more prosperous flourishing state than I have yet seen it.—The supplies we have just received from England & other Places came very seasonably, & it is expected that from this time we shall be nearly able to grow grain to supply ourselves.—The corn (wheat) in general looks promising. We still, however, want livestock both for manure & Labour. The ground is cultivated by the hoe, which is not equal to plow.—The soil in some parts is good, but will soon wear out unless fallowed & manured. The Colony spreads in extent every year. A great number of those whose term of transportation has expired have turned settlers, some of who are doing well, better than many farmers in England.

The Reverend Richard Johnson eventually returned to England in September 1800, his duty done to God, man and woman.

Irish Rebels

The transport *Hercules* arrived in Dublin in September 1801. The Irish convicts taken aboard included rebels from the United Irishmen Rebellion of 1798. They sailed on 29 November, bound for Port Jackson via Rio de Janeiro, an uncomfortable seven-month voyage and, as it turned out, one that was lethal for some.

At around 2.30 p.m. on 29 December, as Captain Luckyn Betts and his officers took a meal, they heard screams from the women convicts. The captain and his men ran from the cabin to find the sentries of the New South Wales Corps overpowered by a group of convicts who were in possession of the quarter-deck. A shot was fired, bringing other sailors and soldiers to the scene. The next forty-five minutes were filled with firing, slashing and battering as the mutinous convicts were driven back below decks and the ship secured.

Thirteen convicts were dead. One of the surviving mutineers, James Tracey, informed the captain that a convict named Jeremiah Prendergass was to be the ringleader of a second attempt if the first mutiny failed. Prendergass, kneeling on the quarter-deck, loudly proclaimed his innocence but was shot dead on the spot by Captain Betts. For the rest of the voyage, all the convicts were locked down in filthy conditions, deprived of adequate food, water, ventilation and sanitation.

When the *Hercules* arrived, many convicts were 'dreadfully emaciated', as Governor King wrote to Lord Hobart. Including the fourteen killed in the mutiny, the *Hercules* lost forty-four convicts. The surviving convicts were too badly debilitated to ever be of much use to a frontier colony.

At the trial of the mutineers, Tracey, along with several others, appeared against their former comrades as witnesses for the Crown. Surprisingly, the defendants were found not guilty. Captain Luckyn Betts was also tried for the murder of Prendergass but found guilty of the lesser charge of manslaughter. He was ordered to pay the very large sum of 500 pounds to the colony's orphan fund and held in jail until the money was paid.

The odd outcomes of this affair persisted. Not long after the trial, James Tracey took to the bush with John Lynch and others, some of whom were known rebels, including James Hughes. They robbed and assaulted the Hawkesbury Valley settler Samuel Phelps, taking a silver watch, jewellery, clothing and other items of value, including a land title. Except for Hughes, whose bones were found at the foot of the Blue Mountains three years later, they were arrested, tried and sentenced to hang at Castle Hill on 26 September 1803.

According to the *Sydney Gazette,* Tracey remained defiant to the end, in contrast to his condemned companion:

> One of the unhappy men, Lynch, seemed sensibly affected at his situation; and with a fervor suited to his circumstances, attended to the exhortations of the Minister, acknowledging himself guilty of the offence he was about to expiate. Tracey, on the contrary, assumed an air of sullen hardihood, denied his being accessory to the fact of which he had been convicted, and reproached the penitent, whose deportment was contrasted to his own.

There were no elaborate gallows with a trapdoor drop. The condemned men were bound and stood in a cart with a noose around their necks:

> Shortly before the cart was driven off, Lynch addressed the spectators in a becoming manner, and hoped that his melancholy fate would operate on the minds of others as a caution against falling into similar vices: but in this last voluntary effort of contrition he was interrupted by his unrelenting companion who harshly desired him not to gratify the spectators and shortly after they were both launched into Eternity!

The report of the execution revealed that Tracey had been the instigator and ringleader of the *Hercules* mutiny:

> He was foremost in the insurrection on board the Hercules on her passage hither, and was the first who dared attempt to surprise the Officers; but receiving a wound through the arm instantly turned upon the wretched companions of his guilt and rashness; and in consequence of his informations many afterwards suffered exemplary punishments, and too late repented of a precipitancy whose object merited no better fate. His companions had formerly nick nam'd him 'The key of the works', by which appellation he was generally distinguished.

In what was then the usual style of newspaper accounts of executions, Tracey was described as 'an abandoned unrepentant sinner'. The hope was expressed that a public execution would be a warning to others: 'We ardently hope therefore, that the ignominious end of these sufferers, whose vices death alone could put a period to, will deter all others from imitating them.'

These were not empty moralising slogans. There was a deeply prejudiced fear of the Irish convicts throughout the colony. As well as the rebellions that led to many of them being transported, Irish convicts were involved in escapes, attacks and a violent rising. Their large number and the insurrectionary experience of many were deeply troubling to the shaky government of the colony, to other convicts and to the small but growing community of free settlers.

As early as 1798 Governor Hunter was writing to the Duke of Portland about 'the problem of the Irish convicts':

> I have to inform your Grace that the Irish convicts are become so turbulent, so dissatisfied with their situation here, so extremely insolent, refractory, and troublesome, that, without the most rigid and severe treatment, it is impossible for us to receive any labour whatever from them. Your Grace will see the inconvenience which so large a proportion of that ignorant, obstinate and depraved set of transports occasion in this country by what I shall now state.

He went on to complain about escape attempts, delusions of a colony of white people 'in some part of this country' and 'their natural vicious propensities'.

The government's darkest nightmares were realised in March 1804 when the Irish and some other convicts did rise up at Castle Hill. The insurrection was brutally but efficiently put down by Major George Johnston and his 'Rum Corps' at a place later to be known as 'Vinegar Hill' (near Rouse Hill), named after an earlier rebel battle in County Wexford, Ireland. The convict rebels' battle cry was 'Liberty or Death'. None received liberty and more than thirty received death, either under the musketry of the soldiers or at the gallows. The rest were flogged and shipped to the Coal River (Newcastle).

That was not the end of the colony's Irish troubles, which were an extension of British repression since Oliver Cromwell's time and before. Many disaffected Irish convicts were prepared to operate, like Tracey, as 'the key of the works', not only in New South Wales and Van Diemen's Land but also during Western Australia's later period of convict transportation.

The Fever Ships

In 1814 Governor Macquarie was horrified at the arrival of three transports in 'a calamitous state of disease'. The emancipist William Redfern was working in the colony's rudimentary hospital and was told by Macquarie to investigate the fever ships. Redfern's eventual report revealed their tragic tales.

After picking up her human cargo from the hulks at Woolwich, Sheerness and Portsmouth, the *General Hewett* sailed for New South Wales in August 1813. Aboard were 300 convicts, seventy soldiers, fifteen women, eight children and more than a hundred sailors, as well as several passengers. Many convicts had been confined below decks for almost a month by this time.

While they were at sea, the prisoners were allowed on deck in rotation but were again confined whenever the ship was in port.

After nine days below decks at Madeira, the first sign of disease appeared. By the time the ship reached Rio de Janeiro, illness 'had increased to an alarming degree', though Redfern found that some attempts had been made to cleanse and purify the foul conditions:

> The decks were swept every morning, scraped and swabbed twice a week; they were sprinkled with vinegar weekly, until they made Rio Janeiro, when this was discontinued. The ship was also fumigated once a week for 6 weeks, but was afterwards much neglected. That three weeks previous to their arrival at Rio Janeiro, their bedding was thrown overboard in consequence of having been wetted; from the want of which the convicts, when they came into a cold climate, suffered exceedingly.

To make matters worse, the captain was profiteering from the supplies intended for the convicts' rations, apparently purchasing them and then selling them to his charges at 'shamefully enormous prices'. At least the convicts were now allowed on deck for the rest of the voyage, but 'It was now, Alas!, too late. No care, no exertion, however it might lessen, could now remedy the evil'. By the time the *General Hewett* reached Port Jackson thirty-four convicts had died from dysentery and typhous fever. Many of the survivors had to be hospitalised.

The *Three Bees* sailed from Cork on 27 October 1813 with 219 Irish convicts aboard. They were allowed on deck but suffered from extreme cold in Rio de Janeiro where the first convict died of fever. Despite efforts to cleanse the ship, by the time she arrived and disembarked her cargo in May 1814, '55 were sent to the hospital in a dreadful state'. Nine convicts died during the voyage. (Not long afterwards, the *Three Bees* was destroyed when her store of gunpowder exploded near the present site of the Opera House.)

The third fever ship, the *Surry,* left England with 200 transports early in 1814:

> On the 7th of March, John Stopgood sickened, the first that laboured under a well defined case of Typhus or common ship

fever. On the 12th John Ransom died of fever, and another fatal termination of fever occurred on the 22nd May. No attempt appears to have been made towards ventilating the prison and neither the Surgeon's representations nor his efforts met with that attention or assistance from the Captain and his officers, which it was their duty to have afforded him. On the 22nd of May, Isaac Giles died of fever, and on the 9th of June, Aaron Jackson died of fever, from which period the deaths became awfully frequent.

By July, so many officers were ill that the ship could not be manned. Fortunately, the transport *Broxbornebury* hove in sight and was hailed. When some of her sailors boarded the *Surry,* they found that 'the Captain, two Mates, the Surgeon, 12 of the ships' company, 16 convicts and 6 soldiers were lying dangerously ill with fever. Captain Paterson died the same day'.

They finally reached their destination with the assistance of crew from the *Broxbornebury* in late July:

> The sick were landed and taken into tents prepared for their reception on the north side of Port Jackson. Every plan was adopted and carried into effect, that had a tendency to cut short the progress of contagion. The measures adopted proved so effectual, that but one case of infection took place after the sick were landed.

Of those aboard the *Surry,* casualties totalled thirty-six convicts, four soldiers and seven seamen, including the captain, both mates and the surgeon.

William Redfern's report made recommendations on improving hygiene, nutrition, ventilation and fumigation, as well as allowing prisoners to access fresh air and sunlight. Macquarie agreed, reporting to Earl Bathurst back in England:

> Out of those landed, it has been necessary to send fifty-five to the Hospital many of them being much affected with Scurvy and others labouring under various complaints. On enquiring into the cause of this mortality and sickness, it appeared that many of

them had been embarked in a bad state of health, and not a few infirm from lameness and old age.

Together with Macquarie's representations to the British government, Redfern's report led to significant improvements in conditions aboard future transport ships. Scurvy and other diseases such as smallpox would still plague convict transports after the three fever ships of 1814, but if Redfern's sound advice was followed they were more effectively minimised and contained.

Despite his abilities as a doctor and manager, Redfern would be refused promotion to the position of principal surgeon, largely because he was an ex-convict. He resigned and went on to establish a small farming empire in the colony and was a founding director of the Bank of New South Wales, becoming a leader in the efforts of the emancipists to assert their rights as free citizens. His wealth allowed him to continue to support the poor, including Aboriginal people. He is commemorated in the name of the Sydney suburb of Redfern.

Attacked by America

The dangers of voyaging from Britain to the other side of the world in small ships were many. One transport experienced storm, sickness, a riotous crew and an attack by the United States of America.

The transport *Francis and Eliza* sailed from Cork, Ireland, in December 1814. She carried more than fifty male convicts and around seventy female convicts bound for New South Wales. Separated from the convoy in a storm off the island of Madeira a month later, she had the misfortune to meet with the American privateer, *Warrior*. Britain and the United States were at war again and American ships were given the legal right to harass and plunder British merchant ships. That included convict transports carrying armed soldiers.

The *Warrior* was a heavily gunned warship carrying more than one hundred and fifty armed soldiers and crew under the command of Captain Champlin. It did not take the Americans long to capture the lightly armed transport, defended with only four guns. Captain Harrison of the *Francis and Eliza* was taken aboard the *Warrior* and held for some hours while the Americans plundered his ship. According to a report in a colonial newspaper:

> [The *Francis and Eliza* was] stripped of all her arms, rigging, provisions, medicines, charts, stores, and in short of everything necessary for pursuing her voyage to NSW. These marauders even plundered the Captain and passengers of their clothes. They then put on board the master and crew of the brig Hope, Robert Pringle, from Greenock to Buenos Ayres, and, after setting the convicts at liberty, and throwing their irons into the sea, left the Francis and Eliza to her fate. The scenes of horror that ensued, it would be impossible to describe. They were everything that depravity, desperation and inebriety could produce. The Captain's life was repeatedly attempted, and conspiracies to scuttle and blow up the ship and to set her on fire, were happily discovered and frustrated.

The Americans also transferred aboard the crew of another ship they had previously captured. Harrison was returned unharmed to his ship but several crew members deserted, leaving the *Francis and Eliza* in a dangerous situation. The convicts were no longer confined and discipline among the crew and soldiers evaporated:

> The Crew almost a score in number seized upon the spirits and other liquors, which were treated as common plunder, and the most dreadful scenes of riot and intemperance prevailed, until their arrival at Santa Cruz, five days later. But for the steady conduct of the Male Convicts, it is certain that the Females on board would have received the unwelcome and lewd attentions of the debauched seamen, who on several occasions set the Ship on fire during their drunken frolics.

According to one account of this incident:

> One of the female prisoners, distinguished for her personal charms, passed herself off to the captain as the well known Mrs. M.A. Clarke. Her attractions conquered the heart of the American, who implicitly believing the story she told of having been convicted upon a false charge of swindling, he took her on board, presented her with 2000 dollars in cash, besides linen, clothes, &c.; nor did he discover the imposture until he returned to port, when the lady eloped from him with a sailor, and shortly after sued him for the payment of a promissory note for 5000 dollars, which he had unthinkingly assigned her.

The 'well known' Mrs M.A. Clarke was the mistress of Frederick, Duke of York.

At Santa Cruz, the commander of the British sloop *Harrier* received a letter from Captain Harrison detailing his troubles and requesting him to bring his men aboard and help him restore order:

> [The commander] immediately boarded the vessel with three of his officers, and a party of marines, when he found the ship in the full possession of the convicts, and every thing in the greatest disorder and confusion; that upon the representation of the master of the violent and disorderly conduct of the chief mate and four of the seamen . . . removed the said five persons from the said ship to his own sloop, and ordered a court-martial upon such of the soldiers as had been most guilty of mutinous and unsoldierlike conduct, and which court-martial awarded a severe punishment, which they accordingly underwent.

The broken bulkheads of the convict prison below were restored and the convicts returned to their confinement. From Tenerife, the *Francis and Eliza* received a naval escort and at Senegal a military guard of the Royal African Corps. In convoy, the transport proceeded to Sydney via the Cape of Good Hope, arriving in early August 1815. Here, the extent of the captain's and other losses was revealed:

> His private losses are very severe indeed, as are those of Mr. West, ship's Surgeon, from whom an investment of a thousand pounds was wholly taken, together with most of his wearing apparel, surgical instruments, and the ship's medicine chest, which latter loss, but for the favour of Providence, might have been followed by the most fatal consequences to the numerous persons on board.

Not surprisingly, this incident was greeted with outrage by the British:

> The case of the convict ship Francis and Eliza affords a new proof of the total disregard in which the Americans hold the rights and usages of civilized nations, while in a state of hostility with one another. Their conduct towards the above mentioned vessel would disgrace a Barbary corsair, and violates every principle of international faith, generosity, and forbearance which their magnanimous President so clamorously affects to advocate.

But the American version of events was very different:

> Captain Champlin assures us, that so far from releasing the convicts, (as there stated) he found them in a state of mutiny and insurrection, and supplied the captain with a guard to suppress it. He also put a crew on board of her, (of British prisoners he had captured) which made her number of seamen superior to that of the convicts. No plunder, whatever, was permitted, and she was left with a bountiful supply of everything, proper for a three months' voyage, with Madeira only 50 miles to leeward, where any succors could have been procured.

While claim and counterclaim echoed across the Atlantic and the Pacific, justice still had to be served. Around eight people died of sickness during the fraught passage of the *Francis and*

Eliza and others needed medical attention when they arrived. The male convicts were taken to work at the settlements of Windsor and Liverpool and many of the women went to the Parramatta Female Factory.

The *Francis and Eliza* was the last ship to transport both men and women to Australia.

The Might-Have-Been Mutiny

We did give them all a dinner that they could not swallow. Four and six dozen lashes to every man on Saturday; our sailors had no mercy in flogging them. We have all the ringleader[s] on deck chained down, several have since confessed the affair.

So an unidentified sailor described the aftermath of a murky series of events aboard the transport *Chapman* in 1817. The official story was that the mostly Irish convicts aboard plotted and prepared a mutiny even before they boarded the ship taking them to Port Jackson. Each prisoner took an oath, willingly or not, 'to be true and loyal, and not to deceive each other'. Any who refused were 'To be stiffled with blankets, quartered, and hove out of the port-holes'. The plan was to murder the sailors, soldiers and officers, sparing the first mate and a few sailors who had assisted the convicts in their design.

According to evidence given by convict Michael Collins, there was a secret password and, at the appointed time:

One part of the convicts to force the fore-scuttle, with a view of drawing the attention of every one on deck to that part; while the main body was to rush aft and force their way into the guard-room, for the purpose of getting possession of the arms, and go to the powder magazine, which they intended to set on fire, if they could not make their way back to the deck, as it would be as well to be blown up, as shot by the guard.

This was to be coordinated with another manoeuvre on deck:

> There were 17 men allowed to wash on deck, who were selected
> out of the convicts for that purpose, all the stoutest men, besides
> three cooks and four swabbers, altogether 24; they were to watch
> the opportunity when the ship's company went down to dinner,
> when the sentinels were to be knocked down, and their arms
> taken, and then come aft, and take possession of the quarter-deck,
> and cut every body down that attempted to come from below.

When the plot had succeeded they planned 'a grand dinner; the dinner was to be roasted turkey, roast pigs, geese, with a glass of brandy; after the goose, Port and Madeira wine'. Then the convicts would sail their prize to America and freedom. If they were unable to sail for America, they would revert to the ship's original course and sail to Australia where, according to one of the ringleaders, 'sworn on their arrival at Botany, with the PILOT'S people, and as many as they could get there, to join them, to take Botany Bay'.

The *Pilot* was another transport crammed with Irish convicts travelling with the *Chapman*. In this version of the story, the plotters aboard both ships planned to join together when they landed and take over the colony. An unidentified sailor aboard the *Chapman* gave his account of what happened when the convicts launched their plot just a few days into the voyage:

> On Thursday evening they made their attempt forward, first by
> forcing up the fore scuttle; finding they could not succeed, they
> all made a rush to force the aft hold bulk head, we then began
> to fire at all the hatchways, they still persisted, and sung out
> that they wanted no quarter; we kept firing until we found them
> all quiet, singing out for mercy. I went down with a party of
> the Guard, and demanded the dead and wounded. We found
> nine dead, and twenty-four wounded, who have since died of
> their wounds.

But that was not the end of the affair. Three days later, on Sunday evening:

> We heard them consulting in a body below, the sentry fired, we
> then commenced for a little time until we found them all quiet.
> Killed one wounded six. We have not got half of them to the
> chain-cable, so there is no fear of their doing any more harm; if
> they do, we do not intend to leave a man of them alive. It was
> planned in Dublin prison, that whatever ship they embarked in,
> they would take and murder all hands.

This sailor, who would presumably have been a victim if the mutiny succeeded, was looking forward 'to see them all hung at Botany Bay'.

After severe floggings, most of the convicts were chained up for the rest of the long voyage. One man, William Lea, was tied to a rope then thrown astern and towed along by the *Chapman*. Later he was chained to the poop deck for fourteen weeks. Others were whipped and severely treated.

The *Chapman* reached her planned destination with 186 of the original convict complement of 198. Seven had been shot dead, two died of dysentery and nobody seemed to know what happened to the remaining three. Suspicions were raised but an official inquiry concluded that the officers, crew and soldiers were guilty only of a misdemeanour. Governor Macquarie was not satisfied with this and sent the ship's surgeon and three soldiers back to England, under guard, to answer to murder charges. Eventually the master, some officers and several soldiers of the *Chapman* went to trial at the Old Bailey in January 1819. They were all acquitted. The jury decided that the defendants' fear of the convicts excused the killings, even if these concerns were unjustified.

This peculiar verdict has always left open the question of whether there actually was a mutiny aboard the *Chapman*. Or were the officers, crew and soldiers so fearful of the rumours that they attacked their charges before anything happened—or might have happened? There were accusations that two prisoners had given false information to the captain and doctor, fuelling their fears. In this interpretation, all the elaborate details of plots, oaths and passwords were merely invented to justify what might have been a massacre of defenseless men.

A Melancholy Mystery

Few people have ever been quite sure what really happened aboard the *George III* in the D'Entrecasteaux Channel between the southeast mainland of Tasmania and Bruny Island in April 1835. She left London's Woolwich Pier on 14 December 1834 with more than three hundred souls—crew, guards, convicts and free. By the time she reached Van Diemen's Land fifteen men, women and children were dead. This was not an unusual death rate for convict ships at the time. But the figure was about to rise dramatically.

In bright moonshine on the night of 12 April, the *George III* hit an uncharted rock while taking a shortcut through the channel to Hobart. Almost immediately the decks were awash. The main mast and mizzen top-mast soon fell, entangling the deck in rigging and sweeping away one of the ship's boats. Two remaining boats picked up those still clinging to the upper deck and thirty-six survivors were safely put ashore. The captain with five men returned to the wreck to rescue those still aboard, including the convicts.

The convicts were locked down below on the prison deck, and according to the *Hobart Town Courier,* they were 'screaming in a most violent and agitated manner to be let out—they put their hands through the grating and seized the surgeon by the hands, saying "You promised to stand by us".' The ship's surgeon, Dr Wyse, had promised to stay with the panicking convicts. As the waves battered the ship, the barricade erected to keep the convicts secure began to give way. Trying to save themselves, men began testing the barrier.

But then an order was given: 'A considerable body of the military formed a compact guard round the hatchway with their muskets levelled in intimidation. It was at this period, that the sentries over the main hatchway, in obedience to the positive orders they had received, to keep the men below, fired.' At least one convict was killed. 'By this action the prisoners remained subdued, but they kept crying out that the water was gaining on them, and the crashing of the rocks through the ship's bottom, was dreadful to hear.'

The justification for this extraordinary act was that the convicts would have overcrowded the ship's longboat then taking off those above. According to the official account, as soon as the boat was safely away, the convicts were released to save themselves as best they could. Close to sixty were disabled with scurvy in the ship's hospital and all of them drowned except for two lucky men. Of those convicts who made it to the chaos of the upper deck, thirty or more, including twenty boys, were washed to their deaths or died from exposure as they shivered through the long, cold night awaiting rescue.

When the rescue ships arrived from Hobart: 'The scene of desolation was appalling. The waves had made a complete passage through and through the vessel—the masts overboard—the sides and bottoms gone—and the decks and other parts that still hung together floating up and down with the waves—while the anchors were resting on the rocks.'

There was nothing aboard but the body of an old lag on his third transportation. John Roberts, unable to swim, lashed himself to a ring bolt in the surgeon's deck cabin, hoping he might be floated to shore if that part of the ship broke away.

In the end, more than 130 lives were lost from the wreck of the *George III*. Eighty-one convicts survived. A board of inquiry was held. Convict James Elliott testified: 'I was in the hatchway several minutes before I could get up. The soldiers kept me down and threatened to fire; I heard two shots fired: the first shot killed Robert Luker, and about three or four minutes after another shot was fired and I saw another man fall.'

The inquiry nevertheless concluded that, 'The conduct of all was most praiseworthy and entirely free from blame of any description'.

But then there were reports of bodies washed up bearing

evidence of gunshots and sword cuts, leading to the exhuma-
tion of seventeen of the dead. The coroner decided that the
wounds were the result of the bodies being washed against the
rocks.

Among convicts and in the free community there were dark
rumours. A poem appeared, said to have been written by a
convict survivor of the tragedy:

> A dreadful wreck we did sustain,
> Near Derwent River's mouth;
> On a reef of rock we there did strike—
> The wind being then due south.
> The dreadful sufferings to relate
> Would take a scholar's skill,
> To see us in the hold secured—
> The water rushing in;
> A guard was round the hatchway plac'd,
> To shoot us if we mov'd,
> When death was making rapid strides,
> 'Mong some of those we lov'd . . .

The belief that many more of the prisoners were shot
grew with each telling, rolling down the years until it became
accepted fact. Passed on to the descendants of convicts, the
legend lived on and is still echoed in the local folklore of the
region. A monument to the disaster was erected near the site in
1839. The inscription reads:

> Near this place are interred the remains of many of the sufferers
> who perished in the wreck of George the III, convict ship,
> which vessel struck on a sunken rock near the Actaeon Reef on the
> night of the 12th April, 1835: upon which melancholy occasion
> 134 human beings were drowned.
>
> This tomb is erected by the desire of His Excellency Colonel
> George Arthur, Lieut. Governor, to mark that sad event,

and is placed on this spot by Major Thomas Ryan,
50th Regiment, one of the survivors of the occasion.

Skeleton Island

At 5 p.m. on 13 May 1835 the lookout aboard the barque
Neva, a convict ship travelling through Bass Strait on its way
to Melbourne, sighted a reef dead ahead. The master ordered
evasive action:

> The ship came head to the wind, and while in stays, struck and
> carried away her rudder—the wheel fell on deck, and the vessel
> being unmanageable, payed off before the wind. In a few minutes
> she took a reef on her larboard bow, and struck violently. A sea
> hove her broadside on, and bilged her—the next that followed,
> made a fair breach over her, and swept many of the unfortunate
> women overboard.

The 150 convict women on the stricken ship were being
transported to New South Wales from Cork. They left Ireland
in January with twenty-six crewmen, nine free women and
fifty-six children. After a long voyage via St Pauls Island rather
than the usual Cape of Good Hope, the transport was quickly
breaking up on a reef off King Island in Bass Strait, trying to
take the dangerous shortcut to Melbourne known as 'threading
the needle'. There was panic as passengers, crew and convicts
rushed the only two boats and two rafts:

> The pinnace was hove out, and the Captain, Surgeon, and several
> women got in, but before she could be shoved clear of the wreck,
> so many women rushed into her, that she sank alongside. The
> Captain and two others recovered the wreck. The long boat was
> then launched, into which most of the crew consigned themselves,
> but she had scarcely cleared the wreck, when a sea capsized her,
> and the whole number excepting the Captain and Chief Mate,
> met with a watery grave.

The two sailors managed to get back onto their vessel but she was disintegrating:

> She soon after separated in four parts, the deck leaving her top, and dividing formed two rafts. On one of these the Captain and several of the surviving women held fast; the first officer, with some others, clung to the other. They floated clear of the wreck, and the hapless people, after clinging to them for 8 hours, were drifted upon them into a sandy bay.
>
> The raft upon which was the first officer, being disengaged from the rigging and gear, went well in shore, and most of the people were saved from it. Those upon the Captain's raft were not so fortunate—a large portion of the vessel's foremast stuck through it, and occasioned it to ground, when about ¾ of a mile from it. A tremendous surf rolled upon the beach, which brake upon the raft, and swept from it every individual—the Captain, a seaman, and a woman gained the shore, the rest of this ill-fated little band, perished in the surf. Twenty-two persons in the whole reached the shore alive—seven of whom died the next day, either from over exertion, or injuries received in the melancholy struggle for life.

Only fifteen men and women were saved. They were lucky. They erected a tent from the remains of masts and sails washed ashore, along with few provisions. Living mainly on shellfish, they were found by the survivors of an earlier wreck on the other side of the island. This group had some hunting dogs and they were able to supplement the shellfish with wallaby.

On 15 July, most of the survivors of both wrecks were taken off the island by the owner of the *Tartar*. But three people searching for food on the other side of the island were left behind, two seamen and a convict woman named Margaret Drury. They were later taken off by a government boat and brought safely to Launceston Gaol, while officials decided whether the surviving convict women should stay in Van Diemen's Land or go on to their original destination.

Margaret Drury was still in Launceston Gaol in late November when she was charged with drunkenness. The authorities eventually decided that the surviving women of the *Neva* should serve out their time in Van Diemen's Land. In the meantime, romance had bloomed. Peter Robinson, one of the sailors left behind with Margaret on the island, applied for permission to marry her. They wed in January 1836 and, as usual with such marriages, the convict was assigned to her husband. But it did not go well.

A couple of months after the wedding, Margaret spent three weeks on bread and water for harbouring a convict woman who may have been trying to escape. The next February her husband brought a charge against her of drunkenness and indecent exposure. She spent six months in the Crime class, comprised of the most badly behaved convicts. After her release Margaret seems to have separated from Peter and lived on an island in Bass Strait. In July 1839 she received another six months for re-offending. During this sentence she again spent thirty days on bread and water in solitary confinement for disobeying orders. Despite her infractions, Margaret was freed in 1840 and settled back down with her husband. They had at least one child and later moved to Victoria.

It is thought that 224 people died in the wreck of the *Neva*, mostly female convicts and all the children. It is considered Tasmania's worst shipwreck and one of Australia's greatest maritime tragedies. Skeletons are still being found in the island. Seven turned up in 2010, inspiring Hobart psychologist Catherine Stringer to research the story and to create a unique memorial to the women and girls who died. She collected seaweed from the area, made it into paper and used that to fashion small dresses. The forty-two framed items in the collection are known as 'The Neva Reliquary'.

Other artists and writers have been drawn to the tragedy, their researches raising doubts about the official accounts. There are anomalies in the evidence given to the inquiry and it has been suggested that, with a large cargo of rum, some of the women and the crew were drunk when the *Neva* struck whichever obstruction destroyed her. There is also a possibility that some of the cargo was not lost, as stated, but salvaged and later sold. We will never know if these rumours were true and although the *Neva* story is still not widely known today, it has generated some folklore, including the suggestion that she was carrying 50,000 pounds in wages for the soldiers guarding convicts in Van Diemen's Land.

'A Government Jail Gang, Sydney, N.S. Wales'. Originally published in Views in
New South Wales and Van Diemens Land*, 1830.*

3
The Convict Underworld

The jury guilty found her for robbing a homeward bounder
And paid her passage out to Botany Bay

'Maggie May', street ballad

Wife for Sale

A 'disgraceful transaction' took place at the Hawkesbury River town of Windsor in 1811. Ralph Malkin, transported in 1801, put a rope around his wife and led her down the street seeking a buyer. He found one. Thomas Quire stumped up 16 pounds on the spot, plus a few yards of cloth to be delivered later.

While the better classes of society were outraged at such a 'gross violation of decency', wife-selling was a custom practised throughout Britain since at least the sixteenth century. And not only by the common folk. The 2nd Duke of Chandos is said to have purchased his second wife around 1740 and many recorded cases of the custom involve tradesmen and skilled men as the purveyors of their spouses. While the practice was not legal, it was commonly believed to be so and there was often a reluctance by magistrates to prosecute cases.

By the time Ralph Malkin decided to offer his wife to the highest bidder in Windsor, the custom was increasingly frowned on by public opinion. The writer of the letter in which the event is recorded used words like 'shameful' and 'contemptible' to describe the seller and the buyer of Mrs Malkin.

But all was not as it might seem to contemporary or modern sensibilities. For a wife-selling to proceed, the woman had to agree to be sold. Research on this custom indicates that in quite a few cases the women were sold to men who were already their lovers. It seems that wife-selling was a form of folk divorce at a time when the average person could not afford such proceedings, or even access the legal means to achieve that state.

Prices paid for wives exchanged by this process varied from a high of 100 pounds down to 3 farthings. There are even cases where wives were given away free or for a glass of beer. The price was not as important as the fact that the sale took place in public, usually a market, fair or public house. This ensured the presence of plenty of witnesses to validate the transaction. Popular participation and approval was an important element of the custom. There are reports of magistrates seeking to stop a wife sale being driven away by the crowd.

An occasional reason for sale was that the wife simply tired of her husband, as in the case of a wife sold in Wenlock Market, Shropshire, in 1830. When her husband showed signs of cold feet at the last minute, she reportedly flipped her apron in his face and said 'Let be yer rogue. I wull be sold. I wants a change'.

In the case of the Windsor event, Mrs Malkin (who is never named) was thought to be: 'so devoid of the feelings which are so justly deemed the most valuable in her sex, agreed to the base traffic, and went off with the purchaser, significantly hinting that she had no doubt that her new possessor would make her a better husband than the wretch she thus parted from.' Which was the long-winded nineteenth-century way of saying that she not only agreed to be sold but that she thought the new husband was a whole lot better than the old one.

While everyone involved in this transaction was seemingly perfectly happy with it, the local bench of magistrates investigated and determined that a breach of some law had taken place. And in any case, the three 'base wretches' involved quite readily admitted to their crime, if it was one. Ralph Malkin received fifty lashes and three months hard labour in irons. His wife—or ex-wife—was transported to the Coal River (Newcastle) for an indefinite period. There seems to be no record of any proceedings against Mrs Malkin's purchaser.

Convict Magic

Why were convicts secreting shirts, shoes and the odd dead cat in the walls and chimneys of colonial buildings?

This little-known folk practice has recently received some much-needed attention by researchers in Britain, America and Australia. The custom, which can also involve a variety of other everyday objects and implements, dates to the medieval era at least and there is also evidence that the Romans followed a similar practice during their occupation of Britain.

No official records document this seemingly odd activity but an ever-increasing number of finds suggests that it was once extremely common. To date, the largest Australian cache is in Tasmania. An early nineteenth-century house near Oatlands yielded thirty-eight boots and shoes concealed in voids and cavities. Other sites throughout Australia have harboured garments, religious items, animal bones, toys and mummified cats, as well as miscellaneous bottles, coins and cutlery. Even a few parasols have turned up.

The Moreton Bay Penal Station gave up its secret of a working boot when the commissariat building was being renovated in 1913. The remaining fragment suggests the wearer was possibly fifteen years old, or less, and was engaged in very hard labour. Other finds include convict shirts in Sydney's Hyde Park Barracks (now Sydney Living Museums) and Tasmania, as well as a convict jacket connected to Port Arthur.

The most widely accepted explanation for the careful placing of these everyday items is that they were concealed in buildings as protection from evil forces, for good luck and, as many of the items are associated with children, perhaps as a form of secret household memorial. While this may sound bizarre, in earlier eras it was widely believed that evil was somehow in the air and needed to be constantly warded off. The wearing of amulets and the casting of charms, spells and curses are old practices that reflect the same folk beliefs.

This magic, of course, was not peculiar to convicts. But convicts were mostly ordinary people whose opportunities to acquire book learning were usually non-existent or severely limited. In the void of the unexplainable and the feared, the ritual concealment of significant objects, frequently at the borders of buildings, may have been a way of protecting the inhabitants from whatever nastiness lurked outside, whether supernatural or real.

As well as the concealed objects, researchers have discovered magical symbols in old buildings of the convict era. These marks were traditionally made to avert evil, and may be scratched into stone or wood, usually around doors or windows. A common mark is the six-petalled hexafoil, or daisy wheel. One of these appears on the Norfolk Island gravestone of Michael Anderson, executed in 1834 for his part in the convict mutiny that year.

These practices have also been identified and researched in Britain and the United States. They were presumably taken from Britain to America and, later, to Australia by convicts and settlers who were English, Irish, Scots, Cornish and Welsh. They were never written down or apparently observed by the officials who were supposedly regulating the colonies, but they had powerful meanings for those who carried such venerable folk beliefs across the world to protect them in strange new lands.

Mrs Gravy's Husbands

In the English city of Chester one day in September 1825 'an elderly-looking woman' was brought before a local magistrate and the town clerk to answer a few questions. In those days there were no social security welfare payments and those without other means of support had to apply to the parish for relief. The interview began with the woman being asked her name:

'Well my name, your Honour's, a very ugly name—it's Kitty Gravy, (dropping a curtsey) I come from the Vale of Clwyd.'

Next, they wanted to know if the woman was married:

'Married! O yes; I are be married very often; I have had four husbands, and the last he is in Liverpool Infirmary with a broken leg, and his name's John Joachim Gravy; a very ugly name, isn't it your Worship?'

What His Worship replied, if anything, was not recorded but Mrs Gravy went on to tell the panel that she had been married at Botany Bay. They thought she meant a place in Chester near the canal, opposite Queen Street.

'Pooh, no: I mean Botany Bay—the real Botany Bay, 30 000 miles off, your Honour.'
    'And what took you there?'
    'Pon my word, they transported me for seven years for doing nothing—nothing at all; God knows what for, I can't tell. I never stole anything in my life.'

Kitty then put her hand into her 'sinister pocket' and drew out some papers. They turned out to include what purported to be a certificate from the governor-general of New South Wales dated twenty years earlier. On the back was a description of the 'fair complexion' of a much younger Kitty. When the clerk read it out, Kitty, 'looking very knowing, and with a shrug of her shoulders, exclaimed, "Aye, but it's withered now"'.

Kitty went on to explain that Mr Gravy, a German, had been a free settler in New South Wales, living at Woolloomooloo. It was there that she had, presumably, met and married him.

All this time, Kitty 'appeared to be in high glee'. So much so that she was rebuked for her levity by one of the aldermen. She replied:

> 'Thank your Honour, (curtseying), I'm much obliged: I paid 100 pounds for my passage home, and everyone loves poor Kitty. I'm all fair yea and nay, your Honours.'

It was then suggested by one of the interviewers that Kitty was, in fact, living with a Frenchman in Brighton 'but she repelled the charge indignantly' and went on to catalogue the history of her various husbands:

> 'My first husband was James Miller, and he was a Scotchman; Thomas Wilson was my next, and he was a Hollander in the Navy; my third husband John Grace, an Irishman, from the County of Wicklow; and my fourth was John Gravy, a German. So you see (said Mrs Kitty with all the naivety of an accomplished punster) that for my last two husbands I had Grease and Gravy!'

Of the four, Kitty reckoned the first had been 'worth them all'. When asked when she had first married, she replied: 'Eh! The Lord knows, it's a long while ago.' She told the panel that she had a daughter aged forty-six with six children, and it was eventually decided that Kitty Gravy must have been seventy-six years of age.

The innocent transport said she had arrived back in London two years earlier, where she had 'promptly been robbed of 170 pounds. Her fingers were decked with rings, some silver'. Whether the parish interviewers decided that Kitty was a deserving case for the Poor Books (the papers in her 'sinister pocket' included a number of receipts for relief she had already received from other parishes), we do not know. Her practised arts of flattering and cajoling the system to satisfy her needs, real or contrived, were certainly on display that day in Chester. They must have served her well in the penal system of New South Wales.

Special Treatment

It was early in December 1826 when Robert Newsham—described by the *Sydney Gazette* as 'the spouting Government servant of a gentle man at Windsor, but who resides at a Curry-jong [Kurrajong] farm'—was charged for harbouring and encouraging one Catherine Murphy. He then aggravated the offence by denying that she was concealed in the house.

Newsham, something of a poet, addressed the court in mock-Shakespearian style, obviously not taking the charges very seriously:

> May it please your Worships—thus I bow and plead
> I heard a noise of sorrow at the wicket
> Of our hospitable home, I listened!
> That my affections were estrang'd from rigid
> Duty, proudly I admit I paus'd awhile,
> 'Tis Juliet' said I. I trac'd, thro' crevice,
> With eager glance, her beauty dissolved was
> All rectitude of thought! her gown thrown loosely
> O'er her head and shoulders, screening a modest
> Figure from the vulgar gaze of man: I blush
> And own the rapture of my heart methought the
> Lisping of her faultering tongue a poignard
> Ent'ring my breast! so raised I my head, and
> With a gentle touch of thumb and finger, the
> Latch of door gave way 'Gracious urbanity!'
> Said Kitty Murphy: in she came. 'Give me a
> Drink of milk!'
> Tempus fugit. Up came John Welsh,
> And as Othello dark! but in his hand no
> Dirk! his eye the dagger! Alas! my conscience,
> Not my skin was pierc'd. When thus I said 'Your all
> Relenting wife has here reclin'd.' 'She has!' A
> Constable he sought; and Kitty Murphy fled
> The anger of her lord, leaving Robertus

To himself alone. 'This is the head and front
Of my offending.' Inclin'd to pity one,
Who fled for succour, may I your pity find.

The grandiloquent Newsham was discharged with a stern warning 'not to shelter the runagate wife of any man in future'.

But it seems that Catherine was also busy elsewhere in the area at that time:

John M'Namarra was detected in the brush wood upon Mr Howe's farm at the Curry-jong, by a constable, when in search of Kitty Murphy. The constable conceived a familiarity had taken place which was improper, and therefore lodged the man in custody. The man pleaded he was on his master's ground, and about his mister's business, and that he could not be bound for a runaway trollop not coming upon the estate.

M'Namarra was given a rap over the knuckles and discharged. Finally, Catherine herself was brought into court:

Catharine Murphy in her torn way, brought up to account for repeated drunkenness and other bad habits. To look upon this woman, the impression would be in her favour; to read the depositions taken in the case, the uncontrovertible facts adduced, and then say 'frailty thy name is woman!' would be mild, but to say, Catharine thou art a disgrace to thy sex, would be speaking fact. She had not long been married to a man holding a ticket of leave, who may be said to be close fingered and industrious. By her drunken habits she had become a pest in the neighbourhood, and her misconduct tended also to injure the reputation of her husband.

Catherine Murphy was sentenced to six months in the third class at the Parramatta Female Factory. This was the class supposedly reserved for women who had committed serious crimes but was also used to punish those considered wayward or wanton. Catherine would have passed her time at the factory breaking rocks and possibly suffering solitary confinement and having her head shaved.

Stitches in Time

Tiny specks of blood stain a long lost quilt, now carefully treasured in the National Gallery of Australia. Many unknown hands stitched the quilt as they voyaged to Tasmania aboard the transport *Rajah* in 1841. Some, perhaps most, were not skilled with the needle but they managed to design, cut and sew almost 3000 separate scraps of material into a bright and beautiful handiwork of flowers, birds, lozenges and other shapes. At the lower border of the quilt, cross-stitched in fine silk yarn, is the inscription:

> To the ladies of the convict ship committee, this quilt worked
> by the convicts of the ship Rajah during their voyage to Van
> Dieman's [*sic*] Land is presented as a testimony of the gratitude
> with which they remember their exertions for their welfare
> while in England and during their passage and also as a proof
> that they have not neglected the ladies [*sic*] kind admonitions of
> being industrious. June 1841.

The 'ladies of the convict ship committee' were led by the English Quaker reformer, Elizabeth Fry. Shocked by the appalling conditions of women and children in London's prisons, Elizabeth formed the forerunner of the British Ladies' Society for Promoting the Reformation of Female Prisoners in 1817. The women of this group provided convict women transported to Australia with: 'sewing supplies which included tape, ten yards of fabric, four balls of white cotton sewing thread, a ball each of black, red and blue thread, black wool, twenty-four hanks of coloured thread, a thimble, one hundred needles, threads, pins, scissors and two pounds of patchwork pieces (or almost ten metres of fabric).'

Aboard the *Rajah* was young Miss Kezia Hayter, bound for Van Diemen's Land at the recommendation of Elizabeth Fry to help Lady Franklin establish the Tasmanian Ladies' Society for the Reformation of Female Prisoners. It is thought that she encouraged the convicts to work on the quilt in accordance with Elizabeth Fry's belief in the redeeming and practical value of needlework for otherwise idle hands.

That may be so, though quilts were made by convict women on other ships, including the *Brother* in 1823. If Miss Hayter was the direct inspiration and overseer of the quilting, it is a little odd that the name of the society she represented is not directly mentioned in the dedicatory inscription. Perhaps the women of the *Rajah* organised themselves when provided with the opportunity and the resources?

Whatever its exact origins, the completed work was handed to Lady Franklin after the *Rajah* docked at Hobart on 19 July 1841. Within four years it was sent back to Elizabeth Fry in England, though it is thought that she had died before she could see it. The *Rajah* quilt then disappeared from view. It was not rediscovered until Janet Rea, researching her *Quilts of the British Isles,* stumbled across the *Rajah* quilt in a Scottish attic in 1987. It was acquired by the National Gallery of Australia in 1989. The quilt is so fragile that it is only usually displayed once a year.

The *Rajah* quilt is not the only convict needlework to have survived. Sarah Litherland (Leatherland) was only about sixteen years of age when she was convicted of stealing in Chester and transported for seven years to Port Jackson where she finally arrived in 1801 aboard the *Earl of Cornwallis.* Her trade was listed as lacemaking. By 1806 she had her ticket-of-leave and the following year married James Wall in Parramatta. Wedded bliss, it seems, was short-lived. In 1809 James Wall published a warning in the *Sydney Gazette* against allowing his wife any credit in his name. Where Sarah was or who, if anyone, she was with is not known. All we have is her quilt made in 1811, the earliest known hexagonal quilt in Australia.

No Common Criminal

Not much that Owen Suffolk said or wrote about himself was very reliable. He had the possibly unique distinction of having been exiled twice, once from Britain when transported to Australia and the second time when he was banished from Australia.

A thief, conman, swindler, bigamist, bushranger and adventurer, Suffolk even faked his own death. He was a criminal conjuror, adept at deceit, illusion and eluding capture. These nefarious abilities landed him in a transport to Melbourne at the age of only seventeen in 1847. On arriving at Geelong he was granted a conditional pardon.

It was not long before Suffolk was in trouble again. In 1848 he was sentenced to five years hard labour in a road gang for horse stealing. He spent two years on Cockatoo Island in Sydney Harbour where he endured, at different times, a total of seven weeks in solitary for relatively minor offences. Transferred to Pentridge Prison, Coburg at Christmas 1850, he escaped three months later using a forged document.

With two old accomplices, Suffolk robbed a mail coach, was caught, tried and sentenced to ten years, the first three in irons. Eventually moved to Melbourne Gaol, he became an informer and 'trusty' (a convict who guarded other prisoners), winning a ticket-of-leave after serving less than three years of the original sentence. Suffolk's literary publications and eloquence apparently encouraged Chief Justice Sir William à Beckett to declare that he was 'certainly no common criminal'. The chief justice presumably had something to do with the remarkable commutation of Suffolk's original sentence.

Even more remarkable was Suffolk's next move. He applied to join, and was accepted into, the police detective corps, working on the Victorian goldfields. His criminal investigation career was short-lived. Convicted of some forgery he had performed while in Melbourne Gaol, he was back inside by Christmas 1853. Again using his considerable writing talents, Suffolk petitioned the chief secretary so convincingly that he was granted remissions and he was out again on a ticket-of-leave in December 1857.

But, as ever, he was soon back to crime and was convicted of horse stealing in 1858 with a cumulative sentence of twelve years. He served less than nine of these years, mainly in Pentridge and on the hulk *Sacramento*. During this time he began writing his memoirs. He was given yet another ticket-of-leave in July 1866 and in September was aboard a ship bound for England with a free pardon.

Despite his crimes, and to some extent because of them, Owen Suffolk was a remarkable character. As well as educating himself from the proceeds of his youthful illicit activities, his experiences in many jails and long associations with the underworlds of London and the colonies gave him the ability to walk, talk and write on both sides of society. His autobiography, initially sold to the *Australasian* newspaper for 50 pounds, is full of racy information about thieves' language, or 'Cant', street life and surviving in the underbelly of his time, as in one of his less flowery poems celebrating one of many releases from jail:

> I'm out in the world once more,
> And I mean to run the rig,
> For I've learned from the prison lore
> That the pauper fares worse than the prig.
> I've shivered and starved in vain,
> And been honest for months in rag,
> So if I'm convicted again,
> I think it won't be on the vag.

That might have been the end of the story, but for Owen Suffolk's deep criminality. Once back in England, the eloquent exile from Australia quickly married a wealthy widow, and not for love. In 1868 he was tried for stealing and obtaining money by false pretences. He pleaded guilty and his appeal to the court was that he had care of his brother's nineteen-year-old daughter and her child. This time, though, Suffolk's silver tongue failed. The chief justice did not mince his words:

Don't try and impose on me. I know your career. You were married to a widow, obtained all her property, deserted her, pretended by a fake report inserted in a newspaper that you were drowned, went away with your brother's child, who cannot therefore be your wife (the prisoner here interrupting said, 'She is my wife, my lord.') Then, said his lordship, if you did marry her, you have added bigamy to your other offences, and I sentence you to a term of 15 years penal servitude.

Suffolk went to prison and seems never to have been heard of again. Unless the odd account appearing in an Australian newspaper a few months after his last trial can be believed. According to this report, Suffolk engineered a boating accident involving his niece/wife and managed to fake his own drowning: 'It was ultimately discovered that he escaped to America with his wife's moneys, and the proceeds of the sale of his wife's furniture, which he sold before he left England. By the latest advices he was enjoying himself in New York.'

The Flash

If you were a convict, you might know how to crack this code:

I pulled down a fan and a roll of snow. I starred the glaze and snammed 16 redge yacks. My joiner stalled. I took them to a swag chovey bloak and got 6 finnips and a cooter for the yacks. A cross cove who had his regulars lowr, a fly grabbed him. I am afraid he will blow it. He has been lagged for beaker hunting. Was a mushroom faker, has been on the steel for snamming a wedge sneezer so I must hoop it. Tell swag chovey bloke to christen the yacks quick.

It translates as:

I stole from a shop door a waistcoat and a web of Irish linen. I broke the corner of a window and got 16 gold watches. My fancy girl stood close by and screened me from observation. I took them to a person who buys stolen property who gave me 6 five-pound notes and a sovereign for the watches. A fellow thief who shared the money with me is taken by a policeman. I am afraid he will turn informer. He has been transported for stealing poultry. He used to travel about the country mending umbrellas and has been in prison for stealing a silver snuffbox. As I must run away, tell the person who bought the watches to get the names altered as soon as possible.

This is the flash language. This exchange took place between two transportees in Western Australia some time in the late 1850s or early 1860s. Most of the words and terms are unrecognisable, though *blow it*, meaning to make a mess of something, is still with us. As well there are many other flash terms that passed into the general vocabulary of Australian folk speech, like *gadding* (usually *padding*) *the hoof* for going about barefoot or poorly dressed and *prad* for a horse, a term also heard in British fairground speech. Some surprisingly modern-sounding terms were also in use then, such as *screw* for copulation and *well-hung* to describe an impressive set of male genitalia.

The flash language was a form of the secret underworld language spoken by British criminals since at least the early seventeenth century. Often called 'Cant', it was spoken by those with professional criminal backgrounds who were *bellowsed*, or transported to New South Wales and later to Van Diemen's Land and Western Australia. It consisted of technical terms for the equipment, methods and targets of criminals, as well as the colloquial speech of the urban working classes.

The earliest record of flash speech in Australia was made by Watkin Tench, a captain in the marines who saw convict society at first-hand from its earliest days. He had very definite views on the flash or '*Kiddy*' (after *kid,* the flash term for deceive or mislead, still playfully in use as 'just *kidding*' and similar uses) language spoken by many of the transportees. Tench tells us that it was often necessary to have an interpreter in court to translate the evidence of witnesses and accused who spoke in a language that 'has many dialects. The sly dexterity of the pickpocket; the brutal ferocity of the footpad; the more elevated career of the highwayman; and the deadly purpose of the midnight ruffian, is each strictly appropriate in the terms which distinguish and characterize it'.

A number of Cant dictionaries were compiled by scholars and educated rakes. One of the most colourful was a man said to have been the only convict transported to New South Wales on three separate occasions. His name was James Hardy Vaux, a ne'er-do-well thief, forger, conman and bigamist.[15] He was also an excellent writer whose autobiography is one of the earliest Australian literary works. In it Vaux tells of his adventurous, if mostly nefarious, life.

After a chequered early career that included an apprenticeship to a draper, office work and a spell in the navy, Vaux was transported for the first time in 1801. His skills got him clerical work but after forging the governor's initials on a food order he was sent to a road gang. His way with words got him back in favour and he returned to England as tutor to the governor's children and those of the Reverend Samuel Marsden, also returning home. But his sentence expired during the voyage and he was then forced to join the crew sailing the ship.

Back in England Vaux married a London prostitute, returned to crime and was sent back to Sydney in 1810 after a death sentence was commuted to transportation for life. After once again abusing the trust given him through official appointments, he was soon in trouble and was sent to Newcastle. Here, he compiled his famous dictionary of convict-speak. He tried to escape but was recaptured, flogged and sent back to Newcastle in 1814.

In 1818, Vaux married an Irish convict woman, Frances Sharkey, at Newcastle and by the following year he was back in Sydney working as a clerk. He received a conditional pardon in 1820, converted to Roman Catholicism in 1823 and bigamously married another Irish convict, Eleanor Batman, in 1827.

But the settled life was not for James Hardy Vaux. In 1829 he absconded and made his way to Ireland. He changed his name to James Young and under this alias was convicted of passing forged notes in 1830. This time he was transported for seven years. But he was so well known in Sydney that he was recognised on arrival and his original life sentence reinstated. He was then sent to Port Macquarie on the mid-north coast of New South Wales where he remained until 1837 when he returned to Sydney. Two years later he was charged with assaulting an eight- or nine-year-old girl and sentenced to two years imprisonment. Although Governor Gipps wished to have Vaux serve out his life sentence, he was released in 1841.

And that was the last known sighting of an extraordinary adventurer, criminal and social observer who first recorded the speech of convicts like himself. It would not be until the formation of official police forces in the eighteenth century that a more serious, practical interest in the flash language arose. The police, often recruited from different social groups than those they were to pursue, found the language of the underworld incomprehensible. The necessity to understand this 'code' led to intense collection and study of underworld slang and its codification into police publications and individual notebooks.

In the State Archives of New South Wales is a book kept by an anonymous Sydney policeman from 1841–45 titled 'Registry of Flash Men', a list of criminals known to the compiler and an indispensable tool of the detective's trade, then as now. It included terms like the plural form *flash mob*—a criminal confederacy, which could also refer to a pimp. As it still did back in England, the term was also applied to dandified dressing. A *hocus pocus man* or one who practised *leger de main* prospered by *humbugging* or deceiving others, probably using tricks that were later adapted by magicians. Illegal spirits were sold *on the sly* and illegal goods were redistributed through a *fence* or *fence master*. Implements of the burglary trade were frequently mentioned, including *skeleton keys*, *screws* and the small iron bar known as a *jemmy*. Nicknames were frequent and colourful, including

Scrammy Bill, *Gypsy Cooper* and *Hopping Saul*. One flash man was reportedly '*doing the stallion* to Mrs W'.

The Cant language included such terms as the already-mentioned *lag*, though this referred not only to a convict but also to the sentence received and the act of transportation. To be *lagged* meant being caught and convicted. A *lagging* was a prison sentence. An *old lag* was one who had served out his or her transportation and who might be either free or perhaps serving another. Ned Kelly was still using the term as part of everyday speech in the late 1870s when he referred to being 'lagged innocent' in his Jerilderie Letter, meaning being unjustly imprisoned.

Other flash terms noted in the colony by Vaux included: *bash*—to beat; *blow the gaff*—reveal a secret; *dollop*—a large quantity of anything; *frisk*—to search; *school*—a number of persons met together to gamble; and *snitch*—to betray. Quite a number of these very early convict terms are still part of Australian English, including *turn it up*, to cause or create a *stink*, and to be *nuts* on someone or something, while a *put up affair* has become a *put up job*. The terms *swag, snow-dropper* and *bloke* are derived from Shelta, the language of travellers. Some Cant words well-established in the underworld speech of late eighteenth-century England are also still in use, including *blubber* to cry, *boose* for drinking alcohol and *boosy* for drinking too much of it.

Skin Deep

Many male and female convicts marked their bodies with tattoos. Unlike modern tattoo inks and machines, the markings were often pushed into their skins with needles using the black soot from lamps. Tattoos could simply register personal and family details, such as significant dates of trials or embarking on a transport, but they often also told a deeper story.

Twenty-one-year-old groom Laban Stone married Sarah Burgess in 1828. They had a son named John before Laban was convicted of 'robbing a person' and transported aboard the *Eleanor* in 1831. On Laban's left arm were the initials: LS and SS, followed by a sun, the initials JS, a tree, then the date 1831 and finally a heart. The message of connection, family and constancy was clearly expressed in these few signs, with the sun being a phonetic equivalent for 'son', the tree standing for strength and endurance, and the heart, of course, for love.

Some tattoos were simply obscene. Others might be heavily symbolic. A butcher from Cork named Denis Barrett sported Masonic emblems, a harp and the words 'Erin Go Bragh' (Ireland forever) on his left arm, suggesting strong nationalist belief. An anchor was a frequent symbol and not necessarily connected with sailors. An anchor by itself meant hope and commitment. A man carrying an anchor meant that the bearer was carrying hope, while a man near an upside-down anchor would be someone who had lost hope. An anchor and a crucifix could signify a hope for salvation. Many symbols had more or less common meanings and so could be assembled in a kind of crude code to form meaningful statements.

Popular symbols that made up this more or less secret language included hearts, fish, mermaids, bugles, ships, flags, darts, crowns, rings and crosses. One symbol that appeared frequently on convict skins was a flowerpot. What it might be meant to convey is not known, unless it was meant to convey the idea of confinement, a plant trapped in a pot struggling towards the sun, a crude allegory for the life of a convict?

Tattoos also made it easy for the authorities to identify convicts and careful records were made of the markings that appeared on individuals when they arrived in jail, boarded a transport or stepped ashore. It was not unusual for convicts without previous tattoos to be tattooed aboard ship on their way to exile. When a convict absconded, the authorities simply went to their register and advertised the tattoos carried by their quarry. A female escapee from Launceston was easily described by a distinctive set of markings, including the anchor, heart and darts on her right arm, together with the letters 'TRHCDAWT'.

On her left arm appeared: 'JJ', a heart with dart, 'I love John Johnson' and 'JBWH'.

Convicts sometimes wore tattoos with clandestine or obscure meaning. Ann Corbett carried on her right arm the letters 'MWW HMDBDSDSDEDBDLDSDR'. It is thought that lines as lengthy as these might be a cypher for biblical or political messages. Only those in the know would understand their import. The more personal and perhaps subversive the meaning of the tattoo, the more likely it was to be on a part of the body not usually visible. Some male convicts were tattooed on their penis.

A system of dots was also in use. In 1839, Elizabeth Williams was recorded as having five blue dots on the back of her hand, arranged as the four corners of a square with the fifth dot in the centre. Historians are not sure of the meaning of this or other arrangements of dots, but as it usually appeared on a visible part of the body, it was presumably meant to communicate a meaning. It is thought that the five dots represent the four corners of a cell, with the convict imprisoned in the centre. This arrangement was still being seen in the 1870s on convicts transported to Western Australia.

Whatever the motivations of convicts to mark their skin with painful images, messages and codes, the practice was significant for them, personally and within the convict world. Tattoos were a way to defy a system that literally owned their bodies for the term of their confinement and even after. It was common practice for executed felons to be examined for biological signs of criminality, including head size and shape, as well as any other bodily indications of nefarious propensity. Heads might be removed from bodies and death masks made in pursuit of this pseudo-science known as 'phrenology'. Only after these indignities would the body be released for burial and then often in unhallowed and unmarked ground.

The Jury Guilty Found Her

Tempting drunken sailors to sin and robbing them before or after the promised sexual favours was a steady source of income for prostitutes. It was a method employed in every sailortown and usually ended up with no consequences for the woman, who was long gone by the time the matelot woke up and found his pockets empty. But sometimes the woman was unlucky, like the heroine of this mildly ribald ballad. Its rollicking chorus has made it a favourite in one version or another, possibly since the 1830s. This one hails from the English seaport town of Liverpool and is much less bawdy than many versions sung at sea.

Oh come along all you sailor boys and listen to my plea
And when I am finished you'll agree
I was a goddamned fool in the port of Liverpool
The first time that I came home from sea.
We was paid off at The Hove from a port called Sydney Cove
And two pound ten a month was all my pay
Oh I started drinking gin and was neatly taken in
By a little girl they all called Maggie May.

Chorus
Oh Maggie, Maggie May they have taken you away
To slave upon that cold Van Diemen shore
Oh you robbed so many sailors and dosed so many whalers
You'll never cruise down Lime Street any more

'Twas a damned unlucky day when I first met Maggie May
She was cruising up and down old Canning Place
Oh she had a figure fine as a warship of the line
And me being a sailor I gave chase.
In the morning when I woke stiff and sore and stoney broke
No trousers, coat, or waistcoat could I find
The landlady said 'Sir I can tell you where they are
They'll be down in Stanley's hock-shop number nine'.

To the bobby on his beat at the corner of the street
To him I went to him I told my tale

He asked me as if in doubt 'Does your mother know you're out?'
But agreed the lady ought to be in jail.
To the hock-shop I did go but no trousers there I spied
So the bobbies came and took the girl away
The jury guilty found her for robbing a homeward bounder
And paid her passage out to Botany Bay.

Flogging prisoners, Tasmania. Pencil drawing from the 1850s by James Reid Scott, an explorer and politician who was part of a committee tasked with inquiring into Port Arthur and which recommended its closure and the redistribution of prisoners to other sites.

4
The System

Excessive tyranny each day prevails

'The Convict's Lament', c. 1830

The Hulks

When transportation to the American colonies ceased after the War of Independence, British jails soon overflowed with prisoners. This situation rapidly created a new form of penal horror.

To ease the pressure on prisons, the government allowed old ships to be anchored in the River Thames (and at Portsmouth, Plymouth and elsewhere) to hold prisoners awaiting banishment across the seas. These 'hulks' were supposed to be a stop-gap measure, but like many temporary arrangements they became permanent. Many prisoners would endure years aboard the rotting hulks, doing hard labour on the docks and in the naval arsenals, until they were finally transported.

The *Dunkirk* hulk moored at Plymouth was notorious even before the First Fleet set sail. Prisoners were sometimes without any clothing and in 1784 the abuse of the female convicts by the marine guards led to a 'Code of Orders' that was supposed to protect the women. Mary Bryant, later an almost successful escapee from Port Jackson, was held on the *Dunkirk* before sailing with the First Fleet. She became pregnant on the hulk.

Another infamous hulk was the *Leviathan*, moored at Portsmouth in the 1820s. She had seen better days when convict James Tucker (alias Rosenberg) was held there in 1826:

> This vessel was an ancient '74 [1774] which, after a gallant career in carrying the flag of England over the wide oceans of the navigable world, had come at last to be used for the humiliating service of housing convicts awaiting transportation over those seas. She was stripped and denuded of all that makes for a ship's vanity. Two masts remained to serve as clothes props, and on her deck stood a landward conceived shed which seemed to deride the shreds of dignity which even a hulk retains.

Conditions aboard the *Leviathan* were better for the convicts, but were designed to strip them of whatever dignity they retained and subdue them into the system. When taken aboard, the prisoners were paraded and mustered on the quarter-deck:

> Their prison irons were then removed and handed over to the jail authorities, who departed as the convicts were taken to the forecastle. There every man was forced to strip and take a thorough bath, after which each was handed out an outfit consisting of coarse grey jacket, waistcoat and trousers, a round-crowned, broad-brimmed felt hat, and a pair of heavily nailed shoes. The hulk's barber then got to work shaving and cropping the polls of every mother's son.

Fettered and shaven prisoners were then marched below 'where they were greeted with roars of ironic welcome from the convicts already incarcerated there'. The lower deck was a prison of wooden cells, each one holding between fifteen and twenty convicts.

Edward Lilburn, a pipe-maker from Lincoln, described his experience of the Woolwich hulks around 1840:

I was led to think there was something dreadful in the punishment I had to undergo, but my heart sank within me on my arrival here, for almost the first thing I saw was a gang of my fellow unfortunates, chained together working like horses. I was completely horror-struck, but every hour serves now to increase my misery; I was taken to the Blacksmith and had my irons, the badge of infamy and degradation rivetted upon me, my name being registered and my person described in the books of the ship; I was taken to my berth, and here new sufferings presented themselves, as the great arrival of convicts had crowded the ship so much, that three of us have but one bed, and this the oldest prisoner claims as his own; our berth is so small, we have no room to lie at length, thus I passed a wretched, a half sleepless night; at the dawn of day we have a wretched breakfast of skilley, in which I cannot partake, and though suffering dreadfully from hunger I subsist wholly on my dinner, at present live on one meal a day!!

Lilburn had the cheek to complain but was told that he was 'brought here for punishment and that I must submit to my fate'. He finished with a warning:

Whether I speak of my present situation in reference to daily labour, daily food, or the rigorous severity of the system under which I suffer, I can say, if there is a Hell on earth, it is a convict-ship. Let every inhabitant of the City and County of Lincoln know the Horrors of Transportation, that they may keep in the path of virtue, and happily avoid a life like mine of indescribable misery.

After 1844 convicts were transported directly from the prisons where they were held rather than being sent first to the hulks. But the old ships still operated as jails. By the time the journalists and social reformers Stephen Mayhew and John Binny visited the Thames hulks in the early 1860s, public outcry against the conditions and horrors of the hulks as described by Lilburn and others had already brought about reforms to the system, allegedly at least. Mayhew described conditions aboard the hospital ship *Unité* just a few years earlier in 1849:

> The great majority of the patients were infested with vermin; and their persons, in many instances, particularly their feet, begrimed with dirt. No regular supply of body-linen had been issued; so much so, that many men had been five weeks without a change; and all record had been lost of the time when the blankets had been washed; and the number of sheets was so insufficient, that the expedient had been resorted to of only a single sheet at a time, to save appearances. Neither towels nor combs were provided for the prisoners' use, and the unwholesome odour from the imperfect and neglected state of the water-closets was almost insupportable. On the admission of new cases into the hospital, patients were directed to leave their beds and go into hammocks, and the new cases were turned into the vacated beds, without changing the sheets.

Mayhew and Binny interviewed one of the warders who served under the previous 'hulk regime' and reported, 'He well remembers seeing the shirts of the prisoners, when hung out upon the rigging, so black with vermin that the linen positively appeared to have been sprinkled over with pepper'. By the time this survey was conducted, there was regular medical treatment available on the hulks, a lending library and education for the man who could not read or barely so. The food provided had also improved dramatically, at least according to the regulations:

> We now followed the chief warder below, to see the men at breakfast. 'Are the messes all right?' he called out as he reached the wards.
>
> 'Keep silence there! keep silence!' shouted the officer on duty.
>
> The men were all ranged at their tables with a tin can full of cocoa before them, and a piece of dry bread beside them, the messmen having just poured out the cocoa from the huge tin

vessel in which he received it from the cooks; and the men then proceed to eat their breakfast in silence, the munching of the dry bread by the hundreds of jaws being the only sound heard.

Each prisoner received a breakfast of 12 ounces of bread and a pint of cocoa. For dinner they were allowed 6 ounces of meat, 1 pound of potatoes and 9 ounces of bread; for supper, 1 pint of gruel with 6 ounces of bread. Wednesdays, Mondays, and Fridays were 'Soup Days', when the dinner was 1 pint of soup, 5 ounces of meat, 1 pound of potatoes, and 9 ounces of bread.

For punishment, the luckless convict was reduced to 1 pound of bread and water each day. Those on the sick list were fed 1 pint of gruel and 9 ounces of bread for breakfast, dinner and supper. But an enhanced diet was given to the very sick, as the master of the hospital told the journalists:

> The man so bad, up-stairs, has 2 eggs, 2 pints of arrowroot and milk, 12 ounces of bread, 1 ounce of butter, 6 ounces of wine, 1 ounce of brandy, 2 oranges, and a sago pudding daily. Another man here is on half a sheep's head, 1 pint of arrowroot and milk, 4 ounces of bread, 1 ounce of butter, 1 pint extra of tea, and 2 ounces of wine daily.

The trades and occupations of convicts in the 1850s included carpenters, blacksmiths, painters, sawyers, coopers, rope makers, bookbinders, shoemakers, tailors, washers and cooks, even the occasional doctor. Convicts received 'gratuities' for the quality of their work and general conduct. They wore badges which indicated their duration of sentence, period in the hulks and levels of good or bad behaviour, updated monthly, the details entered into the 'character book' of each hulk.

Mayhew also described the work performed by those whose labour was now at the control of the state:

> The work of the hulk convicts is chiefly labourers' work, such as loading and unloading vessels, moving timber and other

materials, and stores, cleaning out ships, &c., at the dockyard; whilst at the royal arsenal the prisoners are employed at jobs of a similar description, with the addition of cleaning guns and shot, and excavating ground for the engineer department.

Mayhew saw the working parties in the dockyards:

Only the strongest men are selected for the coal-gang, invalids being put to stone-breaking. In the dockyard there are still military sentries attached to each gang of prisoners. We glanced at the parties working, amid the confusion of the dockyard, carrying coals, near the gigantic ribs of a skeleton ship, stacking timber, or drawing carts, like beasts of burden. Now we came upon a labouring party, near a freshly pitched gun-boat, deserted by the free labourers, who had struck for wages, and saw the well-known prison brown of the men carrying timber from the saw-mills. Here the officer called—as at the arsenal—'All right, sir!' Then there were parties testing chain cables, amid the most deafening hammering. It is hard, very hard, labour the men are performing.

Most closely regulated of all was convict time. From the moment of waking—5.30 a.m. in summer, half an hour later in winter—the prisoners of the hulks ate, worked, washed and prayed to a strict timetable. All were in their beds or hammocks at 9 p.m.

This strictly regulated world of servitude, obedience and hard labour was theoretically replicated in Western Australia, by then the only colony taking Britain's transported convicts. But the reality of frontier servitude had always been very different.

The Dogline

At Port Arthur even the animals guarding the convicts were in chains. Located on the Tasman Peninsula, the narrow isthmus known as Eaglehawk Neck was the only means of land access and from 1832 was guarded by a detachment of military guards and a pack of up to eighteen dogs. The animals were housed in wooden barrels or small huts and kept chained under the care of a convict handler.

The artist and author Harden S. Melville described the beasts in the late 1830s: 'There were the black, the white, the brindle, the grey and the grisly, the rough and smooth, the crop-eared and lop-eared, the gaunt and the grim. Every four-footed black-fanged individual among them would have taken first prize in his own class for ugliness and ferocity at any show.'

Twenty years later the commandant, James Boyd, noted, 'Many of them have not been off the chain for years and are consequently very savage.'

This 'dogline', as the network of guard posts, lights, dogs and semaphore stations was known, was part of a broader security and signalling system connecting the Port Arthur establishment with Hobart. The messaging stations were tall land-bound masts with moveable arms that could send messages by sight quite efficiently with the use of an elaborate code book for reading the position of the arms. If it was dark or cloudy, warnings that an escape was in progress were made by firing two musket shots in rapid succession. The arrangement worked very well, most of the time. Its existence, combined with the belief fostered by the authorities that the surrounding waters were full of sharks, deterred all but the most desperate and resourceful escapees. The annals of Port Arthur are full of stories about escape attempts that ended in death or recapture and flogging.

In 1859 fourteen prisoners made a rush for liberty through the tower entry. It was a cloudy evening and the semaphore could not be used, so a written note was rushed by a runner up to Eaglehawk Neck. Most of the escapees were soon recaptured. Another fabled attempt was made by a man named Billy Hunt who wriggled inside a kangaroo skin and tried to hop to freedom. The guards, eager for a kangaroo stew, began taking pot shots and he was forced to reveal himself.

But there were some successes. The most celebrated was that of Martin Cash, Lawrence Kavanagh and George Jones. Cash, the longest lived and most celebrated of the Van Diemen's Land bushrangers, and his accomplices encountered the dogline in 1842 but decided to try a different way:

At the dusk of the evening we came in sight of Eagle Hawk Neck, when we could see the line literally swarming with constables and prisoners. I here enjoined my mates to preserve the strictest silence, observing that one false move might frustrate what we had already achieved, and pointed to the place we should cross. We took a circuitous route through the scrub until we arrived at a spot where we could scan the line for about a mile on either side. We lay here for the next three hours, and having made a fair division of the bread which remained, trusted that it would be the last we should ever eat on Tasman's Peninsula. On finishing our temperate meal, we started on the forlorn hope, moving as silently as possible, as the slightest noise might bring half-a-dozen constables about our ears. The most perilous part of the adventure was in crossing the road, where constables might be lying in ambush in the scrub which lined the opposite side and up to the water edge.

They reached the water, then silently followed each other into the ocean:

It was then blowing fresh, and the night being very dark, I lost sight of my mates; on getting to the centre, the waves broke clean over me, at the same time carrying away my clothes, which I had fastened in a bundle on my head, and thinking it useless to try and recover it, owing to the darkness of the night, I continued my course. As I could neither hear or see my companions, the horrible idea occurred to me that they had been eaten by the sharks, a similar circumstance having previously taken place about a mile lower down the gut, I being the first who ever attempted to cross so convenient to the 'Neck.' I by-and-by touched the bottom, and remained for some time standing, expecting to hear or see my mates. I had not remained more than five minutes, however, when I could distinctly hear them conversing, and apparently coming to where I stood. Jones now said to Kavanagh, 'Martin's drowned', on hearing which I sprang on to the bank, and observed that I was worth half-a-dozen people in that situation. We were obliged to indulge in a laugh when we found that we were all situated alike with regard to clothing, as my mates as well as myself had lost theirs on the passage.

This escape around the dogline made Cash a hero among the convicts. He and his companions proved that it was possible to get free of the supposedly inescapable prison. When Port Arthur was closed in the late 1870s, so was the dogline. It would be nice to think that the dogs were then freed from their chains.

Canaries and Magpies

The traditional picture we have of convict garb is of broad arrows printed on a nondescript grey sack. The arrow was certainly used on convict uniforms but there were many variations, some of them quite odd.

At first, the lack of supplies in the colony that would become Sydney meant that convicts dressed in whatever they could find, augmented if they were quick, with a set of basic work clothes known as 'slops'. By Macquarie's term of governorship, extra trousers were distributed for those relatively few convicts attending church to appear respectable. In 1819, newly landed male convicts received 'a suit consisting of a coarse woollen jacket and waistcoat of yellow or grey cloth, a pair of Duck [canvas] or cloth trousers, a pair of worsted stockings, a pair of shoes, two cotton or linen shirts, a neck handkerchief and a woollen cap'.

The cabbage tree hat was the favoured headgear. It was quickly and cheaply made by those with the skills and was comfortable to wear, protecting heads and faces from the harsh sunlight. These locally produced items were preferred to the official issue models, which were uncomfortable and unsuitable for the climate.

Re-offending New South Wales convicts were punished by being made to wear parti-coloured suits, one side black or grey and the other side yellow, usually with broad arrows on the trousers. They were known as 'canary men', or 'canaries', the absurdity of their appearance intended to add some public shaming to their other punishment.

A similar striking garb known as a 'magpie' was worn by Van Diemen's Land male convicts. The outside seam of the trousers was held together by twelve buttons to allow them to be pulled on over chains. According to one recollection, from convict W. Gates, 'The suits were all of a size, or with but a slight variation, and were distributed to us as we stood in rank, without regard to their fitting our person. The consequence was, we got all sorts of fits'.

Even clothing could provide an opportunity for some convict resistance. When the cosy grey coats that had previously been issued in Van Diemen's Land were replaced with the magpie suits, the prisoners knew that they were being made to wear these clothes 'for the purpose of humbling and mortifying our spirits'. Taking their cue from the absurdity of their 'motley, grotesque' garments, the convicts 'danced about and sung songs as though we were in a real perfect delirium of joy,' Gates said. 'A few cursed and swore like madmen possessed' and 'succeeded in some measure in making our masters ashamed of the matter'.

Yet these elaborate costumes were in demand, not only as prison and work clothing but also as money spinners for imprisoned entrepreneurs. Two sets of these cloths could be taken apart and re-stitched into one grey and one yellow set. Using dye made from bush plants and some stolen military scarlet, the rebirthed suit could be unloaded on soldiers. The buttons were used as currency within the prison system.

Female prisoners were dressed in various ways, or not.

Many of the First Fleet women transported aboard the *Lady Penrhyn* arrived half naked, their rotting and worn-out clothing hanging from their emaciated bodies. Women clothed themselves as best they could in the early years of the colony. From 1804 most were sent to the Parramatta Female Factory where they were employed in sewing, spinning or domestic tasks.

By 1826 all new entrants to the factory were made to bathe and inspected by the matron. Their clothing was a blue or brown gown, jacket and a coarse white apron. The beginnings of the class system had by now been introduced and women of the first, most obedient class, were given a white cap, a long dress frilled with muslin, a red calico jacket, two checked handkerchiefs, petticoats, aprons, shifts, stockings, shoes and a straw bonnet. These were for wearing mainly on Sunday. For weekdays they had calico caps, a serge petticoat, a jacket and one apron.

From 1829 the inmates of female factories generally received a cotton petticoat, jacket, two aprons, two shifts, two caps, two handkerchiefs, two pairs of stockings and one 'common straw bonnet of strong texture'. Women were usually graded into three classes—first class were good prisoners, second class relatively minor re-offenders and third class were the frequent troublemakers. The second class was made to wear a large yellow letter 'C' on the jacket sleeve, while third class inmates wore it on the right sleeve and on the back of their jacket and petticoat. Women in the third, most refractory class, could be made to work breaking stones on the roads.

There is more than a touch of irony around elaborate clothing provided to female and male convicts. In those days clothes were worth a great deal of money and it was not uncommon for poor people to dress in rags, or sometimes less. The largest class of crime for which convicts were transported involved stealing clothes, or the materials for making them. Now, no matter how strangely, they were dressed at the expense of the state.

Obtaining a Wife

Even well into the 1830s it was possible, and often necessary, for men to marry convict women. There was a decidedly unromantic bureaucratic process available for this necessity at the Parramatta Female Factory:

> A man desiring a wife, and being unable to suit himself elsewhere, proceeds to the female factory at Parramatta, and presents himself to the matron and master of that institution. The certificate of a clergyman or magistrate is produced; setting forth that the applicant is a proper person to have a wife given to him, from the many under charge of the matron. The applicant is then introduced into a room of the building, whilst the matron proceeds to the class department, that contains the best behaved of the female convicts. Notice is here given that a wife is required, and such as are willing to be married step forward, and are marshaled in batches into the presence of the would-be Benedict. On they pass, the man speaking to individuals as they attract his attention, inquiring their age, etc. till some one is met with who pleases his taste, and possesses the required perfections.

The couple then negotiated. Had the other been married? How many sheep, cattle and how much land did the man possess? If both parties then agreed, 'the matron is acquainted with the fact, and a day named for the marriage'.

> All the time, this lady is present, and has frequently to witness strange and ludicrous scenes; scores of females passing for review, between whose personal and other claims, the applicant balances his mind, sometimes leaving it to the matron to decide whom he shall take. When this knotty point is settled, the authorities are informed of the fact; the clergy of the place publishes the banns, and if no impediment intervenes, on the appointed day, the parties are married; the woman leaving the factory, and returning to a state of freedom in the colony, during good conduct.

Marriage through this process was frequent and was reportedly how thousands of lonely men obtained wives. It was also a way out of the severe restrictions of the female factory for the women. Through much of its early history, Australia was plagued by a serious disparity between the number of males and the number of marriageable females. This early solution to the problem was an effective matchmaking arrangement long before speed dating and internet partnering agencies.

Marriage between female convicts who were assigned servants and ex-convicts could be more complicated, if we can believe James Mudie, a notorious flogging magistrate. In his heavily biased *The Felonry of New South Wales*, Mudie described an event he claimed was true.

A young man who had recently completed his sentence established himself on 30 acres along with a few pigs. He was a long way up the country but set out for the Parramatta Female Factory to find himself a wife. On the way he stopped at Mudie's extensive property, known as 'Castle Forbes', and was told by one of the female servants that the master had a young convict woman named Marianne as an assignee. If she was willing, he could get a good wife without going any further. 'Celebs', as Mudie contemptuously calls the young man, asked to see Marianne. The couple hit it off and agreed to proceed. But first they had to obtain the consent of the master. Marianne volunteered to make the request.

Entering the breakfast room of her master with an unusually engaging aspect, and having made her obeisance in her best style, the following dialogue ensued:

> *Marianne.—I wish to ask you a favour, your honour.*
> *His Honour.—Why, Marianne, you have no great reason to expect particular indulgence; but what is it?*
> *Marianne (curtsying and looking still more interesting).—I hope your honour will allow me to get married.*
> *His Honour.—Married! To whom?*
> *Marianne (rather embarrassed).—To a young man, your honour.*

His Honour.—To a young man! What is he?

Marianne (her embarrassment increasing).—I really don't know!

His Honour.—What is his name?

Marianne.—I can't tell.

His Honour.—Where does he live?

Marianne.—I don't know, your honour.

His Honour.—You don't know his name, nor what he is, nor where he lives! Pray how long have you known him?

Marianne (her confusion by no means over).—Really, to tell your honour the truth, I never saw him till just now. Mrs. Parsons sent for me to speak to him; and so we agreed to be married, if your honour will give us leave. It's a good chance for me. Do, your honour, give me leave!

His Honour.—Love at first sight, eh! Send the young man here.

At this point in the story, Marianne leaves and the young man enters to face his interrogation:

His Honour.—Well, young man, I am told you wish to marry Marianne, one of my convict servants.

Celebs (grinning).—That's as you please, your honour.

His Honour.—As I please—Why, have you observed the situation the young woman is in? (Marianne being 'in the way ladies wish to be who love their lords.')

Celebs (grinning broadly).—Why, your honour, as to that, you know, in a country like this, where women are scarce, a man shouldn't be too 'greedy!' I'm told the young woman's very sober, and that's the main chance with me. If I go to the factory, why, your honour knows I might get one in the same way without knowing it, and that, you know, might be cause of words hereafter, and she might be a drunken vagabond besides! As to the pickaninny, if it should happen to be a boy, you know, your honour, it will soon be useful, and do to look after the pigs.

After checking on the young man's situation and whether or not he was free, permission was graciously given for the union.

The author claimed only to be giving 'some idea of the nature of rustic courtship in New South Wales, and of the relations towards each other of the two sexes of the felon population, as well as of the charming prospect attendant upon a convict wedding'. Mudie concluded with the observation that this was 'a state of things difficult to be conceived in England, and certainly unparalleled in any civilized country'.

The Convict's Lament

Perhaps the most powerful of all the convict ballads, this song is also known as 'Moreton Bay' and 'The Exile's Lament'. It is generally thought to have been written by Francis MacNamara, or 'Frank the Poet'. If he did not compose it, he certainly knew it, as did many other old lags.

Many 'places of condemnation' are mentioned, but the main action centres on the death of Captain Logan, commandant of the Moreton Bay penal station around fourteen kilometres north of present-day Brisbane from 1826 to 1830. Logan was hated by the convicts as a cruel flogger. He was killed by Aborigines in October 1830 and when his body was brought back to the settlement, those who had suffered under his floggings 'manifested insane joy at the news of his murder, and sang and hoorayed all night, in defiance of the warders'. And someone wrote this song.

> One Sunday morning as I went walking,
> By Brisbane waters I chanced to stray,
> I heard a convict his fate bewailing,
> As on the sunny river bank I lay.
> I am a native from Erin's island,
> But banished now from my native shore,
> They stole me from my aged parents,
> And from the maiden I do adore.
> I've been a prisoner at Port Macquarie,
> At Norfolk Island and Emu Plains,

At Castle Hill and at cursed Toongabbie,
At all these settlements I've been in chains.
But of all places of condemnation,
And penal stations in New South Wales,
To Moreton Bay I have found no equal,
Excessive tyranny each day prevails.
For three long years I was beastly treated,
And heavy irons on my legs I wore,
My back from flogging was lacerated,
And oft times painted with my crimson gore.
And many a man from downright starvation,
Lies mouldering now underneath the clay,
And Captain Logan he had us mangled,
All at the triangles of Moreton Bay.
Like the Egyptians and ancient Hebrews,
We were oppressed under Logan's yoke,
Till a native black lying there in ambush,
Did deal this tyrant his mortal stroke.
My fellow prisoners be exhilarated,
That all such monsters such a death may find,
And when from bondage we are liberated,
Our former sufferings will fade from mind.

'The Convict's Lament' lived on among convicts and ex-convicts. It was passed on by word of mouth and in handwritten form to the free-born generations in the prison system. Ned Kelly knew it well, as did his family, probably learned from their father 'Red' Kelly who was imprisoned in Port Arthur at the same time as Frank the Poet. The song is still sung today, its stark poetry and fine tune evoking the evils of the convict system.

The Ironed Gang

Work. Who did it, when, where and how? These questions were at the base of Governor Phillip's plans for a colony. He assumed that the convicts would work to provide the necessities of survival and to build the infrastructure to develop the economy and the society. But they had other ideas.

Convicts did not want to work. Nor did the circumstances of their imprisonment in the early years of New South Wales encourage it. Basically roaming around almost as free men and women, they came and went as they pleased, malingered, hid their tools and generally bludged, as we might say today. The only way the colonial authorities could make transportees perform the work required was to force them to it.

Men were formed into labour gangs to carry out specific tasks, such as erecting public buildings and making roads. A road gang or 'party' was the most common form of labour unit and the easiest. Men received reasonable rations, could cook for themselves, even if it was, as described by one ex-convict, 'often a straggling piece of meat with about as much fat on it as would grease the eye of a packing needle'. They also had the small but coveted freedom to find their own beds for the night, even if only 'a sheet of ti-tree bark'.[14] Men who committed crimes in the colony, or were considered troublemakers, or simply fell foul of an official could end up in an ironed gang.

The road gangs were paradise compared with the hard labour of the ironed gang. The work was just as arduous, usually involving hacking through bush and mountain rock, but was carried out in full chains. The exact nature and weight of the chains varied from place to place and over time, but they usually consisted of an iron collar around each ankle joined by a chain. Weighing perhaps 6 kilograms, these irons were placed on each man by a blacksmith. The collars cut into the prisoners' flesh, making exertion even more painful. At night the gang was fettered together, usually to a convenient tree, and each individual had to make himself as comfortable as possible. Rations were generally poorer and those who attempted to escape might have extra chains loaded on them during the day and the night. Even if they went to hospital, chains might not be removed from a sick convict and, it was said, some were even buried in their shackles.

In 1835 an educated convict in the ninth year of his sentence wrote home to a 'Gentleman in London'. The writer of the letter said that discipline had become increasingly severe during his time in the colony:

Every year has increased its severity since I have been here.—Disobedience or insolence is fifty lashes—first offence not less than twenty-five; second offence seventy-five or a hundred lashes; third offence twelve months to an Iron Gang. Absconding—or Taking-the-Bush, as we term it—is fifty lashes first offence; second time TWELVE Months to an IRON GANG, and increased each offence.

The letter went on to describe the iron gangs:

Nothing is more dreaded by the men than Iron Gangs; as when their sentence is expired they have all that time spent in irons to serve again, as every sentence is now in addition to the original sentence. If a man is nearly due for his ticket of leave, and is flogged, he is put back for a certain time, unless for theft, and then he forfeits every indulgence. If an iron-gang man has served any number of years in the country, he must begin again; he is the same as a new hand; he has to wait the whole term of years before he receives any indulgence.

The work of the iron gangs was hard and long: 'The delinquents are employed in forming new roads, by cutting through mountains, blasting rocks, cutting the trees up by the roots, felling and burning off.' Their labour was made more difficult by the appalling conditions:

They are attended by a Military Guard, night and day, to prevent escape; wear Irons upon both legs, and at night are locked up in small wooden houses, containing about a dozen sleeping places; escape is impossible; otherwise they live in huts surrounded by high paling, called stockades; they are never allowed after labour to come without the stockade under penalty of being shot; so complete is the confinement, that not half-a-dozen have escaped within the last two or three years; they labour from one hour after sunrise until eleven o'clock, then two hours to dinner and work until night; no supper. The triangles are constantly at hand to tie up any man neglecting work, or insolent. Iron-Gang Men [are] not allowed to be hut keepers, cooks, or other occupation, as such is considered an indulgence; nothing but hard labour. Not one day of liberty will he ever enjoy; he will have all his sentences in addition to his original sentence to again.

The letter concluded:

Picture to yourself this hot climate, the labour and the ration, and judge for yourself if there is laxity of discipline. It is to places such as I have described, that the Judges now sentence men from the English bar—poor wretches! did they know their fate, be assured, respected Sir, it had been well for them had they never been born.

The Innocence of Thomas Drewery

In September 1847, Thomas Drewery, a chemist from Kingston Upon Hull, arrived at Geelong aboard the *Joseph Somes* under the Pentonville scheme. Convicted of stealing a horse and gig in York, he was given a seven-year sentence, all the while maintaining his innocence. He had already spent eighteen months in prison when he embarked for Australia to serve the rest of his time.

On arrival at Geelong, Thomas received his conditional pardon and was immediately offered a job but turned it down as he considered the salary 'beneath my notice'. He travelled to Melbourne where he soon found suitable employment as the business manager of the Melbourne Medical Hall.

Continuing to protest his innocence through a solicitor and the efforts of his wife and friends in England, Thomas had an almost unbelievable stroke of good luck. A convict in Van

Diemen's Land confessed to the crime for which Thomas was suffering. Convicted of an unrelated crime and transported to Van Diemen's Land, John Webster heard about Thomas Drewery's plight and had an attack of conscience. He provided a full and convincing confession to the religious instructor. This was forwarded to the British government but they would not believe it.

Agitation by Drewery's solicitor, local newspapers and parliamentarians eventually brought his case to public attention and he secured a pardon in January 1848, together with passage home paid by the government. His troubles were over. He wrote home to his wife, Elizabeth:

> My dear, here are fresh proofs of your husband's innocence . . . I hope you will give this publicity in the press, to erase any stigma my position may have brought upon you and friends.
>
> The only compensation I ask is that government will send you and my dear children out to me respectably, not as the wife of a convict.

Elizabeth and the five children had been in severe financial difficulties during Thomas's imprisonment. They also suffered the social stigma of Thomas's fall from middle-class respectability to convict. Thomas decided that his prospects, and those of his family, would be better in Australia. He requested that Elizabeth and the children have their passage paid by the government, rather than his returning home. Correspondence on this and the payment of the passage dragged on but, eventually, the system delivered a result: Thomas was reunited with his wife and children in Australia.

He went on to run a number of businesses in Melbourne, and to serve as a local councillor. By 1858 the family was in Dunolly, Victoria, where Thomas returned to his old profession. He died soon after and his widow and children moved to Castlemaine, once again struggling to get by. Elizabeth died in 1864, leaving two children in the care of the eldest daughter,

Ann. Two others were taken into care under the *Neglected and Criminal Children's Act*.

Thomas Drewery was one of a significant number of convicts transported to what would be the colony of Victoria and to its capital city, Melbourne. There was an early attempt to establish a penal settlement in what was then the 'Port Phillip district of New South Wales' from October 1803. The settlement was to be near present-day Sorrento. As well as officers, officials and marines, about three hundred convicts were landed, together with the wives and children of a few. Unable to find suitable land and clashing with the local Wathaurung people, the colony was progressively abandoned between January and May 1804. The party returned to Hobart, except for a few convicts who had escaped. One of these, William Buckley, became famous for spending the next thirty-two years living with the Wathaurung.

Victoria did not become a colony until 1851, but between 1844 and 1849 almost 2000 convicts were transported to the Port Phillip district. Mostly sent from Pentonville, Millbank and Parkhurst prisons, these boys and men like Thomas Drewery were officially described as 'exiles' rather than convicts. Although they had been convicted of crime, the idea of the scheme was to provide skilled labour. Quickly dubbed the 'Pentonvillains' by the unhappy free residents of Melbourne and Geelong, these transports were welcomed by farmers desperate for labour. The Pentonvillains were granted conditional pardons as soon as they arrived, allowing them to work and live freely as long as they did not return to Britain until their full sentences had been served.

Whether as a colony in its own right or as the Port Phillip district of New South Wales, Victoria also experienced convictism through work parties sent down from Sydney or across from Hobart in the earlier days of settlement and, of course, through the arrival of ex-convicts in search of work, gold or land. Ned Kelly's father, 'Red', was one of many ex-convicts who made lives for themselves and their families in the 'cabbage patch', as Victoria became known to many in New South Wales.

'The Most Absurd, Prodigal, and Impracticable Vision'

Criticism of convict transportation began early. In 1791 an irritated correspondent calling himself 'Tumbledown' wrote to the editor of a popular journal on 'the new settlement at Botany Bay'. Like most people who had never visited New South Wales, Tumbledown was under the misapprehension that the colony was established at Botany Bay. His argument, such as it was, revolved around the costs of the system and what the writer considered the impracticality of settlement:

> Previous to the 18th of March, 1791, 2,029 convicts have been shipped from England for New South Wales. We also learned that prior to the 9th of February, in the same year, the expences [*sic*] of this establishment amounted to £374,000. Besides this sum, we are told of contingencies that cannot as yet be stated! It was for the Minister's credit to make his project appear as wise as possible, and to suppress a part of this enormous expenditure to serve the temporary purposes of debate. We may safely affirm that the contingencies referred to make no trifling sum. Six additional months fall now to be added to the account, and it is more reasonable to compute the total expences up to this date at £600,000.

Tumbledown calculated that each convict cost 300 pounds sterling. If the average duration of transportation was twenty years, that worked out at 1500 pounds sterling per transportee. A great deal of money. And not only that, what about the cost of developing the country?

> It may indeed be acknowledged that before that time the country will be reduced to a state of cultivation. But a circumstance mentioned by the Governor sufficiently shows the great distance and uncertainty of such a prospect. It cost him and a party five days to penetrate thirty miles into the desert, and the fatigues they underwent during this journey were excessive.

And there was more fearful expense:

> In the same paper you tell us that 1,831 additional convicts were then under orders for shipping. It is impossible to estimate with any degree of certainty what may be the annual expence [*sic*] of this colony before the end of the Eighteenth Century. By a very moderate computation we may suppose that before ten years elapse the colony will receive at least 10,000 additional convicts; and it is but fair to compute that of the whole number by that time transported 10,000 will then be alive, and maintained at the expence of Government. Now, if each of these gentry cost us only £30 a year, the whole annual expence would amount to £300,000. At the end of twenty years it may rise to double that sum. Will the British nation, with its eyes open, walk into such a gulf?
>
> We must infer that the Botany Bay scheme is the most absurd, prodigal, and impracticable vision that ever intoxicated the mind of man. Transportation to North America was in comparison but a ride before breakfast. New South Wales is at the distance of 6,000 or 8,000 leagues, if we include the windings and turnings necessary on the passage. In the former country the price of a felon when landed was sufficient to pay the expence of his voyage; but in the latter, a convict, the moment we set him on shore, is enrolled with many other right honourable gentlemen in the respectable and useful band of national pensioners. There is not an old woman in the three kingdoms who could not have suggested a better plan.

Tumbledown finished his diatribe with the likelihood that the convicts would cut the throats of their jailers and sail away.

There would be many more letters of this kind to many more newspaper and magazine editors in the coming years. People also sent in accounts of corruption and exploitation that the system made possible, even easy, for those so inclined. In November 1791 the master, chief mate and some soldiers and sailors aboard the transport *Neptune* came before a court at Guildhall in England. The accusation was that:

They sailed from Portsmouth in the Neptune, Capt. Donald Thrale [Trail], and William Ellington, chief mate, having on board 500 male convicts, bound to Botany Bay; that during the voyage the captain and chief mate used the unhappy convicts ill by keeping them short in their allowance, allowing only half a pint of water a day; that 171 died on their voyage; that many of them were so hungry that they have seen several take the chews of tobacco from the mouths of the men that lay dead on the deck; that numbers used to steal the provisions from the hogs; and that when they arrived at Botany Bay the captain and mate stopped the boxes of many, took the things out, and threw the boxes overboard; that, soon after they had landed the convicts, the captain and mate opened a warehouse on the island, and sold the provisions which the unhappy convicts ought to have had; that, when landed, they were swarming with vermin; and that, on account of the above persons making complaint, they had been very ill-treated by the captain and mate, and had wounds to shew of the ill-treatment they had received.

Eventually, agitation at home and discontent in the growing colony would bring about a powerful anti-transportation lobby demanding, and receiving, inquiries into the system and its ills. These agitations culminated in two large public protests when the transport *Hashemey* reached Sydney in 1849. Speeches were made, including by Henry Parkes, later to be known as 'the father of Federation', and dire warnings declared.

But feelings had been running high for some years. The number of free settlers and emancipists eclipsed the number of convicts by the 1830s, by which time opposition to transportation had become a major political issue in New South Wales and was making waves back in Britain. In the public debates of the time, poems were often used to argue political points of view. One of these referred to Australia being 'overwhelm'd by streams corrupt, impure/The refuse and the vile', 'Britain's filth and scum', debauched daughters, debased sons and sodomy. Colonists, the males at least, were exhorted in the final verse to righteous rebellion:

Arise, then, Freemen—rise:—
Secure your liberty,
Ne'er rest till Transportation dies;
And Australia's isle be FREE.

If freedom can be equated with the abolition of a harsh
system of penal transportation, then the existing colonies of
Australia received theirs from the day transportation was officially ended.

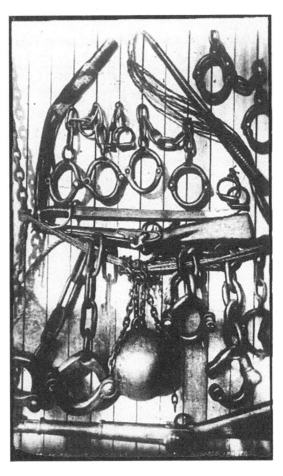

*'Relics of Convict Discipline', J.W. Beattie, Hobart
c.1900. Includes leg-irons, a ball and chain,
handcuffs, whips (one of them a cat-o'-nine-
tails), rifles and a sword.*

5
Pain and Suffering

Lay by your dog and snare to you I do speak plain,
If you knew the hardship we endure you ne'er would
poach again

'Van Diemen's Land'

Hanged Three Times

Joseph Samuels was one of a gang of Sydney housebreakers who stole a desk containing money and other valuables from the home of Mary Breeze in August 1803. The constable who caught up with the thieves the next day was beaten to death. Who actually struck the fatal blows was unclear but Samuels was blamed, tried and sentenced to hang for the crime together with another member of the gang named Hardwicke.

The men were brought to the place of execution around 9.30 on the morning of September 26 where they were comforted by their respective ministers, Hardwicke a Christian and Samuels a Jew. According to the *Sydney Gazette*, 'Both prisoners conducted themselves with becoming decency'. Samuels made a statement in which he threw the blame for the murder on another gang member, Isaac Simmon(d)s. Samuels delivered his accusation 'with mildness and composure' though it was loudly contradicted by Simmonds who was in the crowd, having been brought there to witness the execution of his accomplices. Samuels gained the sympathy of the spectators, most of whom had already decided that Simmonds was the real murderer—'He had escaped condemnation at the Trial, yet he had been arraigned in the Court of Public Opinion.'

At that time hangings were performed from a wooden cart. Samuels and Hardwicke stepped up to suffer their final punishments. All was ready when the provost marshall in charge of the proceedings unexpectedly announced a reprieve for Hardwicke. 'Samuels devoted the last awful minute allowed him to the most earnest and fervent prayer.' A signal was given and the cart was driven away from under him. As the condemned man's body dropped through the air, the rope parted and he was flattened face down onto the ground.

Another rope was fetched. The cart was driven back under the gallows, men lifted Samuels up while the new rope was placed around his neck. 'He was again launched off' but this time the rope simply unwound, leaving Samuels only half suspended between life and death.

Some in the shocked crowd declared that 'the invisible hand of Providence' was at work after hearing the story Samuels told earlier. But the sentence had to proceed. Samuels was unconscious by now so some men lifted him up on their shoulders while the hangman fitted a third noose. Then they gently lowered the body. But as soon as the weight of the body pulled on the rope, it snapped, dropping Samuels immobile to the earth.

This was too much even for the provost marshall. He hastened to the governor and rushed back with a reprieve 'which diffused gladness throughout every heart'. Samuels was still insensible: 'By what he had endured his reasonable faculties were totally impaired' and when he recovered consciousness, 'he uttered many incoherences, and was alone ignorant of what had passed'.

A belated examination was now made of the rope used in the execution. One end was fastened to a wooden beam and seven weights of 56 pounds each were hung from it. One strand gave way, then a second. But the third strand held the full weight placed upon it and should have been easily adequate to hang a man.

As usual with newspaper reports of the time, miscreants were admonished to learn the lessons of their deeds and, in this case, of a remarkable reprieve. But perhaps Samuels' experience addled his mind. He returned to a life of crime and was then sent to Newcastle. Here, he joined a group of prisoners attempting to escape by boat on April Fool's Day 1806. He was never seen again.

The Lash

The 'cat' or whip used for floggings usually consisted of a wooden handle, around 2 feet in length. To this were attached nine or five whipcord lashes, each one knotted six or seven times. There were many variations on the basic design, including the model with lead balls used at Norfolk Island, but they were all fearsomely effective. An experienced superintendent stated that he had never overseen a flogging where the victim's skin was not cut by the fourth blow.

How many lashes could a body bear? In the 1790s three men found guilty of attempted pack rape were sentenced to severe flogging. They had been tried earlier but no verdict had been reached, encouraging others to carry out this crime against women. At the second trial a verdict was reached and as a deterrent to others, the ringleader was sentenced to receive 1000 lashes and his two accomplices 800 each.

Even when the number of lashes was smaller, floggings—always public events—were grisly displays of penal theatre designed to humiliate, wound and demonstrate the complete powerlessness of the victim. An Irish convict named Holt described a flogging he witnessed at Toongabbie when a man named Maurice Fitzgerald was sentenced to receive 300 lashes:

> The unfortunate man had his arms extended round a tree, his two wrists tied with cords, and his breast pressed closely to the tree,

so that flinching from the blow was out of the question, for it was impossible for him to stir. Father Harold was ordered to put his hand against the tree by the hands of the prisoner, and the two men were appointed to flog, namely, Richard Rice, a left-handed man, and John Johnston, from Sydney, who was right-handed. They stood on each side of Fitzgerald; and I never saw two threshers in a barn move their flails with more regularity than these two man-killers did, unmoved by pity, and rather enjoying their employment than otherwise . . .

The very first blows made the blood spout from Fitzgerald's shoulders; and I felt so disgusted and horrified that I turned my face away from the cruel sight . . . I have witnessed many horrible scenes, but this was the most appalling sight I have ever seen. The day was windy, and I protest, that although I was at least fifteen yards to leeward from the sufferers, the blood, skin and flesh blew in my face as the executioners shook it off from their cats.

As required by law, Doctor Mason occasionally checked Fitzgerald's pulse as the flogging continued:

I never shall forget this humane doctor as he smiled and said 'Go on; this man will tire you both before he fails.' Through the whole three hundred, Fitzgerald 'never uttered a groan.' His only words were 'Flog me fair! do not strike me on the neck.' After he was cut down, two constables took the bloody convict by the arms to help him into the cart. He told them 'Let my arms go' and elbowed each one in the stomach, dropping them to the ground then climbing into the cart without help from anyone. Doctor Mason observed admiringly 'That man has strength enough to bear two hundred more.'

Another prisoner, Paddy Galvin, was then tied to the tree. Around twenty years of age, Galvin was to receive 300 lashes, apparently for taking part in a planned convict rising. He was given the first 100 lashes around the shoulders and 'was cut to the bone between the shoulder blades, which were both bare'. The doctor told the floggers to work lower down, 'which reduced his flesh to such a jelly that the doctor ordered him to have the remaining hundred on the calves of his legs'. Galvin 'never even whimpered or flinched'. Asked where the pikes for the rising were hidden, he said he did not know and would not tell if he did, refusing to give up his companions to the gallows: 'You may hang me . . . if you like; but you shall have no music out of my mouth to make others dance upon nothing.'

By the time Governor Bourke arrived in the colony in 1831, severe floggings had become the knee-jerk response to almost any infraction of the rules, no matter how minor. Horrified by this practice, Bourke tried to have it moderated. But the landholders resisted, appealing directly to the King to continue flogging at will. In response to this, Bourke collected nearly two hundred typical flogging sentences to show the barbarity and terrible randomness of flagellation. These included:

John Green, absconding, 50 lashes. Appeared to suffer much, bled freely, and fainted after punishment.

William Truelove, neglect of duty, 50 lashes. Bled greatly and appeared faint and exhausted.

Calvin Sampson, stealing, 50 lashes. Blood flowed at the 4th; the convict cried out at the 18th and continued crying for succeeding lashes; his skin was terribly torn and blood flowed during the whole of the punishment. This man groaned much and prayed while suffering punishment; and afterwards declared that he would never come again. I am of opinion that he was sufficiently punished at the 25th lash.

Daniel Alone, neglecting duty, 50 lashes. Cried loudly at the second and repeated his cries at every lash; at the 12th blood flowed largely, and the prisoner seemed to suffer intense agony. I am of opinion that this man was sufficiently punished at the 25th lash.

John Denning, neglect of duty, 25 lashes. Cried out at the first lash and continued crying loudly. At the 6th the flesh was lacerated considerably, blood was drawn but did not flow. It is my decided opinion he was sufficiently punished, and that the number of lashes this man suffered had as much effect as 100 lashes would have had.

William Robinson, drunk and making away with part of his dress, 50 lashes. He cried out at every lash; the skin was lacerated at the 12th; the blood appeared at the 20th; the man suffered intense agony. Twenty lashes would have been an ample warning to him.

David Hennan, stolen property in possession, 50 lashes. Had been flogged 12 months before; he flinched much, but neither cried nor spoke.

William Smith, insolent, &c., 50 lashes. This man was flogged two years ago; he flinched much throughout the punishment; the skin was lacerated and the blood appeared at the 24th lash; he seemed to suffer great pain, evinced by his suppressed groans; blood ran at the 45th lash; he cried out 'domino!' when finished.

Bourke's efforts to reign in the excesses of the system were opposed by those who benefitted from it the most. The larger landholders and magistrates—often the same men—worked to undermine his authority, both in the colony and in England. While his reforms had limited effect, these and his other activities contributed to the abolition of transportation to New South Wales from 1840.

The Treadmill

In an early example of hooning, young John Wilson was charged with 'having furiously driven a chaise in the streets of Sydney, to the great danger of the passengers and moreover, with wantonly and cruelly beating the horse he was driving in the said chaise and himself in a great state of intoxication'.

The year was 1825, Wilson was one of the 'larky-boys', usually the sons of one or more convict parents. This group and their descendants would later be known more generally as the 'larrikins' of Sydney and Melbourne.

Wilson was sentenced to ten days on the treadmill. Recently installed at Carters' Barracks, the treadmill was a penal adaptation of corn grinding machinery, with the usual motive power of water or a horse being replaced by a luckless wrongdoer. 'The punishment consists of perpetual climbing without being able to idle away a single moment. It is a kind of hard labour to which everyone would have a natural dislike and yet, such as everyone can perform without previous instruction.'

The machine was all the rage in Britain, where it had been developed a few years earlier by a Mr Cubitt of Ipswich, and first installed at Brixton jail. The punishment was strongly criticised by reformers and was the subject of a satirical popular song suggesting that the treadmill was unlikely to stop crime:

This Brixton mill's a fearful ill,
And he who brought the Bill in,
Is threatened by the *cribbing* coves,
That he shall have a *milling*.
They say he shew'd a simple pate,
To think of felons mending:
As every *step* which here they take,
They're still in crime *ascending*.

A visiting French naval officer described Sydney's version of the new-fangled punishment:

It is a large wheel whose horizontal blades are wide enough to allow a certain number of men to position themselves, each next to the other, on the outside . . . Holding on to a wooden crossbar that is separate from the wheel and attached at the height of the chin, they climb without stopping from one blade to the next . . . this labour continues for forty minutes without a break; the men rest for twenty minutes, then they start up again, and so on, for the whole day . . . It was difficult to imagine an activity more boring and tiring at the same time, by it's [*sic*] monotony and the care necessary to apply to this task, in the fear of missing the blade and having your legs mutilated.

While human labour was used to power mills in the colony, the penal treadmill was designed specially to allow no respite for those trudging out their sentence. Two of the devices—known to the convicts as 'cockchafers'—were erected at Carters' Barracks, one for ten men and a larger one for fifteen. The government charged farmers to have the convicts grind their grain into flour, so it was seen not only as a deterrent to crime but also as a revenue raiser. It was also an excruciating form of torture, producing cramps, sore joints, broken bones and internal injury. Men also lost body weight drastically. Some lost their lives.

Seventeen-year-old David Simpson had behaved himself well on the voyage to Australia aboard the transport *Minerva*. On arrival he was sent to Carters' Barracks with other juveniles. It was not long before his behaviour changed and for a misdemeanour he committed he was sentenced to walk the treadmill. Now eighteen, David lost some small change into the workings of the machine. He continued his shift until dinner time and then, as reported in *The Australian* in 1825, 'made an attempt to recover his money by thrusting his arm underneath; at this moment the men on the opposite side commenced working the wheel, and his head was drawn in, and crushed to a mummy. Life was extinct before he could be extricated'.

The Iron Collar

In November 1826 Privates Patrick Thompson and Joseph Sudds of the 57th Regiment stole a length of calico from a Sydney shop. They were so dissatisfied with their soldiering lives that they committed the crime with the deliberate aim of being tried and sentenced to transportation. At the end of the five- or even seven-year terms that each would serve, the men would be dismissed from the army and free. Whatever failures of intellect or unpleasant experience drove the men to this extreme, the consequences of their actions were far greater than they could possibly have imagined.

The plot went as planned and the two men received a

sentence of transportation. But then Governor Ralph Darling stepped in. He was a strict disciplinarian and incensed at the actions of the soldiers. He amended the sentence to hard labour in chains of a very special kind. What happened then is told by Patrick Thompson while held aboard the *Phoenix* prison hulk:

> After I received my sentence, I was taken to the gaol; I remained in the gaol till the 22d November. The gaoler then came for me, and Joseph Sudds, who had been convicted the same day with me for the same crime, and had received a similar sentence; I and Sudds were conducted by Wilson, the under gaoler, and two constables, to the military barracks. The clothing which I and Sudds had on were taken off, and a suit of regimentals put on each of us; we were then taken to the parade ground, and the regimentals taken off us, and a suit of yellow cloth put on each of us, and a General Order read to us by Brigade-Major Gilman, by the order of his Excellency Gov. Darling.

After the order was read, each man was fitted with chains:

> The irons consisted of a collar, which went round each of our necks, and chains were fastened to the collar on each side of the shoulder, and reached from thence to the basil [iron bar], which was placed about three inches from each ancle. There was a piece of iron which projected from the collar before and behind, about eight inches at each place. The projecting irons would not allow me to stretch myself at full length on my back. I could sleep on my back by contracting any legs. I could not lie at full length on either side, without contracting my legs. I could not stand upright with the irons on. The basil of the irons would not slip up my legs, and the chains were too short to allow me to stand upright. I was never measured for the irons, and Sudds' collar was too small for his neck, and the basils for his legs, which were swollen.

Dressed now in the 'canary' yellow convict garb and in their ill-fitting irons, the men were escorted from the barracks:

[We] were drummed out of the regiment, the rogue's march being played after us by two or three drummers and fifers. We were not drummed out in the usual way, which is, to put a rope about the neck, cut off the facings, and place a piece of paper on the back, with a description of the offence which the party may have committed. Instead of this, we had the chains on and the yellow clothing. We were drummed to the barrack gate, and from thence conducted to the gaol by constables and soldiers, with their usual arms.

The chains were already cutting into the men's ankles by the time they reached their cells:

I believe that Sudds could lie at full length with his irons, either on his back or sides. Sudds did not complain of the irons being too short for him; but he complained that the collar was too tight for his neck, and the basil too tight for his legs. I do not know that his neck was swollen beyond its ordinary size; he was naturally a thick-necked man; but I do know that his ancles were swollen after his return to the gaol; I think the swelling of his ancles arose from the marching; I heard of his having had a swelling in his legs about six or seven days before the chains were put on him. The collar put on Sudds, was so small, that it would not admit anything to be between it and the neck but a cotton handkerchief; the collar was so small, that Sudds would not allow it to be turned round, so as to allow him to lay upon his back, saying, 'that it would hurt him if it was stirred.'

Sudds complained of illness and his condition became worse and worse. At one point he said, 'They had put him in them irons until they had killed him'. He was taken to hospital but eventually died. His condition pre-existed the trial and was diagnosed as 'dropsy', though Thompson, who had served with him for some years, had never heard him mention it. The surviving prisoner was taken in irons to Penrith and then to 'No. 1 iron gang road party, on Lapstone hill, being the first hill of the range of Blue Mountains'. He was immediately put to work:

> At three o'clock the same day I was taken out to work with the gang, and remained at work there about eight days, having my irons on all the time. At the end of eight days I became unable to work; it was very hot weather; and the heat of the collar used to become intolerable, and compelled me to sit down frequently, in order to hold it with my hands off my neck. On these occasions the overseer of the gang would come up to me, and order me to return to my work. I told him that I could not, and would not; that he might take me to gaol, where I could get a rest from work, and the heat of the sun. He ordered me to gaol accordingly.

Thompson was moved to a gang at nearby Emu Plains, sometimes in irons, sometimes not. He became too ill to work though the doctor ordered him sent back to the ironed gang. He refused and was tried but remanded at the governor's pleasure. By now he was convinced that his treatment was illegal and his case was becoming a political issue in the colony, and beyond. He contracted dysentery and almost died but recovered sufficiently to be taken back to Sydney and then imprisoned in the *Phoenix* hulk as a public political controversy raged.

The governor then had Thompson transported to the notoriously harsh penal settlement at Moreton Bay, where he again refused to work. He was flogged several times but eventually pardoned and returned to Sydney. But his ordeal was not yet over. Darling now commanded Thompson to return to his regiment and resume his military duties. Thompson refused, saying he had already 'been drummed out of the Regiment, and punished for his faults, and he would not do duty'. Now the governor banished Thompson to England, a tactical mistake as his case and the controversy about it in faraway Sydney soon came to the attention of the House of Commons. This confirmed that Darling's action in countermanding the court's original sentence of transportation was illegal and fuelled the local controversy. Despite this, Darling survived his term as governor with his reputation intact. He sailed home from Sydney in October 1831.

Forty years later Marcus Clarke, author of the convict classic *For the Term of His Natural Life*, wrote about the incident in his book *Old Tales of a Young Country*. He finished his account of the peculiarly vindictive case with a plea: 'If some official in Sydney Gaol will turn up the records for 1826, he may solve the mystery of poor Thompson's fate.'

Whipping Boy

The boy was a troublemaker, no doubt about it. His 'master', a Mr Thompson, charged him in Sydney with absconding in October 1830. William Turner had escaped from his position as an assigned servant and turned himself in to the authorities, claiming ill treatment. Thompson claimed that he treated the boy only with kindness. This was contradicted by Turner who said his back was 'cut almost to pieces from the number of lashes he had received' and offered to remove his shirt and display the evidence.

At this point the magistrates consulted the records of Turner's assignment. In the period from March 1829 to the present, he had been punished twelve times:

1st. 10 days to the tread-mill—2d. 50 lashes 3d. 36 lashes—4th. 25 lashes—5th. 25 lashes—6th. 50 lashes—7th. admonished and discharged—8th. 7 days to the tread-mill—9th. 14 do. do.—10th. 20 do. do.—11th. 7 do. do—12th. 3 months to an iron gang.

That litany of pain worked out to 186 lashes, fifty-nine days on the treadmill—often feared more than a flogging—and thirty days in an iron gang.

Turner then gave evidence that the extent of his bad treatment made him fear he might do something with serious consequences. In return, his master threatened to send him to Newcastle where he did not own a farm and where Turner probably feared he would be forced to work in the dreaded coalmines.

By now, the magistrates seem to have made up their minds about the rights and wrongs of this case. They asked Thompson if he was willing to give Turner back to the custody of the government. 'By no means' was his response.

The magistrates then delivered their decision. Considering the numerous times Thompson had dragged the boy before the courts 'frequently on very frivolous charges', they would recommend the governor to revoke Turner's assignment to Thompson. While they awaited the governor's decision, William Turner would be taken out of his master's custody and lodged in the 'barracks'. 'Very proper', concluded the editor of the newspaper reporting this rare convict triumph over the barbarities the system all too often fostered.

But the sufferings of this whipping boy may not have been over. The 'barracks' to which the magistrates sent him was almost certainly the institution for juvenile convicts known as Carters' Barracks, where boys were supposed to receive some basic education, moral instruction and trade training. Edward Scandrake was one of the unhappy inmates:

> Edward Scandrake, feigning sickness, 25 lashes. He received 50 lashes last Monday week, but was never flogged before; his breech was sore from the last punishment; blood came at the first stroke; he screamed dreadfully at every lash, blood streaming from the old wounds; complained bitterly of the treatment at Carter's [sic] Barrack's (Mudie's place) and wished someone would examine into it; indeed, all the Carter's [sic] boys make the same complaint.

Established at the Brickfields end of Pitt Street in 1820, Carters' Barracks was an accommodation and training institution for convicts under the age of sixteen. In the mid-1830s the barracks ceased to operate as a boys' reformatory though a debtor's prison, men's prison and, later, a charitable facility for women occupied the building.

The Hanged Boy

Fifteen-year-old John Gaven (or Gavin) came from Parkhurst to the Swan River as an 'apprentice' early in 1844. He was assigned as a servant to the Pollard family of Dandalup, around seventy kilometres south of Perth, and all seemed to be going well at first. He formed a close friendship with George, the eldest of the three Pollard boys, and the older boy usually took John's side when he was in trouble with Mr or Mrs Pollard for minor infractions or not performing his work well enough. George even saved John's life when they were swimming together. George enjoyed singing and had a book of music from which he often sang.

One day in February Mrs Pollard was not feeling well. John was going about his chores in what she later described as an unusual manner and did not seem himself. At one point he appeared in her room with a length of wood. Mrs Pollard ordered him out and told him to leave the board somewhere else until her husband returned. She then tried to sleep but was disturbed by John's singing in the next room to hers, though she could only make out a few words. Mrs Pollard did not know the song, a Protestant paean on the barring of Londonderry against the Catholic army of James II in 1688, the main themes being resistance to oppression. The full chorus that John sang was:

> These walls still held by valiant men,
> No slave shall e'er subdue
> And when we close these gates again
> We will be all true blue.

The singing stopped and Mrs Pollard got up to find John in the kitchen drinking from a basin. She asked him what he was doing and he said he was filling a barrow with straw at the door of George's bedroom. Mrs Pollard went on preparing her dinner and then wondered where George might be as she had not seen or heard him for some time. In her testimony, Mrs Pollard recalled the events in detail:

> I went out of the kitchen towards the deceased's door, when I saw the prisoner rush out of that door looking wild as if in distraction. He began to stoop, and look down and about him, I asked him what he was looking for, he said nothing; I said he could not look for less. He continued walking about in the same way for a minute or so, when I said, 'Why Gaven, you are like one losing your senses; are you losing your reason, or what ails you, boy?' he made no answer that I heard. He was then going towards the carpenter's shop. I then went to the door of deceased's room, and saw him lying on his bed, with his back to me. I called him two or three times, and no answer was given. I went in and shook him and was surprised at his being so fast asleep in so short a time. There was a coat over, and tucked under his head, I removed the coat, and saw him in a gore of blood, and thought it might have been from bleeding at the nose. I put my left hand under his face, and my right hand under the back of his head, to raise it up, and my hand sunk into the back of his head. I raised his face a little, and he breathed a few times. I clapped my hands and said 'my child is smothered in his own blood.' I screamed, 'George, my jewel, tell me your murderer.' I am sure he was not dead when I first raised his head.

Michael Pollard heard his mother's cry and came running to find her going in and out of his brother's room. He saw an adze covered with hair, blood and brains, lying on the floor halfway between the bed and door. Thomas Pollard arrived shortly after. His mother told him brother George had been murdered and showed him the bloody adze. He went for help to the nearest neighbours, two miles through the bush. Thomas recalled that, 'All the time I had kept calling out, "Murder! Murder! Johnny Gaven! Johnny Gaven!"'

Mrs Pollard then saw John Gaven coming towards the house. He was wet and said he had gone to the river for a drink and fallen in. She accused him of killing George, he denied it, saying perhaps a native had done it:

> He then said, perhaps he had murdered himself; I said, 'you murdering villain, why should you belie my dead child—he could not take an adze and murder himself on the back of the head.' He then went into deceased's room and said, George won't say I murdered him; I answered, you did not give him leave to breathe. He then called out 'George, George,' and I went to push him away from the bed, he said 'don't put a drop of blood on me; you said I murdered your child, don't put a drop of blood on me.' I then took notice of his shirt being wet, and said, 'you villain, did you go and wash the blood of my dear child off your clothes?'

Mrs Pollard tied John's hands together and took him into the only room with a single door, guarding him with a stick. There was a struggle, which she won and then he suddenly knelt down and repeatedly said:

> 'Do forgive me, ma'am, and don't say I murdered your son, and I'll pray for George.' I said he had not given George time to pray. After that, he said at different times, 'do ma'am, blow my brains out.' I said I would not imbrue my hands in his blood, as he had done his in my son's, and that I would deliver him to the law. After this he became more case hardened, and said he did not regard what I could do, as I did not see him do it. He kept coming up to me, and placing his hands against me, and saying 'I didn't' in an impertinent way.

The soldiers arrived and John Gaven was arrested. The next day Mrs Pollard went into George's bedroom where she found the songbook. The page bearing the song she heard Gaven singing was stuck together with another page by George's blood.

At the trial the committing magistrate described the scene he found at the Pollard house on the day of the murder:

I found the head cleft to pieces, a continuation of wounds, quite a mash of skull, brains, and hair. I gave directions for the body to be washed. Early next morning I returned to Pollard's, and, with Sergt. Burrell, examined the body again. I found two wounds on face, one across the cheek bone and nose, the other across the temple, part of three fingers severed, one cut behind left ear, several blows on back of head, smashing the skull into a number of pieces, in a slanting direction, 9 inches long.

Gaven pleaded not guilty and had the benefit of a lengthy defence by his counsel. Nevertheless, the jury took only half an hour to return a verdict of guilty. The boy was sentenced to death. He subsequently confessed.

His plan was to murder Mrs Pollard but he then realised that George would probably overpower him once the deed had been done. So he decided to kill his friend. He claimed he had gone to the river not to wash the blood from his clothes but to drown himself, but his courage failed him. Gaven was unable to state why he wanted to kill Mrs Pollard.

Other than the officials, there were few to witness the end of the Parkhurst boy. The local papers reported that 8 a.m. on 6 April 1844, by the Fremantle Roundhouse:

The prison bell then began to toll, and the melancholy procession set out from the condemned cell to the scaffold: the Sheriff and his deputies and constables, the Rev. G. King, reading appropriate passages of Scripture, the prisoner, supported by Mr. Schoales, and lastly, more constables closed the train. The boy was deeply affected, and was assisted up the steps to the platform.

At ten past eight the cart beneath the scaffold was driven away and John Gaven was 'launched into eternity'. His body was so small and light that heavy weights had to be tied to his legs to make sure he was strangled.

They let the tiny corpse swing in the air for an hour before cutting him down. A cast of the face and skull was made 'for the purpose of furthering the ends of science'. The boy's head was said to be 'of extraordinary formation; the anterior organs being very deficiently developed, while the posterior organs are of an enormous size'. A group of convicts carried the body to the sandhills where they buried him in an unmarked and unhallowed grave 'without rite or ceremony'. John Gaven may be lying there still.

One Hundred Lashes

The most famous novel of convict life and death is Marcus Clarke's *For the Term of His Natural Life*, based on the author's extensive interviews and research into the convict experience. Chapter 15 concerns the flogging at the triangle of a convict named Kirkland by the hero of the novel, Rufus Dawes. Events take an unexpected turn.

The morning sun, bright and fierce, looked down upon a curious sight. In a stone-yard was a little group of persons—Troke, Burgess, Macklewain, Kirkland, and Rufus Dawes. Three wooden staves, seven feet high, were fastened together in the form of a triangle. The structure looked not unlike that made by gypsies to boil their kettles. To this structure Kirkland was bound. His feet were fastened with thongs to the base of the triangle; his wrists, bound above his head, at the apex. His body was then extended to its fullest length, and his white back shone in the sunlight. During his tying up he had said nothing—only when Troke pulled off his shirt he shivered.

'Now, prisoner,' said Troke to Dawes, 'do your duty.'

Rufus Dawes looked from the three stern faces to Kirkland's white back, and his face grew purple. In all his experience he had never been asked to flog before. He had been flogged often enough.

'You don't want me to flog him, sir?' he said to the Commandant.

'Pick up the cat, sir!' said Burgess, astonished; 'what is the meaning of this?' Rufus Dawes picked up the heavy cat, and drew its knotted lashes between his fingers.

'Go on, Dawes,' whispered Kirkland, without turning his head. 'You are no more than another man.'

'What does he say?' asked Burgess.

'Telling him to cut light, sir,' said Troke, eagerly lying; 'they all do it.'

'Cut light, eh! We'll see about that. Get on, my man, and look sharp, or I'll tie you up and give you fifty for yourself, as sure as God made little apples.'

'Go on, Dawes,' whispered Kirkland again. 'I don't mind.'

Rufus Dawes lifted the cat, swung it round his head, and brought its knotted cords down upon the white back.

'Wonn!' cried Troke.

The white back was instantly striped with six crimson bars. Kirkland stifled a cry. It seemed to him that he had been cut in half.

'Now then, you scoundrel!' roared Burgess; 'separate your cats! What do you mean by flogging a man in that fashion?'

Rufus Dawes drew his crooked fingers through the entangled cords, and struck again. This time the blow was more effective, and the blood beaded on the skin.

The boy did not cry; but Macklewain saw his hands clutch the staves tightly, and the muscles of his naked arms quiver.

'Tew!'

'That's better,' said Burgess.

The third blow sounded as though it had been struck upon a piece of raw beef, and the crimson turned purple.

'My God!' said Kirkland, faintly, and bit his lips.

The flogging proceeded in silence for ten strikes, and then Kirkland gave a screech like a wounded horse.

'Oh!. . .Captain Burgess!. . .Dawes!. . .Mr. Troke!. . .Oh, my God!. . .Oh! oh!. . .Mercy!. . .Oh, Doctor!. . .Mr. North!. . .Oh! Oh! Oh!'

'Ten!' cried Troke, impassively counting to the end of the first twenty.

The lad's back, swollen into a lump, now presented the appearance of a ripe peach which a wilful child had scored with a pin. Dawes, turning away from his bloody handiwork, drew the cats through his fingers twice. They were beginning to get clogged a little.

'Go on,' said Burgess, with a nod; and Troke cried 'Wonn!' again.

The surgeon, North, who was supposed to be overseeing the flogging slept late that morning after too much grog the night before.

As he entered the yard, Troke called 'Ten!' Kirkland had just got his fiftieth lash.

'Stop!' cried North. 'Captain Burgess, I call upon you to stop.'

'You're rather late, Mr. North,' retorted Burgess. 'The punishment is nearly over.'

'Wonn!' cried Troke again; and North stood by, biting his nails and grinding his teeth, during six more lashes.

Kirkland ceased to yell now, and merely moaned. His back was like a bloody sponge, while in the interval between lashes the swollen flesh twitched like that of a new-killed bullock. Suddenly, Macklewain saw his head droop on his shoulder. 'Throw him off! Throw him off!' he cried, and Troke hurried to loosen the thongs.

'Fling some water over him!' said Burgess; 'he's shamming.'

A bucket of water made Kirkland open his eyes. 'I thought so,' said Burgess. 'Tie him up again.'

'No. Not if you are Christians!' cried North.

He met with an ally where he least expected one. Rufus Dawes flung down the dripping cat. 'I'll flog no more,' said he.

'What?' roared Burgess, furious at this gross insolence.

'I'll flog no more. Get someone else to do your blood work for you. I won't.'

'Tie him up!' cried Burgess, foaming. 'Tie him up. Here, constable, fetch a man here with a fresh cat. I'll give you that beggar's fifty, and fifty more on the top of 'em; and he shall look on while his back cools.'

Rufus Dawes, with a glance at North, pulled off his shirt without a word, and stretched himself at the triangles. His back was not white and smooth, like Kirkland's had been, but hard and seamed. He had been flogged before. Troke appeared with

Gabbett—grinning. Gabbett liked flogging. It was his boast that he could flog a man to death on a place no bigger than the palm of his hand. He could use his left hand equally with his right, and if he got hold of a 'favourite', would 'cross the cuts'.

Rufus Dawes planted his feet firmly on the ground, took fierce grasp on the staves, and drew in his breath. Macklewain spread the garments of the two men upon the ground, and, placing Kirkland upon them, turned to watch this new phase in the morning's amusement. He grumbled a little below his breath, for he wanted his breakfast, and when the Commandant once began to flog there was no telling where he would stop.

Rufus Dawes took five-and-twenty lashes without a murmur, and then Gabbett 'crossed the cuts'. This went on up to fifty lashes, and North felt himself stricken with admiration at the courage of the man. 'If it had not been for that cursed brandy,' thought he, with bitterness of self-reproach, 'I might have saved all this.' At the hundredth lash, the giant paused, expecting the order to throw off, but Burgess was determined to 'break the man's spirit'.

'I'll make you speak, you dog, if I cut your heart out!' he cried. 'Go on, prisoner.'

For twenty lashes more Dawes was mute, and then the agony forced from his labouring breast a hideous cry. But it was not a cry for mercy, as that of Kirkland's had been. Having found his tongue, the wretched man gave vent to his boiling passion in a torrent of curses. He shrieked imprecations upon Burgess, Troke, and North. He cursed all soldiers for tyrants, all parsons for hypocrites. He blasphemed his God and his Saviour. With a frightful outpouring of obscenity and blasphemy, he called on the earth to gape and swallow his persecutors, for Heaven to open and rain fire upon them, for hell to yawn and engulf them quick. It was as though each blow of the cat forced out of him a fresh burst of beast-like rage. He seemed to have abandoned his humanity. He foamed, he raved, he tugged at his bonds until the strong staves shook again; he writhed himself round upon the triangles and spat impotently at Burgess, who jeered at his torments.

North, with his hands to his ears, crouched against the corner of the wall, palsied with horror. It seemed to him that the passions of hell raged around him. He would fain have fled, but a horrible fascination held him back.

In the midst of this—when the cat was hissing its loudest—Burgess laughing his hardest, and the wretch on the triangles filling the air with his cries, North saw Kirkland look at him with what he thought was a smile. Was it a smile? He leapt forward, and uttered a cry of dismay so loud that all turned.

'Hullo!' says Troke, running to the heap of clothes, 'the young 'un's slipped his wind!'

Kirkland was dead.

'Throw him off!' says Burgess, aghast at the unfortunate accident; and Gabbett reluctantly untied the thongs that bound Rufus Dawes. Two constables were alongside him in an instant, for sometimes newly tortured men grew desperate. This one, however, was silent with the last lash; only in taking his shirt from under the body of the boy, he muttered, 'Dead!' and in his tone there seemed to be a touch of envy. Then, flinging his shirt over his bleeding shoulders, he walked out—defiant to the last.

'Game, ain't he?' said one constable to the other, as they pushed him, not ungently, into an empty cell, there to wait for the hospital guard. The body of Kirkland was taken away in silence, and Burgess turned rather pale when he saw North's threatening face.

'It isn't my fault, Mr. North,' he said. 'I didn't know that the lad was chicken-hearted.' But North turned away in disgust, and Macklewain and Burgess pursued their homeward route together . . .

To Plough Van Diemen's Land

An undeclared war raged in rural England in the eighteenth and nineteenth centuries. Small groups of men went out at night to steal game—pheasants, hares, rabbits—from the private lands of the well-to-do. Illegal though this was, it was not generally considered a crime by poachers and their dependent families and communities. Land once belonging to all was gradually 'enclosed'—effectively privatised—over the centuries, depriving the poor of a vital source of food. As far as most were concerned, they were simply following common law and asserting their common rights.

Not all poachers were feeding their families. Game was in demand in the restaurants of the fast-growing cities of London, Manchester, Liverpool, Birmingham and Leeds, and criminal gangs were formed to supply that demand. Whether professional poachers or people in need, the law made no distinctions and many were caught, convicted and transported for crimes against the draconian Game Acts.

There were many ballads about poaching. This one was especially popular in Britain and also sung in Australia; it tells a tale that many experienced. Typical of commercial street ballads, it has a moralising conclusion at odds with the popular attitude towards poaching. But people sang it anyway.

Come all you gallant poachers that ramble free from care,
That walk out of a moonlight night with your dog your gun and
    snare,
Where the lofty hare and pheasant you have at your command,
Not thinking that your last career is on Van Diemen's Land.

There was poor Tom Brown from Nottingham Jack Williams
    and poor Joe,
Were three as daring poachers as the country well does know,
At night they were trepanned by the keeper's hideous hand,
And for fourteen years transported were unto Van Diemen's Land.

Oh when we sailed from England we landed at the bay,
We had rotten straw for bedding we dared not to say nay,
Our cots were fenced with fire we slumber when we can,
To drive away the wolves and tigers upon Van Diemen's Land.

Oh when that we were landed upon that fatal bay,
The planters they came flocking round full twenty score or more,

They ranked us up like horses and sold us out of hand,
They yoked us up to the plough, my boys, to plough Van
    Diemen's Land.

There was one girl from England Susan Summers was her name,
For fourteen years transported was we all well knew the same,
Our planter bought her freedom and he married her out of hand,
Good usage then she gave to us upon Van Diemen's Land.

Often when I am slumbering I have a pleasant dream,
With my sweet girl I am sitting down by some purling stream,
Through England I am roaming with her at my command,
Then waken broken hearted upon Van Diemen's Land.

God bless our wives and families likewise that happy shore,
That isle of sweet contentment which we shall see no more,
As for our wretched females see them we seldom can,
There are twenty to one woman upon Van Diemen's Land.

Come all you gallant poachers give ear unto my song,
It is a bit of good advice although it is not long,
Lay by your dog and snare to you I do speak plain,
If you knew the hardship we endure you ne'er would poach
    again.

'Female Factory, Cascades', Hobart, Tasmania, from glass plate negatives and photographs collected by E.R. Pretyman, 1870–1930.

6
Troublemakers

I'll give the law a little shock, remember what I say,
They'll yet regret they sent Jim Jones in chains to Botany Bay

Latter day convict ballad

Botany Bay Hero

Convicts transported to New South Wales did not only come
from Britain. In 1820 ex-private Michael Keane (Kain), drum
and fife player late of Her Majesty's 59th Regiment, landed at
Sydney Cove aboard the *Seaflower*. He came from India. His
sentence was for life.

What had he done to deserve spending the rest of his life as
a convict? It all began when the 25-year-old Irishman enlisted
in the British Army in 1805:

I very soon fell in with companions that lead me into all kind
mischeiff, which brought me sooner to feill the affecttes of
punishment then I should have dun if I had kep my owne
companey; I was indused by two of them to stop out of Barrack's
a day and a night, and losing a fife, I recavid seventy five lashess
on the britche; then went to Formoy, and on my routh there 1806,
for losing a bealt and drum, which was stoel from me at Broff,

I recavid one hundred lashess on the britch, and this I got through a yeoman drummer takeen them from the house I was billited at; the went to Charealfield and Dowearalle, I stopet at the halfe way house, and for getting drunk the drum major struck me, and I struck him with the fire poker, It was tryad at Charealfield, and sentaince to receive three hundred lashess, but I got one hundered and and fifty on the bak and britch; I often thought to desart, but I did not, this hapened in the yeare 1807.

Between then and his trial and sentence of transportation, Michael Keane lived a harsh life as a soldier in constant trouble with his comrades and officers. While still in Ireland he was court-martialled for being absent from his guard post, receiving 175 lashes, though originally sentenced to 300. He sailed with his regiment to the West Indies where he fought the French in Martinique: 'I underwent a good dail of hardship there for three months in the field, three days and nights without eating any thing only the duice of sugear cane.' After stealing rum, flour and beef from a native, Keane was tied to a tree and given 250 lashes. A few hours later he was in battle and wounded in the knee.

In 1810 Keane again fought the French and Dutch on Guadalupe and other islands. Accused of drunkenness by a sergeant, Keane was flayed with 400 lashes. He was wounded twice in the engagements and eventually went into hospital at Guadalupe in 1811. Caught outside the hospital grounds without a pass, Keane was sentenced to a mammoth flogging of 900 strokes, though received only 700. In 1813 a dispute led to Keane striking a sergeant with a bayonet and abusing the sergeant-major. A court martial awarded him 800 stripes, of which he received 700.

But by 1814, the well-whipped soldier had been promoted to sergeant and drum major. After a boozy day and night at a Guadalupe tavern, he stole a ring from a native woman and was again court-martialled. Reduced to the ranks, Keane only received a 'light' 300 lashes this time. He was later given another 200 lashes for drunkenness and abusing a sergeant, and then in 1815 Keane was discharged and returned to England. But without means to support himself he soon re-enlisted in a regiment bound for Bengal. It did not take long for the old pattern to re-appear. On the voyage to India he was—as always, by his claims—wrongfully accused of drunkenness and threats. He was sentenced to 300 lashes, receiving 225.

After months of fighting, Keane took to 'desarting'—again and again. On the first three occasions he suffered 900 lashes. The fourth time he was thrown into solitary confinement for ninety-three days with no pay. Then he deserted once more but was recognised in Calcutta, arrested and court-martialled. Perhaps exasperated with the recalcitrant soldier, the army sentenced him to transportation for life. In his autobiography, Keane wrote:

> I landed in Sydney the 2nd May 1820 wheare the mother of misfortuane kep close to me, and still remains a companion of mine, for I had not been long in Sydney before I was taken before the Magistrates, and recavid 50 lashes for stoping out of barracks one night. In a very short time after I was sent to the police for gone oute of the ranks to buy some tubacoo and for not tipping the overseer when I joynd the gang, he took me before the Magistrates, and I was sentaince to be put in the solitary cells for 14 days, for the above crime, which I served and when I came out of the cells, I went to wheare I had my cloths and I came to the Dog and Duck on the Brickfield Hill where I remaind drinking untill six o'clock in the evning and then came to the Barracks.

Keane went to work the next day but was soon arrested and tried for stealing an iron axle tree—which he did not do. He was sent to the Newcastle area for two years and ended up in a lime burning gang.

> And then I begone my hardship at that place. I never dun any work in my life before, I did not no how to get on, I was sick and I was

> sent to the Hospital, and the place the Dacter put me was in the
> dead house, wheare I remaind for five days upon halfe pound a
> bread and one pint of grual a day. I was almost dead in this place
> for the two years that I was at Newcastle I underwent a grate dail of
> hardship—through starvation neakedness and solitary confinement
> sometimes on the bar for 7 days and some times in the cells for 14
> and 21 days at a time without any kind of covering only on the
> coald flagg stone withaut any kind of clothing.

While he was at Newcastle, Keane received a total of 1475 lashes, and spent 123 days in the cells on a pound of bread a day.

Then it was back to Sydney and then to 'joyne a gang up the country'. True to his character, Keane was soon in trouble again and was sent to Port Macquarie where, after two years, he was brought 'all most to deaths door through flogging and starvation'. During this time, he suffered 1525 lashes and twenty-eight days in the cells on bread and water.

Transferred back to Sydney, his drunkenness earned him four painful days on the treadmill. Then, wrongly accused again of theft, he was sent to the ironed gang to work in chains for three months. But here 'I could not stop through the tyranny of the overseer and half starved'. He absconded and received fourteen days on the treadmill after recapture. Michael Keane summed up his astonishing life of soldiering, petty crime, drunkenness and flogging:

> I have been cruley used in this countary, through tyrints of overseers
> and constobles that was at Newcastle and Port Macquarie that
> I was under; and now for life in the countary, after been 15 years
> in the army, foure time wounded in the field of Battle, and now
> poor and miserable and despised by every one above me. The
> corproal punshment that I recavid since the 5th June, 1805 untill
> the 26th September 1826, is sevean thousand two hundered and
> fifty lashess, and three hundered and foure days in the solitary
> cells between the army and been a prisoner.

This 'Botany Bay hero', as he wryly called himself, finished his life story with what must surely be one of the great understatements: 'I still remain, the same Michael Keane, Altho' not so well in health and strenth, as I would wish to have beane.'

Thrown Unpitied and Friendless Upon the World

Wages for agricultural workers in southern England were dropping fast through the 1820s. The introduction of mechanical threshing machines quickly made many manual tasks obsolete. Faced with starvation, farm labourers rose in a spontaneous and uncoordinated rebellion known as the 'Swing Riots' in August 1830. The insurrection was a serious shock to the established order. It was quickly and brutally put down and many of those arrested were executed or were transported to Australia over the next few years.

In the aftermath of these disturbances the formation of a union by a group of Dorset agricultural workers was seen by the local authorities as another threat to social order. While the organisation of a union was no longer illegal, the taking of secret oaths was an offence. New members were blindfolded while they swore allegiance on a Bible. The blindfold was removed to reveal a macabre painting of a large human skeleton holding a scythe in one hand and an hourglass in the other. These clandestine actions were enough for the arrest and trial of brothers George and James Loveless, father and son Thomas and John Standfield, James Brine and James Hammett. They all came from the village of Tolpuddle and all except James Hammett were devout Methodists. Their sentence was transportation for seven years. They were held in prison in Dorchester until the morning of 27 March 1834, when:

> We received orders early this morning to prepare ourselves for the coach bound to Portsmouth. After we were ironed together the coach drove up to the castle door and we mounted: the officer in charge was a Mr. Glenister. We arrived at Portsmouth about

eight o'clock in the evening, and were instantly conveyed to the York hulk; the irons that we wore from Dorchester being struck off, and fresh ones put on.

After a few days of preparation and changing of irons:

On the 11th April we weighed anchor and bore away for New South Wales. I then began to feel the misery of transportation.— confined down with a number of the most degraded and wretched criminals, each man having to contend with his fellow or be trodden under foot. The rations, which were served out daily, were of the worst quality, and very deficient in quantity, owing to the peculations indulged in by those officers whose duty it is to attend that department. In addition to this, the crowded state of the vessel, rendering it impossible for the prisoners to lie down at full length to sleep, the noxious state of the atmosphere, and the badness and saltness of the provisions, induced disease and suffering which it is impossible to describe.

Added to all this, in the case of myself and brethren, the agonizing reflection that we had done nothing deserving this punishment, and the consciousness that our families, thus suddenly deprived of their protectors, and a stigma affixed to their names, would probably be thrown unpitied and friendless upon the world.

They arrived in Sydney on 17 August and were marched to Hyde Park Barracks. 'We had all been assigned to our respective masters previous to coming on shore, and we had not been in the barracks more than three hours when James Brine was called for by the messenger to proceed to his master.'

James Brine takes up the story:

I was assigned to Dr. Mitchell, Surgeon of the Government Hospital, and in a short time proceeded to the farm of Robert Scott, Esq., at Glindon, Hunter's River. I went on board the steam-boat, and reached the green hills the following day. I had then about thirty miles to travel on land before reaching the place of my destination. My master had given me at starting, a small bed and blanket to take with me, and one shilling to bear my expenses, besides a suit of new slops.

On landing, being weary and fatigued, I laid down to take rest under a gum-tree. During the night the bushrangers came upon me and robbed me of all I possessed, excepting the old clothes I had on, which were given me at Portsmouth. On Sept. 7th I arrived at the farm at Glindon, exhausted from want of food, having had but one meal for three days.

I was instantly taken by the overseer to the master, who asked me where my slops and bedding were. I told him the bushrangers had robbed me; but he swore that I was a liar, and said that he would give me a 'D-d good flogging' in the morning. 'You are one of the Dorsetshire machine-breakers,' said he; 'but you are caught at last.' He gave me nothing to eat until the following day. In the morning I was employed to dig post-holes, and during the day he came and asked how I was getting on. I told him I was doing as well as I could, but was unable to do much through weakness, and that having walked so far without shoes, my feet were so cut and sore I could not put them to the spade.

'If you utter another word of complaint,' said he, 'I will put you in the lock-up; and if you ask me for another article for six months to come, or if you do not do your work like another man, or do not attend to the overseer's orders, whatever they may be, I will send you up to Mr. Moody, where no mercy shall be shown to you.'

I afterwards got a piece of an iron hoop and wrapped it round my foot to tread upon, and for six months, until I became due, I went without shoes, clothes, or bedding, and lay on the bare ground at night.

Brine then spent seventeen days up to his chest in water dipping sheep. He caught a bad cold and asked his master for something to cover himself at night, even a piece of horsecloth. He refused:

'I will give you nothing until you are due for it. What would your masters in England have to cover them if you had not been sent here? I understand it was your intention to have murdered, burnt, and destroyed everything before you, and you are sent over here to be severely punished, and no mercy shall be shown you. If you ask me for anything before the six months is expired, I will flog you as often as I like.'

He then asked me to explain to him the designs of the Union, and said if I would tell him it would be a good thing for me, as he would try to get me a ticket of indulgence. I told him that I knew nothing of what he was talking, and that the Unions had no idea of murdering, burning, or destroying. 'You know all about it,' said he, 'and it will be better for you to tell me.'

I still replied that I had nothing to communicate. He then said, 'You d-d convict, if you persist in this obstinacy and insolence I will severely punish you! Don't you know that not even the hair on your head is your own. Go to your hut or I will kick you.' My master was a magistrate!

Back in England the Tolpuddle men were popular heroes but their families were suffering. When they applied for parish relief, they were refused as the local landowners still feared the power of organised labour. In a letter to the supporters, the martyrs' wives wrote: 'Tolpuddle have for many years been noticed for tyranny and oppression and cruelty and now the union is broke up here.' Fortunately, the issue was the object of intense political agitation. Funds for the support of the families were donated.

The Tolpuddle Martyrs were conditionally pardoned in 1835 and received full pardons in 1836. They returned to England where all except James Hammett continued to fight for what was then considered the radical cause of universal male suffrage, the right of every adult to vote and other significant political reforms. Eventually, still harassed, all but Hammett emigrated with their families to Ontario, Canada, where they began new lives. Today they are remembered as heroes of the early trade union movement.

The Beast of Goat Island

Poor 'Bony' Anderson was mad. It wasn't his fault. Orphaned at an early age he was brought up in the workhouse and sent to sea in a collier at the age of nine. It was a tough apprenticeship and when it was over he went aboard a man-o-war as a British sailor. Badly wounded in the head at the Battle of Navarino, he became a violent young man, easily provoked by drink or offence. The inevitable happened and he was involved in a brawl with other drunken sailors during which several shops were looted. Charles Anderson was arrested, tried and sentenced to seven years in New South Wales. He was eighteen.

After arriving in the colony in 1834 Anderson was sent to the tiny Goat Island in Sydney Harbour to work in the stone quarry. According to an account based partly on Anderson's testimony:

> He remained there about two months under treatment so severe that, to escape it, he absconded. Apprehended and taken to Sydney Barracks, he there received 100 lashes for this offence; and upon being returned to Goat Island he received 100 more lashes, and was to wear irons for twelve months, in addition to his original sentence. Before completing it he had received 1,200 lashes for trivial offences, such as looking round from his work, or at a steamer in the river, &c. He again absconded, was reapprehended, taken back to the island, and received 200 lashes; afterwards he was tried for the same offence and was sentenced to 100 lashes more, and to be chained to a rock for two years with barely a rag to cover him.

Anderson was fastened to the rock with a 26-foot chain secured to his waist. His legs were weighted with irons. A hollow was chiselled out of the rock just big enough for him to squeeze into. At night a wooden lid pierced with holes was secured over his head until the next morning. In this living grave, he was fed like a zoo animal, meagre meals pushed to him by a long pole. None were allowed to come near him or communicate with him on pain of flogging. A convict mate managed to get the chained man a quid of tobacco and received a hundred lashes for his mercy.

> Regarded as a wild beast, people passing in boats would throw him bits of bread or biscuit.
>
> Exposed to all weathers, and without clothing on his back and shoulders, which were covered with sores from repeated floggings, the maggots rapidly engendered in a hot climate feeding upon his flesh, he was denied even water to bathe his wounds, such denial being not an unusual portion of the punishment to which he had been condemned; and when rain fell, or by any other means he could obtain liquid, he would lie and roll in it in agony.

After some weeks of this inhuman treatment, Governor Bourke offered Anderson his freedom if he would agree to work—'but he answered he would not; adding, that if he worked, he would be punished, and if he did not work, he would be punished the same'. The governor had him sent to Port Macquarie for life. Here, Anderson carried lime from the quarry to the barges, burning the skin off his back. Anderson then escaped and lived with Aborigines until recaptured and returned to 200 lashes.

Later Anderson agreed to kill the overseer at Port Macquarie, saying he would rather be hanged than live as he was. He smashed in the overseer's head with a spade and was bayoneted near to death by the guards. But he lived. Taken to Sydney and tried for the murder, he was sentenced to life on Norfolk Island, in double chains according to one account.

On Norfolk Island Anderson was tormented by other prisoners, goading him to acts of violence and insubordination just to see what would happen. By the time the new Superintendent Maconochie arrived in 1840, the wretched man had been punished ten times for violent assaults and many times for refusing to work and general insolence. He was now twenty-four years old, but looked forty. When the reforming Maconochie asked why Anderson was so incorrigible, he was told the man was 'cranky'. The superintendent ordered the baiting to stop and Anderson was given responsibility for managing a group of bullocks. This kept him away from the other convicts and provided him with responsibility. The change was marked and Anderson was later put in charge of the new signal station on Mount Pitt. Here, dressed in a sailor's uniform again, he had responsibility for keeping watch, slowly regaining his self-confidence, assisted by his particular love of gardening.

As well as rehabilitating such a lost character, Maconochie used his case as an example of the value of his penal reforms. When Governor George Gipps visited Norfolk Island three years later, he noticed Anderson contentedly going about his tasks dressed in a trim sailor suit and carrying a telescope. 'What little smart fellow may that be?' asked Sir George. 'Who do you suppose? That is the man who was chained to the rock in Sydney Harbour,' the superintendent replied. 'Bless my soul, you do not mean to say so!' was Sir George's astonished rejoinder.

But although much reformed, Anderson's underlying mental health issues continued. Although he regained his self-respect and ability to socialise, he was eventually transferred to a Sydney asylum. This was around the time that Maconochie was recalled, his reforms deemed too permissive in official circles. When a mutual acquaintance visited Anderson in the asylum, 'the poor fellow recognised his visitor, and spoke of nothing but Captain Maconochie and his family'.

Anderson was later sent to another asylum where, amazingly perhaps, he was eventually declared sane. He was freed in 1854, his story providing ammunition for the many opponents of transportation. Charles Anderson's mind was, perhaps, healed. But the marks on his body, tattooed with sun, moon, stars and Christian and nautical symbols of all kinds, as well as the scars of countless lashes, could never be erased.

Nymphs of the Pave

Young George Boothroyd fell right into one of the oldest tricks in the world. His father sent him to cash a substantial cheque at the Yorkshire Bank in Huddersfield, presumably for his business. George got the money and began a pub crawl that ended up at the Green Dragon where he stayed the night. On Sunday morning, still woozy, he found himself in the house of Ruth Richardson. Ruth and her friends Lydia Clay, Mary Anne Wentworth and Elizabeth Quarmby were 'nymphs of the pave', as the press often described women who needed to make their living on the streets in 1845.

The women soon got foolish George gambling and very, very drunk. They knocked him down and took the money he was unwisely carrying. Somehow George managed to stagger back to the Green Dragon, where they had to put him to bed for a few hours before he was sober enough to report on his misadventure and identify his assailants.

The exact details of how much money was involved, as well as where and when George was parted from it, are murky but the four women were arrested, tried and convicted. They were sent to Van Diemen's Land for ten years in 1846 and entered the Cascades Female Factory in Hobart. Established in the late 1820s, the Cascades was a prison, a workhouse and a nursery for the children of convicts. Women laboured for up to twelve hours a day in summer and were subjected to severe regulation, as laid out in the rules of 1829:

> Females guilty of disobedience of orders, neglect of work, profane, obscene, or abusive language, insubordination, or other turbulent or disorderly or disrespectful conduct, shall be punished by the superintendent with close confinement in a dark or other cell, until her case shall be brought under consideration of the Principal Superintendent.

At the Cascades Female Factory, the four Huddersfield 'nymphs' were incorporated into the system like all the other female convicts. As well as their trade and place of origin, the state noted every personal detail—height, age, complexion, the size and shape of the head, hair colour, 'visage' or face shape, angle of the forehead, colour of eyes and eyebrows, size and shape of the nose and chin, as well as any marks, blemishes or other distinguishing bodily characteristics.

Lydia Clay was described as a 'house maid' of thirty-six years, and five and a quarter inches tall (without shoes). Her complexion was dark and her hair black, as were her eyes. With oval face, low forehead, long nose, large mouth and round chin, she was more than adequately catalogued as a creature of the state and easily identifiable. In case of any possible doubt, she had a mole on the inside of her right arm.

Short, dark and feisty, Lydia quickly became a troublemaker who refused to buckle to the system. She was insolent, insubordinate and sometimes absent without leave. On one of these occasions she was 'found in bed with a man' and sentenced to six months hard labour. After a good deal of time in solitary and at hard labour in the first few years of her sentence, Lydia settled down and was granted a ticket-of-leave in 1851 and a conditional pardon two years afterwards. Lydia married in 1850 but was widowed four years later when her husband was killed. A year later she remarried but in 1858 at the age of forty-eight, she was dead from an 'abscess on the brain'.

Elizabeth Quarmby caused almost no trouble and was free in December 1855. She was married by this time and produced three children by 1860. It seems that the grog got the better of her. There was a separation and although Elizabeth took her husband to court, he refused to pay to support her. She had some satisfaction, though. Years later, her husband bigamously remarried and was jailed for three months. Elizabeth lived a pauper's life until her death of 'senile decay' in 1893. She was seventy-two.

Mary Anne Wentworth and Ruth Richardson were well-behaved prisoners. Mary Anne married well while still serving her sentence, and then again after her first husband died. She lived comfortably until her death at the age of ninety-one in 1911. Ruth married a farmer, dropping her age on the marriage certificate by about fifteen years to twenty-one. She died of consumption, or tuberculosis, in 1858.

Flash Mob at the Cascades

Sodomy and lesbianism were among the great paranoias suffered by the respectable classes of colonial society. 'Unnatural' practices among male convicts were endlessly highlighted in the press and official reports and inquiries, if not necessarily with a lot of evidence. Less frequently mentioned, because even more feared, was lesbianism among female convicts. When the press did get hold of such a story, they became quite obsessed with it, which is how the Cascades Female Factory in Hobart became notorious in the late 1830s for the activities, real or imputed, of the 'Flash Mob'.

According to the press, the gaudy, party-loving Flash Mob was the main cause of 'a system of vice, immorality, and iniquity, which has tended, mainly, to render the majority of female assigned servants, the annoying and untractable animals, that they are'. And this was only for starters. The article went on to outline the vile nature and activities of the convict women who made up the Flash Mob:

The Flash Mob at the Factory consists, as it would seem, of a certain number of women, who, by a simple process of initiation, are admitted into a series of unhallowed mysteries, similar, in many respects, to those which are described by Goethe, in his unrivalled Drama of Faust, as occurring, on particular occasions, amongst the supposed supernatural inhabitants of the Harz Mountains. Like those abominable Saturnalia, they are performed in the dark and silent hour of night, but, unlike those, they are performed in solitude and secrecy, amongst only the duly initiated.

With the fiendish fondness for sin, every effort, both in the Factory, and out of it, is made by these wretches, to acquire proselytes to their infamous practices; and, it has come to our knowledge, within these few days, that a simple-minded girl, who had been in one and the same service, since she left the ship—a period of nearly six months—very narrowly escaped seduction (we can use no stronger term) by a well-known, and most accomplished member of this unholy sisterhood. This practice constitutes one of the rules of the 'order' and we need not waste many words to show how perniciously it must act upon the 'new hands,' exposed to its influence.

Another rule is, that, should any member be assigned, she must return to the Factory, so soon as she has obtained (we need to say by what means) a sufficient sum of money to enable herself and her companion to procure such indulgences, as the Factory can supply— or, rather, as can be supplied by certain individuals, connected with the Factory. This sufficiently accounts for the contempt, which the majority of female prisoners entertain for the Factory, while it shows, also, why the solitary cell is considered the worst punishment.

Unable to decide 'whether horror or indignation prevails most in our mind', the journalist suggested the Cascades Female Factory should be called 'The Valley of the Shadow of Death' and speculated breathlessly on the effect the mob was having on the moral fabric of the colony through the system of assigning convict women to work in the homes of settlers:

Good God! When we consider that these wretches in human form, are scattered through the Colony, and admitted into the house of respectable families, coming into hourly association with their sons and daughters, we shudder at the consequences, and cannot forbear asking the question: 'Are there no means of preventing all this?' Is the Superintendent of the Female House of Correction (!) afraid of these harpies? Or is he too indolent and too good-natured to trouble himself about the matter? We cannot think that either is the case; for we believe Mr. Hutchinson to be a righteous man, and not likely to tolerate such rank abomination. If he be ignorant of the practices to which we have referred, we will willingly afford him all the information, that we possess.

In concluding this painful subject, we may observe, that a favorite resort of this Flash Mob, when any of its members are out of the Factory, is the Canteen of a Sunday afternoon, and the Military Barracks of a Sunday night, where comfortable quarters

may be procured until the morning! The whole system of Female
Prison Discipline is bad and rotten at the very core, tending only
to vice, immorality, and the most disgusting licentiousness.

Rants of this kind led inevitably to an 'Inquiry Into Female
Convict Discipline' between 1841 and 1843. The inquiry
named a number of women believed to be involved in these
activities, including Ellen Scott.

Ellen was a servant in Limerick, transported for life for
stealing a watch. Only eighteen when she arrived in Van
Diemen's Land, Ellen wasted no time disrupting the system.
Her record catalogues continuing and frequent breaches of just
about all the many rules and regulations applying to convict
women. Her regular absences, thieving and other crimes,
including 'dancing in a public house', earned her long periods
of solitary confinement, a spiked iron collar and plenty of hard
labour. She led an attack on the superintendent Mr Hutchinson
(his wife was the matron) and was once found 'in bed with
her master'. All in all, forty-eight offences are recorded against
Ellen between her arrival in 1830 and 1843 when she was
found guilty of trafficking tobacco into the Launceston Female
Factory, to where she had been transferred.

This transfer probably accounts for her relatively low-key
presence in the inquiry's report. She is mentioned, but no
changes are laid against her, unlike a number of other women.

Whether there was ever a pseudo-Masonic secret society of
lesbians at the Cascades, we will never know. Nor do we now
care. In 1847, after some years without punishment, Ellen Scott
received her freedom. She later married another ex-convict.
Then, like so many others, she fades from the records.

There was still trouble with the rowdy girls at the Cascades
in the mid-1840s and after. Some women simply refused to be
cowed by the system. The records show convicts such as Helen
Leslie, Catherine Owens, Phillis Perry and Mary Cuttle who
were punished every few months for absconding, drunkenness
and various forms of 'indecency' year after year, sometimes

until they died. From the 1850s the institution was gradually dismantled as transportation ceased and the buildings were used for other purposes. But the women's prison did not close until 1877. Today the place is recognised by UNESCO as the most important female convict site in Australia.

The Patriots

It is not well known that a large group of American and French-Canadian prisoners were sent to Australia in the wake of the Patriot War of 1837–38. A rebellion against British rule in Canada led by the French-speaking population drew in volunteer fighters from America. The rebellion was quickly and ruthlessly put down by the British, under the command of Sir George Arthur, previously Lieutenant-Governor of Van Diemen's Land, and the man after whom Port Arthur was named. Almost thirty of the Patriots were executed and the rest had their death sentences commuted to transportation. The French-Canadians were sent to New South Wales and the Americans to Van Diemen's Land.

The French-Canadians arrived in Sydney in February 1840, fearing the worst for themselves in a penal colony operating a regime of hard labour. They were sent to Longbottom Farm, near present-day Concord Oval, and located around halfway between Sydney and Parramatta. The farm was almost derelict by 1840 but was rebuilt as Longbottom Stockade to hold the Patriots. Their status as political prisoners and their good conduct gave them a privileged position, assisted by their Roman Catholic religion which gave them assistance from the church. Father John Brady said mass for the prisoners and also looked out for their well-being. He wrote:

> When I consider the courage of these prisoners, and their spirit of resignation, I cannot conceive how men so gentle, so modest and so good, whose conduct arouses the admiration of all those who are witnesses of it, can have deserved so terrible a punishment.

They have had the misfortune to see themselves snatched from the arms of their wives and children; they have seen their homes and their possessions given over to pillage and to destruction by fire and after months of anguish, fear and shattered hopes, spent in the depths of prison cells, they received the terrible sentence which is to separate them from all they held dear in the world, so as to cast them into banishment in a far distant soil, where they are suffering through being deprived of the most necessary things.

While the French-Canadians avoided forced labour, their rations were the same as other convicts, Brady observed: 'The food that they receive is so bad that the white Irish slave, accustomed to living on potatoes and salt could scarcely put up with it.'

The Patriots were fast-tracked to tickets-of-leave and within two years of their landing were assigned servants, enjoying the comparative liberty of that indulgence. By 1844 all had received free pardons. Most eventually returned home, though two died and one married and remained in the colony. A monument and some place names in the area commemorate this short but intense intercultural moment, including Canada Bay.

The Americans were not so lucky. In the eyes of the British government they were traitors, despite their citizenship. Discrimination against them began from the moment they left Canada. The French-Canadians were allowed to bring their clothes, belongings and money, while the Americans had to make do with whatever they had upon them. Massachusetts-born Samuel Snow wrote an account of the American experience in Van Diemen's Land, which he considered 'on the very south-eastern outskirts of habitable creation'.

When the American Patriots disembarked from the *Buffalo*, Lieutenant-Governor Sir John Franklin, later to perish in the notorious quest for the Northwest Passage, was not certain how the Americans were to be treated. While he waited for clarification from faraway London, he sent them to work on the road gangs where, according to Snow, 'Our work was a mile and a half from the station, and frequently was it our lot, to return to our huts this distance, through the cold and rain after a hard day's toiling, and have to lay down for the night with our clothes drenched with water, and no fire allowed us to dry them.'

As for the French-Canadians in Sydney, the food in Van Diemen's Land was cause for complaint: 'I have seen men driven to the necessity of picking up potatoe [sic] skins and cabbage leaves, which they would boil and eat to quiet their hunger.' There were failed escapes ending in sentences to Port Arthur, though the Americans were spared the usual floggings and hard labour suffered by ordinary convicts. Not everyone in the system agreed with this lenient approach, as Snow recalled:

> Capt. Wright, our superintendent, who succeeded old Bobby Nutman, was an inhuman, overbearing, unprincipled, incarnate devil, he worked us incessantly, would not grant us the least favor if he could avoid it, and made his boast that 'he would subdue that d-d independent Yankee spirit of ours if possible.' If he succeeded in so doing, we have not yet learned the fact.

Eventually the Americans were separated and made to join the standard convict population where they all starved together. Snow found that 'it seemed impossible for our new associates to live without stealing' just to get enough to eat. If they were caught, the convicts were flogged and made to work in irons. Granted their tickets-of-leave, the Americans found themselves in an economy with little demand for labour. Some clubbed together and took over a farm, putting in a good crop and receiving a fine harvest. But the price of wheat and oats dropped and they came out with only a few pounds each, which was soon spent on necessities.

From 1844 the Americans received free pardons and 'were at liberty to leave this country, to which none of us had formed attachments'. The men had to pay their own passages back to America but eventually, in January 1845, 'we left the land with thankful hearts' after five years and 'could say with emphasis':

Farewell, Van Dieman [*sic*], ruin's gate,
With joy we leave thy shore;
And fondly hope our wretched fate,
Will drive us there no more.

The Old Lags' Hero

The short life of William Westwood was wasted mostly in bondage—from most of which he continually escaped. He was born in Essex in 1820 and fell into crime from an early age, serving a year for highway robbery while still in his teens. Arriving in Sydney in July 1837, the seventeen-year-old, already scarred and tattooed, was to serve fourteen years for stealing a coat.

Assigned to Phillip Parker King's property at Bungendore near modern-day Canberra, Westwood was poorly treated and starved by the overseer. He was convicted of stealing wheat in April the following year, serving six months before being returned to Bungendore. He ran away early in 1839 but was soon recaptured and flogged. In September 1840 he again escaped to become the 'gentleman' bushranger known as 'Jackey-Jackey'. Westwood followed the outlaw hero code of courtesy to women and by not offering violence to his victims. He avoided capture and once stole enough money from a mail coach to live the high life in Sydney for a month without being caught. But in April 1841 he was tried at Berrima for some of his bushranging crimes and sentenced to transportation for life.

True to his Robin Hood image, Westwood escaped, even though he was wearing chains. His cool daring won grudging accolades in the colonial press, further gilding his reputation. Recaptured, he was sent to Cockatoo Island and then to Port Arthur. He made repeated attempts to escape but was apprehended and given floggings, solitary and hard labour for punishment. A reforming commandant of Port Arthur gave Westwood a chance to mend his ways. It worked for a while but he eventually fell back into crime. He was tried for being armed and illegally at large in 1845. The death sentence was commuted to transportation for life to Norfolk Island.

Here, in July 1846, the new commandant, concerned at what he considered the privilege of allowing prisoners their own cooking and eating implements, had them secretly removed. This was the last straw. William Barber was serving his sentence on Norfolk at that time and described what happened:

> One of the principal causes which led to that fearful outbreak was the stoppage of the daily allowance of two pounds of potatoes, which, from the saltness of the beef, were in that hot climate almost absolutely necessary. Upon the failure of the potato crop, an equivalent for these two pounds of sweet potatoes was sought, and it was at length determined by the authorities that two ounces of raw salt pork, being exactly similar in money value, should be given as a substitute. The official report says: 'This has created much dissatisfaction among the men generally, from the very small quantity, which could, with due regard to the public purse, be apportioned: and so difficult has it been to make the men comprehend the equity of such an equivalent, that a large number for a long time refused to receive it, in the hope that some other substitute would ultimately be granted them.' The substitution of two ounces of pork for two pounds of potatoes was an exasperating mockery, which the men bore with patience until the sudden seizure of all their pots and cooking utensils, when an outbreak ensued, resulting in a fearful loss of life.

A special commission tried fourteen men for the massacre, including William Westwood. Most of them showed no repentance for their actions:

> Some laughed and jested; others browbeat witnesses in a style quite professional, and, I presume, acquired in a long experience of courts of justice in England. One addressed the Court at considerable length, after having clearly examined the witnesses, speaking fluently and well, enumerating all the weak points in

the evidence against him, and noting every discrepancy in the facts. This man was more deeply implicated than any, except Westwood. Another, an Irish lad of scarce twenty years of age, began his defence by calling a witness, whom, after a careful personal scrutiny, he dismissed without a question, professing 'not to like the look of the fellow.' Having called another witness, who described himself as a 'scourger or flagellator', much merriment ensued among the prisoners, and the Irish lad finally joked him out of the witness-box, and called another, with whom the following dialogue took place:

Prisoner. You're Darker, I believe?

Witness. I am.

Prisoner. You've an extensive acquaintance on the island?

Witness. I know the men on the settlement mostly.

Prisoner. Divil doubt ye! It's the big rogues is best known. Now, Darker, tell me. Didn't ye some months ago say to a man on this island, that you had so much villainy in yir head, that it was a-busting out at yir ears?

Here the judge's patience was exhausted, although such scenes are common on such occasions, and the witness was ordered to stand down.

Twelve of the accused convicts were found guilty. When they heard the death sentence, they became violent 'cursing the prosecutor and all connected with the trial'. But Westwood remained calm and stood up to address the court in an 'unbroken voice':

He seemed contrite, but had lost none of that coolness and air of resolution, which had characterised him throughout. He expressed deep sorrow for his share in the massacre, sensible that he could say but little in extenuation of it. He expected to suffer, and was content to die, but regretted that innocent men should be involved in the punishment. It was observed, however, that he did not mention any names. He went on to say that he entered life with a kindly feeling towards his fellow-men, which had been changed into misanthropy by harsh treatment, fraud, and cruelty. 'Since childhood', he exclaimed, 'I have never known what kindness was. I have struggled for liberty, and have robbed, when in the bush, to supply the cravings of nature but I never raised my hand against a fellow-creature till the present time.'

He complained bitterly of the harsh treatment he had received, not at Norfolk Island, but previously in Van Dieman's [*sic*] Land. It was said by an officer on the Island that, in his case, there was some ground for the complaint; for he had heard that an act of brutality on the part of an overseer was the occasion of Westwood's absconding and taking to those courses, which now . . . brought him to an ignominious end.

On the evening before his execution, Westwood wrote a letter to the religious instructor, Thomas Rogers:

Sir the strong ties of earth will soon be wrenched and the burning fever of this life will soon be quenched and my grave will be heavens resting place for me William Westwood. Sir out of the Bitter cup of misery I have drunk from my sixteenth year 10 long years, and the sweetest draught is that which takes away the misery of living death—it is the friend that deceives no man, all will then be quiet, no tyrant will disturb my repose I hope—Wm. Westwood.

The twelve ringleaders were hanged a few days later, together with five other convicts. The gallows were in such demand that they required the services of two hangmen, both convicts. They were selected from twenty or more enthusiastic convict volunteers for the grisly privilege: 'One of the two men selected stated, in his written application, that having been a notorious offender and now deeply penitent for his past misconduct, he "hoped to be permitted to retrieve his character by serving the Government on the present occasion".'

William 'Jackey-Jackey' Westwood was buried in unhallowed ground, the final punishment for executed felons. He was twenty-six years old. His legend as the 'gentleman bushranger' lived on among old hands and the general public for many years, though he is mostly forgotten today.

The Ghost Poet

He wanders through the records of trials, floggings and bush-ranging. He serves hard time at many places, including Cockatoo Island, the *Phoenix* hulk in Sydney Harbour and Port Arthur. He is recalled in the odd convict memoir as 'the poet'.

A swag of songs, poems and epigrams are attributed to Francis MacNamara, also known as 'Frank the Poet', many more than he probably composed. But he left his mark never-theless and is today regarded as one of the great characters of convictism and as an early martyr of labour. Whether there was just one 'Frank the Poet' or if his legend is an amalgam of other similar figures with ready wits and quick tongues, we do not know. Perhaps it hardly matters. If no such person ever existed in the convict days, we would have invented him anyway.

Frank's story begins in uncertainty. He may have hailed from Cork, Tipperary or Clare. He first comes to light in 1832 at his trial in Kilkenny for breaking a shop window and stealing some cloth. Defending himself, he cross-examined the arresting policemen and the shopkeeper:

> Please your Wordship, as to Mr. Prince the constable, his oath should not be thought much against me. He may know the weight of that book in penny weights, but of the awful meaning and substance he knows nothing, often as he may have kissed it. He should have the eye of a hawk, and the vigilance of a cat, to see me do what he swears. By the virtue of your oath, young man, (to the shop man,) did you get directions from any persons as to what you were to swear against me.

The shopkeeper denied it, then Frank questioned the constable, who also denied the accusation. Frank turned mischievously to the magistrate, again intentionally mispronouncing his title:

> Now your wordship, I must prove them both perjurers: did not
> that decent looking gentleman sitting under your wordship, in a
> loud and distinct manner, that no body could mistake, direct them
> to swear the truth, the whole truth, and nothing but the truth?

This did him no good, of course. Leaving the dock with the expected guilty verdict Frank waved his hand and declaimed loudly:

> I dread not the dangers by land or by sea,
> That I'll meet on my voyage to Botany Bay;
> My labours are over, my vocation is past,
> And 'tis there I'll rest easy and happy at last.

But Frank's future was to be anything but easy and happy. Aboard the transport *Eliza* in June 1832 he was flogged for bad conduct, the officer responsible recognising his abilities as well as his failings:

> Today gave MacNamara (one of the convicts) 2 dozen [lashes]
> for bad conduct. This fellow is a sad scamp and yet far above the
> common herd in some respects. He has considerable abilities, has
> written some very palpable lines on his trial and sentence since he
> came on board and has a very extensive knowledge of the Scriptures.
> He it appears was tried for a very slight offence but his conduct on
> his trial was so bad that he was transported for 7 years. He recited
> a mock heroic poem of his own composing in which he ridiculed
> judge jury and other officers of the Court that had tried him. This
> of course enhanced his offence and added to his punishment.

After disembarking, Frank continued his career of defiance and disruption. Over the next few years he served on an ironed gang on Goat Island, absconded several times, frequently disobeyed orders, refused to work and was found drunk in the cells, among other infringements. For these offences he was repeatedly flogged, worked in chains, placed in solitary confinement, and made to walk the treadmill. In 1842 he was captured with some other armed bushrangers and retransported for life to Van Diemen's Land. He then went to Port Arthur with many other desperate re-offenders, including the famed bushranger Martin Cash, who later recollected Frank's most famous introductory calling card:

My name is Francis MacNamara
A native of Cashell in the county Tipperary
Sworn tyranny's foe
And while I've life I'll crow.

As soon as he arrived Frank was involved in a convict strike against one of the typically cruel practices of overseers. The gang carrying bundles of wooden shingles was led by one convict with an extra light load. This man ran ahead while the rest of the gang, all with full loads, were made to keep up with him. Frank and the others who had just arrived from Sydney refused to play the game and only walked with their loads.

The overseer shouted for them to close up, but they took no notice of him, so that the other men were coming back for loads before they had reached the first resting place. We each had bundles of shingles to carry, and the Sydney men said, 'Now, do you think these bundles are overweight?' Some of them replied, 'Yes'. They then emptied some of the shingles out, and tied them up again, so that by the time they had done that, the other men had been into the settlement with their loads. When they got into the settlement they were marched in front of the office, and the commandant came. The loads were weighed, and found to be underweight.

The commandant called for the triangle and the floggers and a clerk took down the names of the defiant convicts.

Amongst the rest there was the notorious Jackey Jackey, Frank the Poet, and Jones, and Cavanagh. There were upwards of thirty pairs of cats and four flagellators, and the surgeon, a young man named Dr Benson, who kept laughing and joking, and playing with his stick as unconcerned as though he was in a ballroom. When their names were taken, every other man was called out, and received thirty-six lashes. A fresh flagellator giving every twenty lashes, and they try to see who can give it the worst.

But the floggings had no effect. The next day the convicts again refused to run. 'They were then ranked up, and all were flogged and sent to work again; the overseer still snapping at them and if they could have got him in the bush they would have killed him.' On the third day, the same again. This time it was seven days solitary on bread and water. But when they came out and returned to work, the convicts' resolve remained strong and they refused to run. Again they were hauled in front of the commandant. This time he listened to their complaint and ordered an end to the running treatment. A rare win over the system for the convicts.

It was in Port Arthur that Frank's reputation among his peers was established. He managed to keep mostly out of trouble until 1847 when he was given a ticket-of-leave. He received a conditional pardon later that year and his Certificate of Freedom in 1849. In departing he gave his best-known verse nugget:

Land of lags and kangaroo,
Of possums and the scarce emu,
Squatter's home and prisoner's hell,
Land of Sodom, fare-thee-well.

A free man once again, Frank turns up next on the goldfields around Hill End, New South Wales.

Despite his strong start at Port Arthur, the horrors of the place finally broke his spirit and his body. People who knew him in the years leading to his death said he often coughed up blood. He died at the central-west New South Wales town of Mudgee in 1861. The examining doctor pronounced him dead of cold and malnourishment, diplomatically not mentioning the ravages of alcohol.

Frank's many verses were well known among convicts and old lags, their defiance and sharp humour speaking strongly to their attitudes to authority and the system in general. In death his reputation grew. An obituary published shortly after his death by a man who knew him told the story of Frank's assignment to a station up the country:

> The first duty appointed him was to drive off the cockatoos from a paddock of newly sown grain. Frank performed this duty in the following provoking manner; he wrote out a number of threatening notices to the cockatoos, that they were prohibited from crossing the fence to the grain, and these notices he put at the tops of poles which he fastened at regular distances all round the paddock fences. When asked by the Super, what all those papers meant, he replied. 'Did you not tell me to order the cockatoos off the ground?'

The legend of Frank the Poet did not take long to flower. He was previously known mainly among the 'old hands', his songs and verse transmitted orally and in handwritten form. Now his life and work were featured in newspapers in the years immediately following his death and he popped up in the published memories of ex-convicts, including Van Diemen's Land bushranger Martin Cash. His work, rarely published in his lifetime, began to appear in newspapers and he even featured in a play about Martin Cash in 1900.

There are stories of other Irish convict poets. Some of these have probably blended with Frank's potent legend as a witty but determined defier of the system. Historians calculate that he received nearly 600 lashes and endured many days in solitary during his time in various places of condemnation. Others suffered even more, but Frank's ability to express the horrors of the system with his sharp wit made him a convict hero.

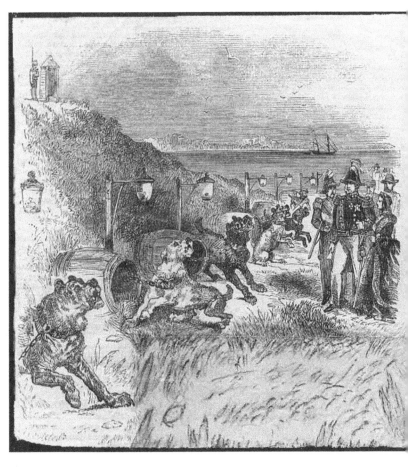

*'Bloodhounds on Eaglehawk Neck to prevent the escape of convicts, Tasmania'.
Eaglehawk Neck was a narrow isthmus connecting Port Arthur to the mainland
of Tasmania.*

7
Places of Condemnation

All those places of condemnation and penal stations in New
South Wales

'The Convict's Lament', c. 1830

Pluto's Land

Convicts named Macquarie Harbour 'Pluto' or Pluto's Land',
a reference to the Roman god of the underworld, or hell. They
feared the prison, on Tasmania's remote west coast, more than
Port Arthur. A 22-year-old convict named John Thompson
scribbled some lines of verse that described the harsh conditions there:

Before the morn has warm'd the east
Each man must early rise
To labour all the day like beast
Till darkness clouds the skies.
In open boat on billows tost
Where raging tempests roar
In heavy seas and vapours lost
To ply the labouring oar.
Then to the lonely woods repair

To swing the axe, or mawls,
Each blow with equal force must bear
Till down the timber falls.
The timber then to form in rafts
With chains and staples bound
To build colonial 'trading crafts'
Men drag it off the ground.
When rain in torrents down does pour
They labour all the day
At night they ply the labouring oar
To drag it o'er the way.
When one day's food, not half enough
Each man will now receive
Of coarsest beef, both lean and tough
Which scarce can he perceive.
With want of food they're driven away,
In woods and mountains lost;
To birds and beasts they fall a prey
Upon the cruel coast.
Their wearied limbs, with hunger prest,
Refuse their weight to bear
Their hearts beat slow within the breast
And death salutes their ear.
And thus in grief afflicted sore
They stretch their limbs and die,
Their wither'd flesh by birds is tore
And scattered through the sky.
Poor exiles here forever lost
And left in deep despair
Upon a wretched cruel coast
With murmurs ring the air.
Three posts triangle firmly stand
Deep stained with human gore
A picture frame for Pluto's land
Where poor men's flesh is tore.
Where men are bound both hand and foot

Fast to the fatal wood,
From mangled flesh that's basely cut
Runs streams of British blood . . .

Thompson was probably one of the fifteen convicts who escaped Macquarie Harbour with the notorious Matthew Brady in 1824. They stole a boat and sailed it to Hobart and began a two-year period of bushranging. Brady was seen by many as a bushranger in the mould of the 'gentleman highwayman' who did not inflict unnecessary violence on his victims. Nevertheless, he and his companions carried out many raids, including taking over the town of Sorell, northeast of Hobart. They released the convicts held there, jailed the soldiers and had a party, in behaviour foreshadowing some of Ned Kelly's exploits half a century later.

Brady's gang grew into a serious threat to the legal authorities and social stability. Lieutenant-Governor Arthur initially offered 20 gallons of rum as reward for the capture of the bushranger. When Brady heard of this, he posted his own reward notice and threatening letter on the door of the Royal Oak Inn in Crossmarch:

> It has caused Matthew Brady much concern that such a person as Sir George Arthur is at large. Twenty gallons of rum will be given to any person that can deliver this person to me. I also caution John Priest that I will hang him for his ill-treatment of Mrs. Blackwell, at Newtown.

Arthur eventually had to raise the ante to the substantial sum of 25 pounds.

Despite his sense of humour and network of sympathisers, Brady could not avoid the usual fate of bushrangers. He was captured in 1826 and hanged for murdering a man who betrayed him. By then Brady was a popular hero. People petitioned against his sentence, many sent gifts to his condemned cell and it is said that the soldiers he locked up in Sorell paid their respects. When asked why he had not surrendered, he replied: 'Because I knew it would end this way and I wanted to live as long as I could.' He shared the scaffold with the cannibal and child killer, Mark Jeffries, complaining bitterly at having to die beside such a monster.

The Rats' Nest

Dutch explorers mistakenly named Rottnest Island after seeing the small marsupials known as quokkas. To the Nyungar people, the same 19 square kilometre rock has for much longer been known as Wadjemup, 'a place across the water', and was traditionally regarded by them as of negative spiritual significance.

From 1838 the island was used as a prison for Aboriginal men and boys transported there from many different parts of the colony. Ten men were reportedly sent there in August 1838, among them Buoyeen, for wounding Charles Hokin, a lad eleven years of age, on the Canning River; Molly Dobbin and Tyoocan, for breaking and entering and stealing a quantity of flour; Helia, an old man guilty of the murder of an Aboriginal woman in the streets of Perth; Cogatt, for stealing butter; and Goodap, for stealing, 'a known bad character'. These six Aboriginal men did not stay long, according to the Western Australian newspapers:

It seems that on the evening of the night they got away they were all made fast together by passing a trace chain through their irons and locking the end with a handcuff: the chain was placed round a cypress-tree [*sic*]. In order to disengage the chain from the tree, they set fire to it, and thus were, comparatively speaking, at large,—the irons having been cut from one leg of each native by Mr. Welch as an act of humanity, on their arrival at the island. It has been remarked as surprising that the falling of the tree was not heard by any of the party; but the tree, although considered sufficiently large for security, could not make much noise, as it fell during a heavy storm of wind and rain which lasted during the night.

It is supposed they were clear from the tree about two or three o'clock in the morning, and made their way immediately to the beach, where Mr. Thomson's boat was lying, and there with some of the iron work contrived to break the handcuff, which united the two ends of the chain. They all got into the boat and pushed off, trusting to the open sea—a most foolhardy and perilous adventure; indeed, it was attended with so much danger, that those who are experienced boatmen would not [have] ventured to have crossed from the island to the main in such a tempest as they must have encountered.

The boat capsized in the surf and Helia drowned, though there was a claim that he was killed by Goodap. Whatever the truth of the matter, the death was avenged with the murder of Goodap by Helia's relatives.

As Rottnest Island developed as an Aboriginal prison the inmates were employed in quarrying and general labouring that built the lighthouse and they also operated a salt works. In the 1850s they were taken back to the mainland in work gangs to build the Perth–Albany road.

Bringing prisoners to the island from distant parts of Western Australia often meant long and hard journeys during which the prisoners were sometimes chained. A Nullarbor Mirning man named Benjamin told the 1883 Royal Commission inquiring into the treatment of Aboriginal prisoners:

I walked from Eyre Sand Patch to Albany naked, with a chain on my neck. My neck was sore from chain. I knocked up from the long walk. Policeman Truslove no good. He hit me for knocking up . . . I came with a bullock chain around my neck from Eyre Sand Patch to Albany. When it rained my neck was very sore from the chain . . . I had no clothes given to me from Eyre Sand Patch to Albany.

Over the years Rottnest held a growing number of inmates, peaking at 170 in 1880. Three years later an influenza outbreak killed more than fifty prisoners. The resulting inquiry, conducted while a deadly measles epidemic raged through the prisoners, revealed lack of clothing, bedding and warmth, and four sleeping in the small cells with each having only 60 centimetres of space. The inquiry led to some improvements to the poor conditions in which the convicts were housed and treated. The octagonal Quod prison was erected as part of these improvements but was inadequate for decent accommodation.

Incidents of violence and probable murder by the father-and-son superintendents, Henry Vincent and, twenty years later William Vincent, were shoddily investigated. The Vincents were both implicated in the killing of a prisoner in 1865. A coroner decided the death of the man was by natural causes rather than William Vincent's violent attack. He was given a sentence of three months hard labour.

As the towns of Perth and Fremantle grew, calls became louder for Rottnest Island to be opened up to holiday-makers. The prison was closed in 1903, though a number of inmates served out the remainder of their time, helping to establish the tourism industry that is now the island's mainstay.

For Aboriginal people, the island is an especially unhappy place. As well as its history of incarceration, 370, perhaps more, deceased inmates were buried in unmarked graves. Most died of disease but at least five were hanged. Hundreds of Aboriginal people travelled to the island in March 1988 protesting the neglect of gravesites. Since then, research has revealed more burials than were previously suspected and there have been attempts to incorporate the story of the prison into the interpretation of the island's history provided to the half a million who visit each year. An Aboriginal tour was established in which the story was told from the indigenous perspective, and the current development plans include a significant emphasis on the Aboriginal aspects of the island's history, despite the difficulty of presenting these in a holiday atmosphere.

Coal River

Coal was found near Newcastle very early in the colony of New South Wales's history. The first attempts to extract it seem to have been in 1801. Convicts were assigned to work in the mines under harsh conditions and about thirty of the Irish rebels from the Castle Hill (later known as 'Vinegar Hill') rising of 1804 were sent there to keep them separate from the main body of convicts in case they fomented further defiance.

In the 1830s the Australian Agricultural Company took over coal mining in the area but by the end of the decade was experiencing severe labour shortages as free workers did not wish to work in the mines and the convicts who had no choice were too broken down to be effective. According to reports written in 1840, this was due to 'the feeble and worn out state of their assigned servants, occasioned by excessive labour and the small allowance of rations awarded them':

> These miserable creatures have every appearance of 'Walking spectres'—such woe begone and wretched objects are scarcely to be met within the colony. An allowance of 3s per ton has been offered these men to perform extra work; but their strength will scarcely carry them through their regular work, setting aside over time labour. They can only be compared with an over worked horse, who, despite all whipping, is unable to job one step farther. We have numerous instances of men belonging to the Company, committing offences for the mere purpose of getting into ironed gangs, in preference to remaining in their service.

Francis MacNamara, or 'Frank the Poet', may have been one of those who preferred being in chains above ground than mistreated in mines underground and penned a poem expressing his resolve not to dig coal and his general defiance of the system:

> When Christ from Heaven comes down straightway,
> All His Father's laws to expound,
> MacNamara shall work that day
> For the Company underground.
> When the man in the moon to Moreton Bay,

Is sent in shackles bound
MacNamara shall work that day
For the Company underground.
When the Cape of Good Hope to Twofold Bay
Comes for the change of a pound.
MacNamara shall work that day
For the Company underground.
When cows in lieu of milk yield tea,
And all lost treasures are found,
MacNamara shall work that day
For the Company underground.
When the Australian Co's heaviest dray
Is drawn 80 miles by a hound,
MacNamara shall work that day
For the Company underground.
When a frog, a caterpillar and a flea
Shall travel the globe all round,
McNamara shall work that day
For the Company underground.
When turkeycocks on Jews harps play
And mountains dance at the sound,
MacNamara shall work that day
For the Company underground.
When Christmas falls on the 1st of May
And O'Connell's King of England crown'd,
MacNamara shall work that day
For the Company underground.
When thieves ever robbing on the highway
For their sanctity are renowned,
MacNamara shall work that day
For the Company underground.
When the quick and the dead shall stand in array
Cited at the trumpet's sound,
Even then, damn me if I'd work a day
For the Company underground.
Nor overground.

The Norfolk Island Suffering of Thomas Cook

Thomas Cook, lawyer's clerk, was only nineteen when he foolishly sent a threatening letter to a local auctioneer. Even though the letter was partly a youthful prank, the judge took a dim view of Cook's actions and transported him to New South Wales for fourteen years in 1831. Cook landed a soft job looking after the stores in Sydney but got into trouble with the superintendent of Hyde Park Barracks and was sent to work in irons on the Blue Mountains road gangs. Here, he experienced want of food, perishing cold and backbreaking labour. He also saw corruption, from the sub-inspector of roads, all the way down to the bottom of the convict pecking order, the status of each man determined by brute force. The well-bred clerk did not do well in such a society.

Cook was transferred to Port Macquarie in 1835 with other educated convicts known as 'specials' but absconded the following year. Recognised as an escapee, he fled once again but was eventually recaptured and convicted on a charge of forgery. He was to be retransported to the notorious Norfolk Island for life.

While awaiting passage, Cook was held with other convicts on the *Phoenix*, a leaking prison hulk almost as unpleasant as Norfolk Island. 'During my stay on board, scenes of depravity which human nature shudders to contemplate were exhibited with apparent delight,' he said. Wrongly accused of smoking tobacco, he and his nine cell-mates were punished viciously by the keeper:

> He sent for ten pairs of Handcuffs, took our shirts, Blankets and clothes away, and manacling each of our hands behind our backs, he reefed the legs, which were very heavily Ironed, to the upper part of the Iron Staunchions of the Cell by means of a Bar outside, with the whole weight of our chains and bodies pressing on our Shoulder blades for the night, in a state of perfect Nudity. By the following morning and for two days afterwards, I could scarcely regain the strength of my Arms.

Cook witnessed the same punishment of other convicts aboard the hulk, with the addition of gags and water dousing. He was then transferred to 'that place of horror', Norfolk Island, with ninety-nine others, already in fear of his life:

> The dreadful picture afforded me the intensity of sufferings and torture to which every Victim to this Island was subjected was most appalling. So much terror had this produced in my mind that during a faint squall on our passage, I most fervently prayed to the Almighty to suffer the Vessel to sink and mercifully receive the Souls of all from a state of endurance worse than death in its most terrific shape.

These forebodings were amply justified. When he reached Norfolk Island, Cook was taken ashore and with the other convicts, stripped and lined up on the beach where they underwent 'a minute and most indelicate inspection', before being marched to the Barrack Yard. For Cook, it was the beginning of the end: 'From this instant, all my hope of happiness was to cease. My beloved Parents, my Brothers, and Sisters for ever lost to me. Shut out from the World for ever to herd with beings in human form, but whose every action excluded their claim to the appellation of "Man".'

The one-time clerk soon discovered the dreadful psychology of incarceration and the extremes to which its victims were reduced. He described the 'Underlings in Office', convicts who sought favours from their overseers by obtaining information from other convicts, as 'despicable Treacherous characters, who passed on to them the daily tittle-tattle'. The Underlings traded the information, true or false, to the authorities in return for preferment or other benefits, even if it was only 'a stinking piece of tobacco'.

But the real moral corruption of this hierarchy of horror was that it was all a cruel game. The hapless convicts who acted as informants to the Underlings were only being strung along. When they had revealed sufficient details about whatever real or imagined plot was being hatched, they were themselves 'suddenly pounced upon', and in a short time 'weighed to the Earth with heavy chains'. According to Cook, 'By these means were the most inoffensive entrapped, cruelly tortured, then placed in the custody of the most brutal overseer, and under him employed at the most harassing descriptions of labour, in whose presence a murmur—nay, an unpleasant look, would again subject the already emaciated wretch to further lacerations and torture. Any who managed to stand aloof from this pitiless play were eventually snared, their aloofness given as proof that they were "artful and dangerous" characters and so, marked men'.

Yet even in this system there was an occasional blip of justice. Cook described an incident in which men were wrongly accused with false evidence of a mutiny. The authorities discovered that the report was fabricated, and the two convicts who sought to implicate their fellows in a nonexistent crime themselves received 300 lashes each. But this was a rarity: 'Human nature could not long patiently endure such dreadful state of suffering, and so treated, men as a natural result became desperate, and in all their passions and actions were Very Devils.' They were, however, devils without hope. Facing a possible lifetime of such constrained savagery 'reduced them to the lowest stage of despair'.

Men were known to commit crimes that would ensure their hanging as the only way to escape Norfolk Island. On Boxing Day 1835 a convict named Thompson was executed for attempting to kill another: 'A baser character than Thompson could not possibly be conceived. He was universally held in hatred as one of the creatures of the Underlings, and was well known as a disgusting wretch; like others on the island, he was given over to propensities abhorrent to nature.' Considered at the time both a moral and legal crime, homosexuality among convicts was often encouraged by overseers as another element of punishment, regardless of individual sexual orientations.

Thomas Cook eventually became a convict overseer. He escaped Norfolk Island, not by sea as a very few did, but by a record of good behaviour and bravery displayed during a boating accident in 1840. He was sent back to Sydney for a while but again ended up in Port Macquarie. He managed to escape from here in 1843 and, as far as the official record goes, was never recaptured.

On the Square, Ever

The Vicar General of Sydney, the Very Reverend William Ullathorne, presided over the fates of the ringleaders of a failed Norfolk Island rising of 1834: 'As I mentioned the names of those men who were to die, they one after another, as their names were pronounced, dropped on their knees and thanked God that they were to be delivered from that horrible place, whilst the others remained standing mute, weeping. It was the most horrible scene I have ever witnessed.'

Norfolk Island's first penal settlement was established shortly after the founding of Sydney. It was abandoned in 1814, only to be re-opened eleven years later as a punishment for 'the worst description of convicts'. These unfortunates, mainly re-offenders, came from many places and by the mid-1840s there were prisoners:

> . . . from every part of the British dominions, and, indeed, from almost every part of the world. Besides English, Irish, Scotch, Frenchmen, Italians, and Germans, there were Chinamen from Hong Kong, Aborigines from New Holland, West Indian Blacks, Greeks, Caffres, and Malays. Among these were soldiers, for desertion, idiots, madmen, boys of seventeen, and old men of eighty. All these were indiscriminately herded together, without reference to age, crime, nation, or any other distinction.

The brutality of the system at Norfolk Island was notorious. Men were flogged for minor offences, left in solitary confinement for lengthy periods and driven to hard labour in an endless routine of backbreaking work. The only way off the island was by release at the end of a sentence, by escape or by death. As a British parliamentary committee heard in 1838: 'Two or three men murdered their fellow-prisoners, with the certainty of being detected and executed, apparently without malice and with very little excitement, stating that they knew that they should be hanged, but it was better than being where they were.'

There were rumours of a secret convict society that organised such extreme actions and generally ran the lives of the convicts and their keepers. These stories were later transformed by writers such as Price Warung and Marcus Clarke into a shadowy freemasonry known as 'The Ring'. This group was forty or more of the longest-serving prisoners who swore to be loyal to each other and take reprisals for punishments against them. They enforced a code of silence, not only among themselves, but obliging every prisoner to keep silent. Informing against any of The Ring's activities meant certain death.

From this basic prison gang, The Ring was over the years inflated into a clandestine criminal cult with its own hierarchy, obligations, oaths and gory rituals that would not be out of place in a Dan Brown thriller. Its initiations involved drinking blood taken from the veins of the existing members and the initiates, accompanied by a dreadful oath of eternal loyalty which began:

Hand to hand,
On Earth, in Hell,
Sick or Well,
On Sea, on Land,
On the Square, ever.

And ended:

Stiff or in Breath,
Lag or Free,
You and Me,
In Life, in Death,
On the Cross, never.

The primary purpose of The Ring was to defy the authority of the jailers and to reverse the power relations of the penal system, most completely played out on Norfolk Island.

Did The Ring exist? Historians doubt that it was ever as lurid as convict writers depicted, though prison gangs are found in most jail populations and it would be surprising if somewhere as brutal as Norfolk Island did not have some form of secret convict confederacy.

The Water Rats

Australia's first organised lifesaving 'club' may not have been Bondi or Bronte, as Sydneysiders might have you believe, but a bunch of convicts on Norfolk Island. At this infamous penal colony, ships had to stand off the island beyond a shallow bar, sending their cargoes ashore in row boats. The waters around Kingston pier were notoriously dangerous and it was very easy for an inexperienced or inattentive helmsman to get his craft into potentially fatal trouble. Boats were frequently swamped, tipping their unfortunate occupants into boiling seas.

By the 1840s the island's convicts had formed themselves into a small band of lifesavers, known as the 'Water Rats'. Whenever a ship arrived, the 'rats' lined up on the rocks, ready for duty. Wearing only cotton drawers, they launched themselves into the waves at the first sign of trouble from incoming boats. Over the years, many incoming soldiers, civilians and convicts were saved from drowning in this way.

In the Norfolk Island Museum lies the diary of Joshua Gregory. In 1842 an American ship hove to off Kingston and lowered a small boat carrying a man and woman. Those on shore tried frantically to warn off the sailors attempting the perilous passage but they were ignored:

> On came the gallant little boat, jumping from wave to wave like a thing of life. When they had got within fifty yards of the bar they could see their danger, but it was too late to retreat, for she

was then in the midst of heavy swells and it was as safe to go one way as the other. The crew showed both strength and skill, but it was all to no purpose for the swells were too much for them. Sometimes she was completely covered with the spray and drenched to the skin the people who were in her. She neared the point and I could see the lady was in great alarm. She looked towards the shore in a most pitiful manner.

Desperately, the crew of the dangerously rocking small boat tried to clear the bar, often hidden by the boiling surf:

When they gained the bar the boat was quite unmanageable and was pitched about from wave to wave like a feather. At last she was thrown by a huge swell, into the air, and came down bottom uppermost whelming the unfortunate people into the rolling waves. Now the Water Rats threw themselves into the water, nobly breasting the surf and in less than five minutes they were all safe and sound on shore.

The convict lifesavers had performed their mercy once again. 'They were certainly the best swimmers I ever saw in my life,' Gregory wrote admiringly.

This was only one of many similar incidents in which the Water Rats dragged people, high and low, from certain death. They became famous, even attracting the attention of Charles Dickens, who wrote about them in his magazine *Household Words* in 1852. Anticipating the development of surf lifesaving more than fifty years later, the Water Rats were by then using ropes to drag stricken souls ashore.

Why did they do it? For successfully saving lives, the convicts were given a reduction on their sentences. For gifting those they rescued more time to live, the Water Rats won less time to serve.

A Running Fire of Curtseys

On New Year's Day, 1851, senior military officer and author Colonel Godfrey Mundy was one of a small group visiting

Hobart's Cascades Female Factory. He was in for a surprise or two.

Mundy described the location of the factory, wedged into a gully at the foot of Mount Wellington, its buildings enclosed in a high wall and its inmates contained by barred gates and sharp-eyed turnkeys—'it is, in short, a gaol in every respect.' The matron, 'a dignified lady who looked quite capable of maintaining strict discipline', greeted the visitors. There were 730 women and 130 infants in the prison. A group of seventy or eighty women were formed up for inspection in one of the squares that made up the establishment. They were available for hire as servants and were 'the better conducted, and the pregnant women'.

Elsewhere, the colonel saw 'more troublesome and notorious characters, who were under restraint and not permitted to go into service'. Their uniform was 'a very unbecoming one' consisting of a white mob cap and a dress of grey duffle. As the visitors passed along the ranks, 'the poor creatures saluted us with a running fire of curtseys, and a dead silence was everywhere observed'.

In the exercise yard were sixty or so women with babies from two days to two years old, all silent. Mundy observed:

> One would have thought them all deaf and dumb;—never was I before in so numerous a nursery;—I hope I never may again! The children were mostly healthy and pretty. As for their mothers— there must, I suppose, be a good deal in dress as an element of beauty—for I scarcely saw a tolerably pretty woman in seven hundred. Some of the females, I found, were the hired nurses of the establishment—not the mothers of the children. Of these latter many, it appears, merely enter the factory to deposit their 'kid forlorn,' and, when sufficiently recovered, return to service in the town or country within the district to which their ticket or pass extends, and not a few re-enter its walls as soon as it is possible for them to require again obstetric assistance.

Mundy knew that 'many of these poor brats will never know their own fathers—their mothers, perhaps, know them no better: and many of the wretched little ones, in the hands of the nurses, will never know either parent'.

The visiting doctor said that the more troublesome women had been put on half rations and dosed with an emetic to induce nausea and vomiting. This kept them quiet and prevented complaints from those with 'fiery temperaments'. Mundy then went to the solitary cells where women were carding and combing wool. The third cell he came to was dark and, he thought at first, empty:

It looked like the den of a wolf, and I almost started back when from the extreme end of the floor I found a pair of bright, flashing eyes fixed on mine. Their owner arose and took a step or two forward; it was a small, slight, and quite young girl—very beautiful in feature and complexion,—but it was the fierce beauty of the wild cat! I am a steady married man, of a certain age,—but at no period of my life would I, for a trifle, have shared for half-an-hour the cell of that sleek little savage; for when she purred loudest I should have been most afraid of her claws!

The heavy cell door was slammed tight and the turnkey said the woman was one of the most unmanageable women in the prison. Mundy reflected:

Beauty is a sad distorter of man's perceptions! Justice ought to be doubly blindfolded when dealing with her. I fear me that the pang of pity that shot across my heart when that pretty prisoner was shut again from the light of day, might have found no place there had she been as ugly as the sins that brought her into trouble. I had no more stomach for solitary cells this day.

Continuing the tour, they reached the laundry where the factory inmates were put to work:

Squads of women were up to their elbows in suds,—carrying on the cruel process of wringing,—or displaying their thick ankles as they spread the linen over the drying lines. The townsfolk may have their washing done here at 1s. 6d. per dozen, the money going towards the expenses of the institution. I was pained to see so many very youthful creatures in this yard—delinquents in their earliest teens; debauched ere the pith had hardened in their little bones.

The next stop was a room full of seamstresses, where most were busy at fine or detailed needlework. 'It was not impossible, the matron stated, that some of the elaborate shirt-fronts we should see at the Government-house ball this evening had been worked in this, and washed and "got up" in the last ward.' The convict women were making garments for the quality members of society.

Colonel Mundy was impressed with the cleanliness and discipline of the establishment, which he dutifully recorded in the matron's visitors book. But his final advice was: 'See a Female Factory once, and don't do so again.'

A Convict's Dream

Charles Ashton was transported to Van Diemen's Land with several hundred others on the *David Malcolm* in 1845. Around thirty-three years old, he was convicted at Chester of stealing money and given a life sentence.

Seven years later, while at Port Arthur, Ashton tried to escape, knocking down a constable. He received a sentence of fifty lashes and thirty days solitary confinement on bread and water in a darkened cell with only one blanket against the cold air. He also served a year of solitary confinement in the pitch dark and soundproof cells and two years wearing extra heavy chains weighing 35 pounds. 'Rather rough on a prisoner?' was his comment on this treatment, together with a poem graphically describing his living nightmare.

I dreamt I saw some prisoners bound,
Standing in heavy chains on the parade ground,
tis true as I do tell this tale,
They marched both in and out of the gaol;
On every morning when the first bell rings
Up from our beds we are forced to spring—
To wash ourselves and brush our hair,
Sweep out our cells we must not dare;
Nor we must not dare a word to speak
Or the silent system rules we break.

Then to the lamp-post we are dragged,
When our mouth is gagged, and our wrist is darbed.
While laboring under a scorching sun
The sweat from off our brow does run;
And whatever labor we are at
We must not look this way nor that,
For the overseer says that will do,
And to the court we are forced to go.
Then the Commandant does at me stare,
'You are charged with idleness, I do declare,
It is true the overseer I must believe,
And fifty lashes you must receive.'

Now I lay my coat, vest, and shirt on the ground,
And to the triangles I am bound,
When the flagellator did behind me stand
With the cat-a'-nine-tails in his hand.
He flogged me till my back was raw
And painted with my crimson gore;
When I awoke with a frightful scream—
It was a reality, and not a dream.

The phrase 'our wrist is darbed' was prison slang, meaning that the men were handcuffed.

Little else is known of Charles Ashton. He died in 1859 and is buried at Fingal.

Not a Bad Man at Heart

An anonymous convict who called himself 'T' published his autobiography in 1867. At fourteen years of age 'I fell into bad company', he wrote. Convicted of robbery, he was transported for seven years to Point Puer on Van Diemen's Land's Tasman Peninsula, a prison for juvenile offenders. He 'suffered at Point Puer the average amount of punishment served out to others of my head-strong and easily-persuaded companions, having received for different attempts to regain my liberty eleven floggings, making a total number of 528 lashes, and 74 days solitary confinement on bread and water'.

T went to Hobart but was unable to find work and, through a misadventure with another ex–Point Puer inmate, he was arrested, tried and sentenced to a further seven years transportation. This he was to serve at Port Arthur. After a few months he attempted an escape from the well-guarded prison:

> I was the leader, rushed the constable, and took away his firelock, and succeeded in getting to Norfolk Bay, nine miles from Port Arthur. But we were still on Tasman's Peninsula. We had to elude not only the constable sent after us and the out-station constables, but the vigilance of sixteen bloodhounds and mastiffs, besides a detachment of military and police at Eagle-hawk Neck before we could reach Forester's Peninsula. We had to pass another constable's station at the Sounds, and another at East Bay Neck before we could reach the mainland. Even then, if successful, we should be in rags and tatters, compelled to hide ourselves in the bush by day, and rob the first farmhouse we came to at night for clothing and food. We resolved to reach the main land, or perish in the attempt.

The escapees had no food and it was getting dark. They needed to get across the Tasman Peninsula's narrow and heavily guarded Eaglehawk Neck or go by sea. There was no time to build a raft so the only option was to swim, a distance of at least 4 miles through shark-infested waters.

The moon rose at about 7 o'clock, and this was against us. There was little wind; the evening was cool—doubly cold to us, for we were still damp with perspiration in reaching Norfolk Bay. Reckless of consequences we threw off our prison-clothing, crawled stealthily down to the water's edge, shook hands with each other, exclaiming softly, 'We agree no succour; liberty or death.'

T was first into the water. All went well for a couple of miles, but then:

Suddenly the hills on the Forester's and Tasman's side of the water reverberated the most unearthly shrieks that ever proceeded from human lungs. One of my mates had been seized with cramp; he knew his case was hopeless, yet he struggled on. He called not for help—no assistance was thought of. Pain, and not fear, produced his agonising screams. Presently he sank with the moonbeams glittering over him.

Then another man began to fall behind the others. They began to slow down for him but suddenly there was 'A splashing—a violent commotion in water behind quickly drew our attention. We heard the words, "Sharks! Sharks! Oh, God!" We saw our companion struggle—we saw him dragged, without a groan, beneath the surface'.

With only one companion, T swam on. Both men weakened and even as they approached the shore, the other man slipped beneath the waves: 'No ear save mine heard his prayer, and he sank, vainly struggling to keep afloat. I would have helped him but I was becoming weak myself.'

T made it ashore but passed out on the beach, only to be found and arrested the next morning. He was sentenced to eighteen months in chains and then sent to Norfolk Island, the last and most feared prison for incorrigibles. Here, the unlucky T endured 544 days of solitary confinement and received 1874 lashes. These punishments were accompanied by beatings and sometimes 'the gag', 'a sort of choking arrangement', probably the torture today known as water boarding. Once, after being an accessory in the attempted murder of an overseer, he was kept for nine months in chains in a confined space to grind chillies to make cayenne pepper, resulting in 'copious bleeding at the nose occasionally'.

While serving these sentences, T was subject to frequent punishments for even relatively minor offences:

> I received intermediate sentences of flogging and solitary confinement, too numerous to particularise. Throwing down my cap at the gaoler, fifty lashes. Having the sign of tobacco in my mouth, fifty lashes. Being in possession of a bar of highly-polished steel, to wit, a needle, fifty lashes. For insolence in looking significantly at a constable, fifty lashes. Fighting, fifty lashes. For unlawfully holding possession of three needlesful of thread, six days solitary confinement. For having possession of a copper button, thirty-six lashes. For talking in school, first offence thirty-six lashes; second offence, fifty lashes, and, so on.

Eventually T decided to murder an overseer with the axe he was issued as a timber cutter. He almost succeeded, and received twelve heavily ironed months in solitary.

Despite almost five years of these conflicts with the system, T was unexpectedly returned to Port Arthur and then to the Hobart penitentiary where he was hired out on the passholder system as a farm labourer. After seven months of near starvation, he stole some potatoes for which he was returned to Hobart and then assigned 'washerman and closet cleaner'. When he failed to clean the toilets one Sunday morning, he received three months on the treadmill. He was then assigned to several other duties but eventually absconded and became a bushranger until apprehended. The sentence this time was transportation to Port Arthur for life.

The same pattern of insubordination, refusal to work, violence and attempted escapes soon appeared and T was punished with shorter or longer periods of solitary confinement and working in heavy irons at the governor's pleasure. During this time, however, the commandant of Port Arthur 'began to notice me, and certainly treated me in a manner that, years before, would have done good. I was now too old, hard, and callous. My spirit had been broken at Norfolk Island. I had no faith in humanity, in kind words I anticipated treachery'.

After eight years T was given probation and once more went to work as a passholder. Again he absconded and made his way to Sydney, living from hand to mouth until he fell in with some old companions and returned to his life of crime. He was arrested and sent to Darlinghurst Gaol for eighteen months where he composed his memoir, claiming that 'I am not a bad man at heart, but troubles have destroyed my temper and my better feelings'.

Moondyne Joe, (Joseph Bolitho Johns). This is the only known photograph of him, taken by Alfred Chopin. He stands holding a tomahawk and wearing a kangaroo skin cape. He was famous for the many times he escaped prison.

8
Desperate Escapes

Will there no gleam of sunshine
cast o'er my path its light?
Will there no star of hope rise
Out of this gloom of night?

John Boyle O'Reilly

A Heroic Struggle for Liberty

It was an unusual case at London's Old Bailey court in July 1792. A woman and four men were on trial for escaping from New South Wales the previous year. Their bid for freedom was desperate and harrowing.

On the night of 28 March 1791 Mary Bryant (née Broad), her husband William and their children Charlotte and Emanuel stole the governor's leaky cutter. With seven other men, they rowed through Sydney Harbour, turning north when they cleared the Heads. Their voyage would take them through unknown waters and past dangerous coasts back to the land from which they had been transported. Most would not survive their epic ordeal.

After two days sailing, the escapees went ashore and camped by a creek. They were visited by the local Aboriginal people who were friendly and happy to accept the clothing and other items the convicts offered. Some days later they needed to repair the cutter and landed in 'a very fine harbor'. But this time contact with the 'Natives' did not go well. They were menaced by 'great numbers armed with Spears and Shields'. Forming themselves into two groups, the fugitives firstly tried to 'pacify them by signes, but they took not the least notice'. Then they fired a musket, but this had no effect and the fugitives were forced to make a rapid retreat to the sea.

They were by now running out of food and feeling the effects of exposure and heavy storms. One of the convicts kept a journal of the voyage in which he wrote: 'the Woman and the two little babies were in a bad Condition every thing being so wet that we could by no means light a fire we had nothing to eat except a little raw Rice at night.'

After weeks at sea, the battered little boat was in the tropical waters of the Great Barrier Reef. Fish and turtle were plentiful and there was rainwater to drink. In the Gulf of Carpentaria they were attacked, probably by Torres Strait Islanders, and were later chased into the gulf by islanders in sailing canoes. They made a fast passage to Arnhem Land and from there reached Timor on 5 June 1791 after sixty-nine days at sea across 5000 kilometres of angry ocean and mostly hostile shores.

On Timor they were well received by the Dutch governor and looked after as shipwreck survivors. But after a few months there was some kind of falling out in the group, leading to the revelation that they were in fact escapees. They were jailed and after a few months taken in chains to the Dutch headquarters of Batavia, modern Jakarta. Batavia was notorious for fevers and here Mary Bryant's son Emanuel died, not yet two years of age. Three weeks later his father died, leaving the dwindling group without a leader.

Three more of the men died while the fugitives were being transferred in separate ships to Cape Town. In April 1792, Mary and Charlotte Bryant, together with the surviving men, were shipped aboard the *Gorgon* bound for England. Despite their trials and recapture, they were pleased to be alive. But the heat of the tropics began to take its toll on the *Gorgon*. Some children of the soldiers aboard died and on May 6 Charlotte Bryant followed them. Mary was now the only survivor of her family and facing a death sentence.

The *Gorgon* docked in June and the escapees were taken to Newgate Prison to await trial. News of their escape and tribulations was now public knowledge and stimulated widespread sympathy. Instead of a death sentence, Mary Bryant and her fellow survivors were only required to finish out their original sentences. For Mary that meant release in May 1793.

The biographer and lawyer James Boswell interested himself in the case. Mary lodged with him in London after her release and before returning to her native Cornwall, though, according to Boswell, 'her spirits were low; she was sorry to leave me; she was sure her relations would not treat her well'. Boswell organised a subscription fund to give Mary a pension, though it seems not to have been very well supported and it is likely that he personally paid her what was then a substantial sum of money. Shortly before his death in 1795, Boswell instructed his financial agents to: 'put into the Banking Shop of Mr Devaynes & Co five pounds from me to the account of the Rev. Mr. Baron at Lestwithiel, Cornwall, and write to him that you have done so. He takes charge of paying the gratuity to Mary Broad.'

That generosity must have been very useful for Mary back home in Cornwall, especially if she was out of favour with her family, locally reputed to be sheep stealers. And she was grateful. In 1930 some documents were discovered in what had been Boswell's Irish estate. With the papers was a package of 'Botany Bay tea leaves', or sarsaparilla, which Mary had evidently sent her benefactor. She must have taken a store of the leaves for drinking and remedy for scurvy on the escape boat. A couple of the leaves are held by the State Library of New South Wales.

The Vagabond of the Woods

It would only take them a week or so. Everyone knew that China lay to the north of New South Wales. A well-supplied group of determined convicts could easily walk to freedom. In

1791 twenty men and women tried it. Seven died and the lucky survivors were found almost naked and near death. They were brought back to Sydney and when they recovered from their ordeal, flogged.

This sorry tale did not deter others from attempting the same hopeless journey. In the following year alone, another forty-four men and nine women were reported to have disappeared into the bush on their way to China. The myth was a powerful one that no amount of actual experience seemed to quell. Six years later a group of Irishmen on the road to China via the Georges River were accidentally discovered and saved from certain death by local settlers. They were lucky.

In 1803 James Hughes, a tall Irish rebel, and fifteen others absconded from Castle Hill, a settlement northwest of Sydney. Robbing settlers as they went, all but Hughes were recaptured, thirteen being sentenced to death. Three years later an Aboriginal told a settler that the bones of a white man were lying with a musket and tin kettle (a billy) beneath the first ridge of the mountains. The settler accompanied the Aboriginal man to the spot and found a long-boned skeleton, presumed to be that of Hughes.

Another belief that gained currency with the convicts came from misinterpreting information gained from Aboriginal people. They told stories of a mysterious colony of white people said to be living several hundred miles to the southwest. As early as January 1788 a group of Irish transports went off in search of the other colony. They were pursued by soldiers and sixteen were taken back to Sydney and punished. This myth would not die either and continued to inspire escape plots, including a mass breakout from the government's Toongabbie farm. Something had to be done. It was, and it involved an extraordinary convict named John Wilson.

Wilson was from Lancashire, where he had been arrested, tried and found guilty of stealing some cloth. He arrived with the First Fleet aboard *Alexander*. At the end of his seven-year sentence, he went bush and lived with the Darug people of the Hawkesbury River area. Together with a runaway convict, Wilson was arrested for attempting to kidnap several young Aboriginal girls. He managed to escape and returned to the Darug, taking a full part in their customs, battles and travels. He worked out how to communicate in a type of pidgin and may even have been initiated, bearing the scars that signified the making of an Aboriginal man. He was also known by his Aboriginal name of Bunboe (pronounced 'Bunbowee').

It was thought that Wilson was among the raiding parties associated with Pemulwuy, the Aboriginal warrior who led a fierce resistance to colonisation. In 1797 Wilson and three others were arrested and charged as 'incorrigibles, rogues and vagabonds wandering at large'. Sentenced to seven years retransportation, he escaped and was outlawed in May. Being legally outlawed meant he must surrender or be shot on sight. Wilson returned to the settlement dressed in kangaroo skins, Aboriginal style. The colonists found the wild white man's accounts of his adventures difficult to credit. But his wanderings had taken him well into the Blue Mountains and likely beyond them, where he had seen many things, possibly including the first sightings of wombats, lyre birds and koalas. He claimed to have also seen the bones of more than fifty convicts who perished in their vain attempts to reach China.

To David Collins, deputy judge advocate, Wilson was 'a wild, idle young man who preferred living among the natives to earning the wages of honest industry'. Despite these criticisms, the 'vagabond of the woods' was known to have a unique knowledge of the country for miles around the settlement. This made him useful to the governor who employed him as a guide for exploring parties. Wilson was with a surveying and exploration party to Port Stephens under Charles Grimes in 1795. He saved Grimes's life by wounding an Aboriginal man attempting to spear him. After his surrender, Wilson promised to reform and in 1798 Governor Hunter sent him with a group of convicts and guards into the bush to search for the rumoured lost colony. When the group failed to find the settlement, the governor hoped that the belief would die out and convicts would stop trying to escape. The party was also accompanied by one of Hunter's servants, John Price, a young man at home in the bush and keen to explore further.

The eleven-strong group set off to cheers of encouragement. It was a very hot summer and at first, the going was thankfully easy through known country but they soon moved into rougher unknown territory. Most of the convicts soon tired of the tough going by the time they reached the present-day Picton area and returned with the soldiers to the settlement. But Wilson and Price pushed on with one of the more determined convicts. They reached a point more than 160 kilometres south of Parramatta where their rations ran out.

Their return journey was almost fatal. They were reduced to eating roots and grubs, tearing up their clothes to provide protection for their feet after their boots disintegrated. The exhausted men were saved only through Wilson's bush craft. Price wrote: 'I thought that we must all have perished with hunger, which certainly would have been the case had it not been for the indefatigable zeal of Wilson to supply us with as much as would support life.'

The governor was pleased with the results of the expedition. They found no mysterious white settlement and also discovered what seemed to be a hill of salt, a valuable commodity for the still struggling colony. Hunter again sent Price and Wilson south to confirm the salt discovery. Once again the leader and most of the group quit, leaving Price and Wilson to forge ahead. This time they got as far as modern-day Goulburn, further than any other known European.

Price and Wilson battled back, again surviving through Wilson's bush skills. Soon after returning from the second expedition, Wilson went bush once again to a life which had taken him far past the limits of settlement and given him a knowledge of the country unmatched by any European. John Wilson's vagabond life came to an end in 1800 when he was speared to death during his attempt to kidnap an Aboriginal woman.

Charlotte the Pirate

The official description of the woman said to be Australia's first female pirate is not flattering: 'Charlotte Badger, a convict; very corpulent, with full face, thick lips, and light hair; has an infant child.' And she had a very bad temper. Various writers have tried over the years to turn chubby Charlotte into a romantic lady buccaneer, dressed as a swashbuckler and brandishing a brace of pistols. But the reality is both more prosaic and more intriguing.

Charlotte arrived in the colony in 1801 with a seven-year sentence to serve for thieving. She became pregnant to a soldier and gave birth to a daughter, Anny. Nothing very unusual. But what happened next has become an enduring mystery spanning Australia, New Zealand, the South Pacific and possibly South America.

In 1806, Charlotte and Anny were aboard the 45-ton brig *Venus* on their way to Van Diemen's Land along with several other convicts and a small crew commanded by Samuel Chace. Bad weather kept the *Venus* at Twofold Bay for more than a month, plenty of time for Charlotte and the other convict woman aboard, Kitty Hegarty, to get to know the sailors and male convicts. At some point Chace had to go ashore for business, leaving the first mate Ben Kelly in command. When Chace returned he found a party in full swing.

From this point in the tale, details vary. According to some accounts, Chace ordered the two convict women whipped but the crew refused, so he did the job himself. He then had the carousers chained up and told Kelly he would be dismissed as soon as the *Venus* landed. But the captain was forced to release Kelly when he sobered up as he was needed to navigate the ship.

When the *Venus* made landfall in the Tamar Estuary in June 1806, Chace went ashore with the official despatches he carried, again leaving Kelly in command. The captain unwisely spent the night visiting another moored ship, returning next morning to see his ship heading out to sea. Kelly and some of those aboard, together with Charlotte and Kitty, had mutinied.

They forced the rest of the crew ashore at the point of swords and pistols.

The *Venus* was carrying a full cargo of stores and so was well prepared for a lengthy voyage as a pirate ship. But where did she go? Nothing was heard for nine months. Then an American whaler reported Kelly and another male mutineer living with Charlotte and Anny in the Bay of Islands, New Zealand. Kitty was dead and the *Venus* was under the command of another crew who were busy pillaging the Maori tribes along the coast. Eventually the Maori killed the crew and burned the *Venus*.

Charlotte and her companions lived in the Bay of Islands alongside the local Maori for eight years or so, until a British ship arrived and captured the two men. Ben Kelly was taken back to England, tried and hanged for piracy. Charlotte is said to have escaped with Anny and—again, accounts vary—either to have remained there, living with a Maori warrior, or to somehow have made her way to Tonga. She either remained there until her death or, in yet another version, formed a liaison with the captain of an American whaler and disappeared into history.

Nobody is sure what happened to Charlotte Badger the pirate and her daughter, Anny. Perhaps yellowing documents will turn up one day with some hard evidence. A Chilean professor is said to have uncovered some new sources in the 1950s that provide an elaborate counter-version of Ben Kelly's survival and subsequent adventures in South America, but this remains unverified.

In New Zealand, though, Charlotte Badger is remembered as the first female *Pakeha*, or European woman, to settle there. She probably was not the first, but this is just one more element of the quicksilver legends about Australia's first female pirate.

A Taste for Flesh

Cannibalism among escaping convicts was not common but it happened. The case of Alexander Pearce is probably the best known.

Transported from Ireland in 1819 for theft, Pearce was soon in trouble in Van Diemen's Land. He was transported a second time to what was then the new penal station in Macquarie Harbour on Tasmania's west coast, known as Sarah Island. Pearce and seven others escaped in 1822 but after a couple of weeks in the bush they ran out of food. They had one axe. Lots were drawn to see who would die and the first convict was killed and eaten. The group broke up shortly after, leaving Pearce with three others.

This group continued their pointless wandering through the bush. Another was killed and eaten, and another died of snake bite and was eaten, leaving just Pearce and the convict with the axe—watching each other closely. Eventually it was Pearce who got hold of the axe, killing and eating his companion. Pearce struggled on alone, sustained by the human flesh in his pockets. He fell in with a group of sheep stealers and was recaptured along with them after almost four months on the run. Oddly, they were hanged but he managed to muddy the waters enough to talk the authorities into taking an extraordinarily lenient view of his crimes. He was sent back to Macquarie Harbour.

It was less than a year before he again absconded with a younger convict named Thomas Cox. Pearce was only on the loose for ten days, not long enough to need to resort to cannibalism. But he murdered Cox at King's River, allegedly when he discovered the man could not swim. Then he ate him.

This time there was no escape. He confessed and was hanged in Hobart on 19 July 1824. In the tradition of alleged famous last words of notorious criminals, he is said to have stated, 'Man's flesh is delicious. It tastes far better than fish or pork'.

The 'greatest monster who ever cursed the earth' was the Van Diemen's Land murderer, rapist and cannibal Thomas (sometimes Mark) Jefferies (Jeffries). From Christmas Day 1825 he and some accomplices carried out a number of callous murders, including that of a five-month-old baby whose brains Jefferies smashed out on a tree trunk. Running short of food, the bushrangers murdered one of their group while the foolish man slept. His flesh kept them alive for four days until they were able to slaughter a couple of sheep. They were still carrying about five pounds of human flesh when captured in late January. The *Hobart Town Gazette* reported:

> The monster arrived in Launceston a few minutes before nine o'clock on Sunday Evening. The town was almost emptied of its inhabitants to meet the inhuman wretch. Several attempts were made by the people to take him out of the cart that they might wreak their vengeance upon him, and it became necessary to send to Town for a stronger guard to prevent his immediate dispatch. He entered the Town and gaol amidst the curses of every person whomsoever.

Jefferies was executed on 4 May 1826, alongside the gentleman bushranger, Mathew Brady, who is said to have protested against dying alongside the monster.

A few years later, another group of Van Diemen's Land absconders served up an even more grisly tale of human flesh. Also from Macquarie Harbour, five men robbed the constable overseeing their labour on a settler's outstation and took to the bush. They had one axe.

Not knowing how to live off the land, they soon ran out of food and drew lots to choose who would slaughter one of their number, Richard Hutchinson, to feed the others. Edward Broughton, a 28-year-old career robber, drove an axe into the unlucky man's head. According to an account of their confessions: 'They cut the body in pieces and carried it with them, with the exception of the hands, feet, head and intestines. They ate heartily on it, as Broughton expressed it.'

When their companion's flesh was exhausted, the four fugitives began to eye each other: 'The greatest jealousy prevailed about carrying the axe, and scarcely one amongst them dared to shut his eyes or doze for a moment for fear of being sacrificed unawares.' Broughton and another man, Mathew Maccavoy, agreed to watch out for each other, one sleeping while the other kept guard.

The oldest man in the group was next to die. While the sixty-year-old known only as 'Coventry' was away cutting wood, the others agreed to kill and eat him. Broughton refused to do the deed as he had already murdered their first victim. So eighteen-year-old Patrick Fagan got the job:

> Fagan struck him the first blow. He saw it coming and called out for mercy; he struck him on the head, just above the eye, but did not kill him; myself and Maccavoy finished him and cut him to pieces. We ate greedily of the flesh, never sparing it, just as if we had expected to meet with a whole bullock the next day.

The three remaining men were still feeding on Coventry's flesh when Maccavoy suggested to Broughton that he should kill Fagan, the only witness to their crimes. Broughton refused. The two men returned to their campfire where Fagan was keeping warm. Broughton recalled:

> I sat beside him, Maccavoy was beyond me; he was on my right and Fagan on my left. I was wishing to tell Fagan what had passed, but could not, as Maccavoy was sitting with the axe close by looking at us. I laid down and was in a doze, when I heard Fagan scream out, I leapt to my feet in a dreadful fright, and saw Fagan lying on his back, with a dreadful cut in his head, and the blood pouring from it. Maccavoy was standing over him with the axe in his hand:
>
> 'You murdering rascal, you dog!', I said, 'what have you done?'
>
> 'This will save our life', he said, and struck him another blow on the head with the axe.
>
> Fagan only groaned after the scream, and Maccavoy then cut his throat through the windpipe. We then stripped off the clothes, and cut the body into pieces and roasted it. We roasted all at once as upon all occasions, as it was lighter to carry, and would keep longer, and would not be so easily discovered.

A few days later 'the remaining cannibals got kangaroo to eat off some wild dogs that killed the animal'. They then 'threw away the remainder of Fagan's body'. Just two days later they turned themselves in. The two men were hanged together at Hobart in 1831. Edward Broughton made a last confession of his grisly crimes as the hangman tied his arms together ready for the drop, concluding, 'I wish this to be made public after my death'.

From Hell's Gate to Chile

On his left arm he sported a tattoo of men boxing. His forehead was scarred and he was blind in the left eye. James Porter was born in London around 1800. He went to sea at fifteen years of age and stayed mostly in South American waters until 1821 when he returned to England and was convicted in 1823 of stealing some silk and fur. Transported for life, he arrived in Hobart in 1824 and soon began trying to escape.

By 1829 he had made at least three attempts to regain his freedom and suffered the ironed gangs as punishment. He was then sent to the grim Sarah Island in Macquarie Harbour. Even by penal station standards, the location was intimidating. Set in treacherous waters and accessible only from the sea through a narrow channel called 'Hell's Gate', Sarah Island was designed to hold the most desperate convicts and re-offenders.

It quickly gained a reputation as the harshest prison in Van Diemen's Land. Floggings, hard labour in irons and solitary confinement were routine as convicts felled timber for a ship-building industry the government hoped to establish. Escape attempts were routine. At one point, out of around two hundred convicts on the island, about one hundred were missing, believed escaped. Many were never seen again. After two years on Sarah Island, James Porter bolted again, only to be caught and punished with the usual flogging.

Finally, as Sarah Island penal station was closing down after a decade of misery, Porter found an opportunity to 'once more chance my life for my liberty'. In 1834, with a group of other prisoners, he seized a brig, the *Frederick*. The convicts overwhelmed the two soldiers left on board and marooned them with the crew. One of the convicts could navigate and some, including Porter, could sail. But there was trouble from the start. One of the escapees deliberately ran them off course and was only just spared 'a short passage over the side', propelled by his irate companions. This incident was a forewarning of what was to come.

With fine weather and a good wind, they sighted the South American coast after little more than six weeks at sea. But the *Frederick* was leaking badly and they decided to abandon her and take to the ship's only boat—'I never left my Parents with more regret, nor was my feelings harrowed up to such a pitch as when I took the last farewell of the smart little Frederick,' wrote Porter. They rowed ashore in the pre-dawn dark and when the sun came up, 'we could see the shore close aboard of us covered with a rich verdure'.

Each of the convicts was armed with a brace of pistols and when they encountered a group of 'indians' they readied for a fight. But there was no need and they were directed to the nearest town and eventually were picked up by the Spanish authorities. Their story was that they were shipwrecked mariners. The governor questioned them but declared: 'Sailors you have come on this coast in a clandestine manner and though you put a good face on your story I have every reason to believe you are Pirates and unless you state the truth between this and 8 o-clock tomorrow morning I shall give orders for you all to be shot—take them away.'

Porter responded with spirit:

> We as sailors shipwrecked and in distress expected when we made
> this port to be treated in a Christian like manner not as though
> we were dogs; is this the way you would have treated us 1818
> when the british [*sic*] Tars were fighting for your independence
> and bleeding in your cause against the old Spaniards—and if we
> were Pirates do you suppose we should be so weak as to cringe to

your Tyranny, never (!) I also wish you to understand that if we were shot england will know of it and will be revenged—you will find us in the same mind to morrow we are in now, and should you put your threat into execution tomorrow we will teach you Spaniards how to die.

The room fell silent. After a few minutes the Spanish summoned a British naval officer and asked if he knew Porter. It turned out that the officer had sailed with him many years before. Porter and the convicts with him were taken back to their quarters. But one of their number was absent. They soon worked out that a persistent malcontent in their group named Cheshire betrayed them in return for the Spanish sparing his life. The men decided to tell their captors the truth, including Cheshire in the confession, to make sure they all hanged together.

The eloquent Porter was spokesman: 'I told him the whole of the circumstance, but also stated that we would rather have died than given him any satisfaction but our motive in so doing was that Cheshire should not escape but share the same fate as us.'

The governor agreed and then released them, keeping Cheshire in custody for his own safety as he knew the other convicts would kill him given an opportunity. Besides, his carpentry skills were useful.

Porter and his companions now settled down as tradesmen and workers in the local Chilean community. Porter made good use of his skills, took up with several women, including a young Indian slave girl, and survived a drunken attack from a 'mad brained sealer'. But he and his companions eventually found themselves back in confinement under the Spanish and awaiting the arrival of a British ship to take them back into custody: 'I then gave up all hope of ever regaining my liberty, we had been Confined above 7 months Chained two and two like dogs.'

Porter managed to get himself separated from his manacled companion; however, 'They put me on a pair of Bar irons, the Bar placed across my instep so that I could not stride or step more than 4 or 6 inches at a time'. Assisted by a woman of his acquaintance, Porter obtained a knife and file, eventually managing to grind through his manacles. Using the change of guards as his cover:

> I shook off my irons, and reared a plank against the wall, I had no shoes on, I went back about 21 yards and on looking behind me saw the door open. I made a spring and ran to the top of the plank and with a sudden spring catched hold of the top of the wall; haul'd myself up, ran down a veranda on the other side and jumped off, being 12 feet from the ground.

He made his way through the darkened streets of the town, across the river in a stolen canoe and into the country, where he was at liberty for a few uncomfortable days. Suffering from dysentery, he was captured by Spanish soldiers. After more failed escape attempts, torture and the threat of being shot, Porter came to no longer care if he lived or died. But somehow he survived and was placed in British custody then returned via several ships to England. After interrogation and the revelation of their true identities as escaped convicts, Porter and his companions were transported once again to Van Diemen's Land.

On the return voyage Porter was, falsely he claimed, accused of fomenting a mutiny aboard the transport. Once again, Cheshire and another of the *Frederick* convicts were the cause of his trouble as they informed against him:

> I was seized by the soldiers lashed to the gratin and a powerfull black fellow flogged me across the back, lines and every other part of the body until my head sank on my breast with exhaustion, as for the quantity of lashes I received I cannot say, for I would not give them the satisfaction to seringe [surrender?] to their cruel torture, until nature gave way and I was senseless.

Chained together with the other bleeding accused conspirators, Porter 'craved for death'. After three weeks of this treatment, the surgeon feared the fettered men were dying from their treatment and lack of food. They were released and the truth, or at least Porter's version of it, came out. Cheshire, 'the monster in human shape', was confined below for the rest of the voyage.

They reached Hobart in March 1837, 'when to the astonishment of all present I was known as one of the men that assisted in Capturing the Brig Frederick'. As they were taken off the ship, Porter managed to get close to the treacherous Cheshire: 'I seized him by the throat and hurled him over my hip and would have throttled him but was prevented by the police.'

The convicts, in heavy irons, were tried for piracy and found guilty. The sentence would have been death but they escaped on a technicality. Porter spent almost the next two and a half years ironed in Hobart Gaol and was then sent to Norfolk Island 'wer Tyranny and Cruelty was in its vigour'. But under a new and reformist commandant, Captain Maconochie, Porter responded to the improved conditions on the island and vowed he would 'live in hopes by my good conduct to become once more a member of good Society'. He was later sent back to the mainland.

It was now twenty-four years after James Porter's original sentence of transportation. He had seen neither his English wife or son in that time. He suffered Macquarie Harbour, Norfolk Island, the Coal River and numerous other jails in Australia, England and Chile. He survived floggings, beatings, torture and hard labour in heavy irons. In May 1847, Porter made his final escape attempt as part of a group who absconded from Newcastle on the brig *Sir John Byng*. He was never seen again.

The Great Escaper

Of the many bushrangers celebrated in folk tradition, Western Australia's 'Moondyne Joe' is probably the least threatening. His clever escapes and non-violent career have given him a Robin Hood aura that is still strong today. But who was he?

The Glamorganshire ironworker Joseph Bolitho Johns was in his early twenties when he arrived in the Swan River colony in 1853. He had a ten-year sentence for larceny but soon earned a conditional pardon in 1855. He took up the business of catching stray horses, returning them to their owners for the rewards offered on such valuable assets. Operating in the Toodyay area, 80 or 90 kilometres northeast of Perth, Joe was eventually arrested on suspicion of causing the horses to leave their rightful owners and then 'catching' them in his horse-traps at a place called Moondyne Springs.

Joe was imprisoned but while awaiting trial he escaped. Recaptured, the horse-stealing charges were dropped but he received three years imprisonment for jail-breaking. Released in 1864 he was returned to jail within a year, this time with a ten-year sentence. The charge was killing an ox with intent to steal the carcass and he was sentenced to hard labour in a working party. By now Joseph Johns was something of a legend among the convicts and settlers, reflected in his nickname 'Moondyne Joe'. As if to prove his legend true, he soon escaped again.

When they caught him this time, the bushranger was given a further year in chains. Bound fast within a cell, Joe almost managed to escape yet again and so was placed in another, supposedly escape-proof cell in the prison refectory. It was only a matter of days before he disappeared from here and enjoyed several months of freedom in his old stamping ground around Moondyne Springs. But in September 1866 he was recaptured and held in a specially constructed escape-proof cell in Fremantle Prison. According to the local paper:

Mr. Hampton is said to have told him, when he saw him put into the cell which had been specially prepared for him, that if he managed to make his escape again, he would forgive him. That cell was made wonderfully strong, as much so as iron and wood could make it, and in it Joe was kept chained to a ring in the floor or wall, allowing a movement of about one yard, in heavy irons, with one hour's exercise daily in one of the yards.

Here, in solitary confinement, on a bread and water diet and in an enclosed space with little light or air, he became so ill that the medical authorities said he would die.

For his health, Joe was taken out of his cell for most of the day and left in the corner of the prison yard by himself, watched closely by a guard and kept isolated from all contact. He was put to work breaking stones and eventually smashed a large pile of rubble behind which it was difficult for the guard to see what was happening. On 8 March 1867, all was normal: the guard watched Joe's pick rising and falling behind the pile of rubble, occasionally checking verbally that the convict was still there. He was.

But what the lazy guard could not see was that Joe's pick was not attacking rocks but a loose stone in the prison wall. As the heat of the day faded, the guard could see Joe's cap over the rubble but could not get an answer from his call—'Are you there, Joe?' Seeing the cap, the guard assumed Joe was having a break and neglected to walk over to check until knock-off time at five o'clock.

Of course, when the guard finally went to get Joe, he found the cap and a broad-arrow jacket propped up on a couple of picks and a large hole in the prison wall. Joe had breached the supposedly unbreachable stone barrier, left his prison clothes behind and wriggled into the garden of the prison superintendent's house. Then he simply strolled through the superintendent's front gate which, fortunately, happened to be open. The West Australian press described Joe's ingenuity in making this escape in delighted detail:

Joe then prepared for his exit, by sticking his hammer upright and with some umbrella wire he had got possession of, he formed a shape something of a man's shoulders and arms; upon the top he placed his cap and having slit up the sleeves of his jacket and shirt, managed to slip out of them and leave them upon the frame he had constructed, then having got rid of his irons, and divested himself of his trowsers, got through his hole in the wall, passed

through Mr. Lefroy's yard and out at a side door to the front of
the prison, whence to a person of Joe's practised sagacity a safe
transit to the neighboring bush became an easy matter.

Pandemonium! Prison authorities and the police scrambled to catch the great escaper once again. Governor Hampton, who had called Joe an 'immense scoundrel' and publicly boasted of the escape-proof cell, was especially displeased, which only increased the pleasure of the broad community of settlers and convicts. For them, Joe had now added another triumphant chapter to his legend and they sang in the streets, to the tune of 'Pop Goes the Weasel':

> The Governor's son has got the pip,
> The Governor's got the measles.
> Moondyne Joe has give 'em the slip
> Pop, goes the weasel.

Moondyne Joe had become a local hero. Not exactly a bush Robin Hood or a Ned Kelly, but an affectionately respected defier of colonial authority nevertheless.

After absconding from his 'escape-proof cell', Joe remained at large for another two years, and was eventually recaptured at a local vineyard on 25 February 1869, drunk according to some accounts. He served another lengthy sentence—without escaping this time—and mostly stayed out of trouble, working around the southwest and in Fremantle as a carpenter, shipwright and bush labourer. He even settled down to married domesticity with the widow Louisa Hearn (Braddick) in 1879. Louisa died in 1893 and Joe succumbed to increasing senility, passing out of life and further into legend seven years later.

Embellished versions of Moondyne Joe's adventures and escapes are still told today. His many unlikely escapes from various jails and hostelries are favourites. So is his alleged crossing of what was then the new Fremantle bridge before the governor had a chance to officially open it in 1867.

Rebel Heroes

He is commemorated with four statues in three countries as one of the great heroes of Irish resistance. Yet outside a small group of enthusiasts and historians, the Irish rebel John Boyle O'Reilly is barely known today.

After joining the clandestine Irish Republican Brotherhood in 1865, trooper John Boyle O'Reilly of the 10th Hussars was arrested, tried and convicted for his part in plotting a rising against the British government. He was to die by firing squad, but his sentence was commuted to twenty years penal servitude. With sixty-or-so other Fenians, as Irish rebels were known at the time, the 23-year-old O'Reilly was transported to Western Australia aboard the *Hougoumont* in January 1868.

When they arrived, the convicts were marched in chains to Fremantle's forbidding limestone prison. They were bathed, cropped, barbered and examined by a doctor. Their physical and personal details were recorded and they were issued with the regulation summer clothing: cap, grey jacket, vest, two cotton shirts, one flannel shirt, two handkerchiefs, two pairs of trousers, two pairs of socks and a pair of boots.

O'Reilly was sent to work on the road gangs around Bunbury, one of more than 3220 convicts in the colony at this time. Later in his life O'Reilly would publish his novel, *Moondyne*, based on his convict experiences. He dedicated this work to 'the interests of humanity, to the prisoner, whoever and wherever he may be'. In the novel, O'Reilly describes the bush and the work of the free sawyers:

> During the midday heat not a bird stirred among the mahogany and gum trees. On the flat tops of the low banksia the round heads of the white cockatoos could be seen in thousands, motionless as the trees themselves. Not a parrot had the vim to scream. The chirping insects were silent. Not a snake had courage to rustle his hard skin against the hot and dead bush-grass. The bright-eyed iguanas were in their holes. The mahogany sawyers had left their

logs and were sleeping in the cool sand of their pits. Even the
travelling ants had halted on their wonderful roads, and sought
the shade of a bramble.

He went on to contrast this with his own situation and that
of other convicts toiling alongside him:

> All free things were at rest; but the penetrating click of the axe,
> heard far through the bush, and now and again a harsh word of
> command, told that it was a land of bondmen.
>
> From daylight to dark, through the hot noon as steadily as
> in the cool evening, the convicts were at work on the roads—the
> weary work that has no wages, no promotion, no incitement, no
> variation for good or bad, except stripes for the laggard.

O'Reilly's education and literary skills soon gained him the
job of clerical assistant to Henry Woodman, the overseer of the
road gangs. In this capacity the young Irishman travelled with
reports and messages to the Woodman family home and seems
to have developed a romantic attachment to Jessie Woodman,
the warder's daughter. This ended unhappily, perhaps before
it really began. In the poetry he wrote, O'Reilly expressed his
despair:

> Have I no future left me?
> Is there no struggling ray
> From the sun of my life outshining
> Down on my darksome way?
> Will there no gleam of sunshine
> cast o'er my path its light?
> Will there no star of hope rise
> Out of this gloom of night?

Just after Christmas 1868, O'Reilly slit the veins of his left
arm. He passed out but was found and saved from death just
before it was too late.

Despite his despair, all was not lost for this transported revolutionary. His case became a popular cause of the day, taken up by those with a political conscience about the activities of the British government in Ireland. A powerful coalition of Irish republicans in the United States of America, elements of the Roman Catholic church and local sympathisers in Western Australia plotted to free the rebel. In February 1869 he was whisked away to freedom by a Yankee whaler. O'Reilly celebrated his twenty-fifth birthday in the middle of the Indian Ocean on his secret voyage back to England from where he made his way to America and freedom.

John Boyle O'Reilly went on to a glittering journalistic and political career in America. He remained deeply involved in Irish patriotic activities and is remembered by some in that country, in Australia and in the country of his birth as a great patriot. He played an influential part in the plot to free his companions still labouring in the West Australian bush. They bore the indignities and sufferings of convict life for seven years more while agitation about their plight and plots to end it slowly developed.

At Easter 1876, the rebels were rescued from bondage by an American whaler, the *Catalpa*, an exploit still celebrated in Irish communities around the world and commemorated in a well-known ballad. The verses tell the exaggerated but rip-roaring story of the bold rescue:

> All the Perth boats were racing,
> Making best tack for the spot,
> When that Yankee sailed into Fremantle
> And took the best prize of the lot.

In fact, the *Catalpa* went nowhere near Fremantle Harbour, laying off Rockingham, far to the south. When news of the escape reached the authorities, they hastily ordered the colony's only armed vessel, the *Georgette*, to undertake an ineffectual pursuit of the Yankee whaler. Approaching the American vessel, the *Georgette* came close enough to hear her captain yell out that if they fired on the 'stars and stripes' he had hoisted in the yards, it would be an act of war against the United States of America.

> The Georgette well-armed with bold warriors
> Went out the poor Yank to arrest.
> But she hoisted the star-spangled banner
> Saying 'You will not board me, I guess'.

The master of the *Georgette* decided that this might be true and allowed the *Catalpa* and her rescued rebels to sail away.

> Now they're landed safe in America
> And there will be able to stay.
> They'll hoist up the green flag and the shamrock
> 'Hurrah for old Ireland', they'll say.

And indeed the Fenians were safe. The British government and the colonial authorities all had egg on their faces and sympathising Irish people everywhere celebrated the escape, just as they had hailed O'Reilly's earlier triumph. Both escapes were accomplished without violence and provided two further stirring incidents in the extensive folklore of Irish resistance to British rule, even more delicious for the American role in the escape.

> Come all you screw warders and gaolers,
> Remember Perth Regatta day.
> Take care of the rest of your fenians
> Or the Yankees will steal 'em away.

'Hobart Town Chain Gang': colonial magistrates could punish convicts for breaches of the rules by sentencing them to work in chain gangs.

9
The Felonry

We left our country for our country's good.

Attributed to George Barrington

The Man Who Invented Australia's Beer

In folklore, the man who invented beer is sometimes known as 'Charlie Mopps', celebrated in a drinking song with the chorus:

> He must have been an admiral, a sultan or a king,
> And to his praises we shall always sing,
> Look at what he's done to us, filled us up with cheer,
> Lord bless Charlie Mopps, the man who invented beer.

The man credited with inventing beer brewing in the colony of New South Wales is still remembered in the name of a popular modern brand of beer. James Squire (Squires) was born in Kingston upon Thames in 1754 or 1755. According to one version of his life, young James was a 'Gypsy' (Romani) who took to the criminal life from an early age. He was arrested for highway robbery in 1774 and sentenced to seven years transportation to the American colonies. As was sometimes the case, he was offered a choice of enlisting in the army rather than being sold off to the plantation owners of Maryland or Virginia. He took the offer and served some years in the British Army, returning to Kingston to manage a local hotel. The hotel became a notorious rendezvous for thieves and smugglers and James was eventually caught stealing. He received a sentence of seven years transportation, this time to New South Wales aboard the First Fleet.

In Sydney his experience in the hotel trade was put to good use in brewing the colony's first beer, which he sold at 4 pence a quart. He also brewed privately from imported English malt for the Lieutenant-Governors Grose and Paterson. In 1789 he was flogged for stealing ingredients used in brewing. By 1792, or possibly earlier, he was free and received a grant of 30 acres near modern-day Ryde where he built a tavern known as 'The Malting Shovel'. He also established a brewery and planted hops from 1806. His brewing business expanded rapidly, as did his interests in grazing and land acquisition.

James left a wife and children behind him in England but wasted no time in forming new partnerships, probably beginning aboard the First Fleet. He had more than one long-term relationship, most of which produced offspring. His son Francis (with Mary Spencer) was placed with the New South Wales Corps at an early age. Francis became a drummer boy, on pay, by the age of eight and went with the corps to England where he later served against Napoleon. He was posted back to Launceston base in 1803 then pensioned off at only seventeen years of age. Francis re-enlisted in 1810 and returned to Van Diemen's Land where he grew barley for his father's New South Wales brewery.

When James Squire died in 1822 he was wealthy and respectable. The former highway robber had served as a district constable in the colony, financially assisted other settlers and even befriended Aboriginal people. The Eora elder Bennelong was buried in an orchard on his property. James Squire's funeral was the largest ever in the colony up to that time:

[He was] universally respected and beloved for his amiable and useful qualities as a member of society, and more especially as the friend and protector of the lower class of settlers. Had he been less liberal, he might have died more wealthy; but his assistance always accompanied his advice to the poor and unfortunate, and his name will long be pronounced with veneration by the grateful objects of his liberality.

At least that was how the artist, forger and alcoholic Joseph Lycett recalled James Squire, though there is no doubt that his astute industriousness made him a successful and popular figure. Like many transports he made a worthwhile new life in the penal colony. His grandson, James Squire Farnell, was the first Australian-born premier of New South Wales.

The Real Artful Dodger

Transported to Point Puer on the Tasman Peninsula of Van Diemen's Land at the age of fourteen, Samuel Holmes had already served time for small offences. With no mother and an alcoholic father, Samuel found lodgings in London's crime-ridden East End. He paid the landlord rent each week and sold him whatever he stole. The landlord apparently lodged a number of other children on a similar arrangement. Young Samuel had fallen in with a shady character who may have even been the basis for fictional young thief, the 'Artful Dodger', in Charles Dickens's famous novel *Oliver Twist*.

Samuel's story certainly reflects elements of the novel: '[I] used to play about in the streets, [my] father tried to keep me at home—has stripped me, taken away my clothes and tied me to a bed post—because the Boys used to come round the House at night and whistle and entice me to go out thieving again with them.'

Two of the boys took Samuel to a house in Stepney:

[It was] kept by a Jew and he agreed to board and lodge me for 2'/6 a week provided I brought and sold to him all that I might steal—He has about 13 boys in the house on the same terms . . . The landlord has also the adjoining House and there is a communication into it from every room—The back kitchen is fitted up with a trap door to help escape—and in a corner of one of the back kitchens is a sliding floor underneath which property is hid.

A coat is hung up in the kitchen of public room and Boys practise how to pick the pockets, the men in the house show them how to manage.—I was about a fortnight in training and afterwards went out to assist and screen the boys where they picked pockets—In a short time I went out on my own account as I soon saw how they did it.

Dickens published *Oliver Twist* a couple of years later and may have come across Samuel's story in his work as a court reporter. We will probably never know, but it seems that Samuel Holmes's story of juvenile offending and learning the nefarious skills required was hardly unique. He was only one of many wild and wicked youths transported to Australia.

Samuel arrived at his place of penance in August 1836. Almost immediately he was in trouble. His record shows an average of four punishments each year up to 1839. In the first year he spent thirteen days underground in the dark and cramped cell known as the 'Black Hole' on suspicion of pilfering buttons. In December he used blasphemous language on the Sabbath and was kept on bread and water for three days. The following January he was flogged for insolence to the superintendent and in April served another three days on bread and water. Three months later, for singing in his cell and other infractions, the boy was flogged again. Another twelve lashes were given in August for resisting his overseer. There were various other visits to the Black Hole and starvation diets over the two year period.

At the age of twenty-eight, Samuel Holmes at last gained his liberty. Where he went and what befell him after his poor start in life nobody knows.

The Botany Bay Rothschild

Rosetta Terry 'dressed in a simple, nay, coarse manner'. Every Saturday she got down on her knees and scrubbed the floors of the unpretentious house in Pitt Street she shared with her husband, Samuel. He spent many hours of most days up to his shirt sleeves salting beef for sale, one of his many businesses. The couple lived on a reasonable but not excessive 500–600 pounds a year, probably less than 100,000 dollars in today's terms.

Lancashire labourer Samuel Terry was transported for seven years, arriving in 1801. He worked as a stonemason and soldier and when the opportunity presented itself, he seized it and started a sly grog and pawn-broking business. In the ever-expanding colony, these enterprises flourished. Although he sold grog and tobacco at absurdly high prices, Terry himself was 'of the most perfectly sober and fruitful habits, he was active and industrious; and his whole philosophy consisted in having made up his mind, to never give value without obtaining value for it'. As early as 1818 he claimed to be worth a staggering 90,000 pounds, millions in today's dollars.

The ex-convict entrepreneur was able to build up a portfolio of land and properties. Through the debts of those who pawned their goods to him and drank his spirits, assisted by some shady legal machinations, he eventually owned streets of Sydney properties as well as farms, the income from which was at least 60,000–70,000 pounds a year.

Terry kept a large portion of his cash in what was known to all as his 'iron chest'. Unable to resist temptation, a young convict assigned to Terry stole 1000 sovereigns. He was apprehended and sentenced to hang, though would not reveal where he had hidden most of the loot. As he awaited trial, Terry visited the young man in his cell and promised to have him pardoned if he would reveal the secret. The youth told Terry where he had buried it in his master's garden. But there was no pardon, the boy was hanged as sentenced. It was said that Terry was 'ever haunted by the sight of the executed, and in moments of acrimony within his family circle, his relations often reproached him with the murder of the lad'.

The miser also defrauded friends and engaged in some dubious but profitable shipping investments. By fair means or foul, he was able to amass a fabled amount of wealth, though his parsimony and guilt eventually caught up with him. He suffered a stroke that paralysed his right side. This left him vulnerable to the mercenary aspirations of his sons and other family members as well as what would today be called 'elder abuse'. He had to be carried around by two men and 'in his open carriage, pale and bloated, he drove about the Domain of Sydney, a silent but impressive example for any one, showing how illusive and worthless, at times, wealth is, especially with a man like him, and if obtained in a low, and even questionable way'.

Terry's health declined and he passed away in February 1838 at the age of sixty-two years. His legacy was 'that of all vulgar misers'. His estate was valued at around 500,000 pounds. His wife received an annuity of 10,000 pounds, passing to his son and his heirs after Mrs Terry's death: 'There is not one word about charity or a house of refuge, or anything of a public bearing; the only provision approaching to such generosity is that all his benevolent subscriptions (perhaps 100 pounds a year), should be continued for ten years to come.'

Although Terry's son died just a year later, Rosetta Terry lived on for another twenty years, long enough to see the family sell to the government the land on which Sydney's Martin Place and the General Post Office now stand.

After his death Samuel Terry was called 'the richest outlaw whom the Australian colonies yet possessed, and ever will possess', and was known as 'the Botany Bay Rothschild'.

This, at least, is some of the folklore of envy and distrust that dogged Terry and his colonial wealth. While he was a determined and tough businessman who was not shy in litigating in defence and expansion of his interests, he was considered to be of good character by Governor Macquarie. He also made significant contributions to the economic and financial development of the colony and to its public life. Even if these activities often furthered his business interests, he did contribute to many good causes and held many public and civic offices. In later life he was a prominent Mason.

Why the marked discrepancy between the official and unofficial records of the Botany Bay Rothschild? That question is answered in the reminiscences of the Reverend Thomas Atkins who arrived in the colony two years before Terry's death: 'On my first arrival at Sydney (1836), a person, who had acquired notoriety for his crimes, his vices, and his wealth, was brought to my notice; that person was named *Sam Terry* (original italics). Both he and his wife had been convicts, and had been whipped for colonial offences.'

Prejudice against 'emancipists', as ex-convicts were known, developed early in Sydney and beyond. Later in life Terry worked to improve the lot of ex-convicts, becoming a prominent representative for legal, political and social reform. His funeral was graced with a military band and Masonic honours and was reckoned the most spectacular such event up to then in the colony's brief history.

The Legend of Margaret Catchpole

The matter-of-fact notice appearing in an English newspaper of 1797 is the unlikely foundation of a story that endures in England and Australia:

> Margaret Catchpole, for stealing a coach horse, belonging to John Cobbold, Esq., of Ipswich (with whom she formerly lived as a servant), which she rode from thence to London in about 10 hours, dressed in man's apparel, and having there offered it for sale was detected.

Margaret Catchpole was then a 35-year-old Suffolk country woman whose employment by the Cobbold family came to an end a few years earlier. She had been a good servant, treated much as a family member and even receiving basic instruction in reading and writing. More than once she had saved the Cobbolds' children from death. Why was she now stealing a valuable steed from her previous master and riding pell-mell for London dressed as a man?

The details are murky, but it seems that a much younger Margaret Catchpole fell in love with a sailor and smuggler named William Laud. In an argument with another suitor for Margaret's affection, Laud shot his rival and became a wanted man. Laud was pressed into the navy. About four years later Margaret was told by a man named Cook that Laud was back in London. Cook persuaded her to steal the horse and ride it to London where he planned to have it sold for his own profit. But she was arrested almost as soon as she arrived.

Margaret pleaded guilty to the charge and was sentenced to death, later commuted to seven years transportation. While in Ipswich prison awaiting passage to New South Wales, Margaret distinguished herself by good conduct until she discovered that William Laud was in the same prison. The two were able to meet and hatch an escape plan. William showed Margaret how she could scale the walls. Then, using money he had given her earlier, she paid his fine. At the pre-arranged time, Margaret clambered over the walls and met her lover. They were waiting for a ship to take them to freedom when the authorities arrived. William was shot dead. Margaret went back to prison and another trial. Again she received a death sentence and again it was commuted to transportation, this time for life.

Margaret arrived in the colony aboard the *Nile* in December 1801. Her domestic skills were immediately put to good use by the commissary and she wrote home to her uncle in her individual spelling: 'I am well Beloved By all that know me and that is a Comfort for I all wais Goo into Better Compeney then my self that is a monkest free peopell whear thay mak as much of me as if I was a Laday—Becaus I am the Commiseres Cook.'

By then, Margaret had found another 'man that keep me Compeney and would marrey me if Lik But I am not for marriing'. The man was probably the botanist James Gordon and, true to her word, Margaret never did marry. Instead she worked for many of the leading families of the colony, becoming a respected and trusted manager. Her letters home reveal many small details of everyday life in early Sydney and along the Hawkesbury River.

Despite the dramatic events surrounding Mary's horse stealing and transportation, she remained on corresponding terms with the Cobbold family in Suffolk. Her letters stress what an upstanding and honest life she led in the colony and are full of observations about the natural world, the state of the colony and the cost of living. In a letter to her previous mistress, Mrs Cobbold, written in January 1802 and beginning 'honred madam', Margaret described the many gardens, which she thought 'very Butteful'. But, in capitals, she also wrote 'I MUST SAY THIS IS THE WICKEDEST PLACE I EVER WAS IN ALL MY LIFE', describing the convicts sent to the Coal River (Newcastle) with their heads shaved and half starved. Others she said were sent to Norfolk Island with a 'steel Corler on thear poor neckes'.

Like most settlers, Margaret was afraid of the Aboriginal people, then waging a fierce resistance: 'Thay are very saveg for thay all wais Carrey with them spears and tommeay horkes so when thay can meet with a wit man thay will rob them and speer them.' She admitted that she did not like the Aborigines and 'I do not know how to Look at them—thay are such poor naked Craturs', though they were well behaved when visiting her house. She was especially afraid of the black snakes which she claimed were up to twelve feet in length and 'will fly at you Lik a Dog and if thay Bit us wee dy at sun dowen'.

While Margaret served out her relatively uneventful sentence, finally receiving a pardon in 1814, she had not been forgotten back in England. Richard Cobbold, the son of the Suffolk farming family who employed and also helped her after her conviction, would write a best-selling book about her. It was a highly romantic version of reality that also inspired popular plays about Margaret. She remained in the public mind into the twentieth century, being the subject of an early Australian feature film directed by Raymond Longford and starring Lottie Lyell titled *The Romantic Story of Margaret Catchpole*. Today, you can enjoy a real ale at The Margaret Catchpole pub in Ipswich and read a recent novel, *Scapegallows* by Carol Birch, based on her life and legend.

In the year 1819 the real Margaret Catchpole, adventurer, convict, servant, midwife and carer, was nursing an elderly shepherd suffering from influenza at Richmond in New South Wales. She caught the disease and died.

The Convict King

Along the convict-built bridge at Ross in Tasmania are a series of carvings. One of these represents perhaps the most extraordinary character ever transported to Australia. His name was Jorgen Jorgenson, one-time King of Iceland.

The son of a high-class Danish watchmaker, Jorgenson took to a roving life of adventure. At the age of sixteen he went to sea and spent the next thirteen or so years sailing the world. His voyages took him to Port Jackson and to Van Diemen's Land and eventually back home by 1807. With the British attacking Copenhagen, Jorgenson was given a hasty commission into the Danish navy. He was captured and became a prisoner of war.

By 1809 he was the interpreter for an English trading expedition to Iceland. At that time it was still possible for merchants to operate as privateers, basically legalised pirates. The man financing the trade expedition managed to take over the government of Iceland and installed Jorgenson as ruler. After a couple of months in which Jorgenson showed himself to be quite good at the business of kingship, a Royal Navy ship arrived and convinced the privateering merchant to relinquish control of the country. Jorgenson was removed from his throne and was taken back to England.

Despite displaying considerable bravery and skill in rescuing all the passengers from a burning ship, Jorgenson went straight into captivity on a hulk for Danish prisoners of war. He was eventually released but took to drink and gambling with enthusiasm. The British employed him as a spy for a while, but he was in constant debt and in and out of prison until he finally received a death sentence after ignoring an order to quit the country. Through the influence of botanist William Hooker, one of the passengers Jorgenson rescued from the burning ship, the sentence was commuted to transportation. In April 1826, he once again arrived on the shores of Van Diemen's Land, twenty-two years after his first visit.

During the voyage aboard the transport *Woodman*, the multi-skilled Jorgenson had taken on and performed the duties of doctor to crew, passengers and convicts. He had hopes of a reward from the government for this service. But Lieutenant-Governor Arthur was a strict disciplinarian and it was much harder to obtain a pardon under his rule. And Jorgenson's internationally colourful career and escapades had preceded him, as he described in his memoirs:

> Strange rumours were afloat which tended to make the Governor somewhat circumspect in his dealings with me. Some said I had been punished for having written pamphlets against the British Government and for having been a spy in England. Others reversed this story and declared that the British Government had employed me as a spy in foreign countries, and Heaven knows what else equally ridiculous and void of truth. The effect of such stupid irresponsible stories was to create a prejudice against me in official quarters. I was told by Mr. O'Farrell that when an application was made to Colonel Arthur on my behalf, the Governor replied: 'I can do nothing for Jorgenson, as he is a violent political character, and a dangerous man in any country.'

Assisted by letters of introduction from his network of influential contacts, it did not take Jorgenson long to distinguish himself. Now free of drink and gambling after discovering Christianity, he worked as a clerk. In this role he exposed a forgery and received the reward of working for the Van Diemen's Land Company as an explorer. He and another convict were the first white men to find a way across the Central Plateau in the rugged Central Highlands of Tasmania. Jorgenson then received a conditional pardon and was made a police officer. In this and related roles he played a part in the inglorious 'Black Wars' in which the government sought to rid the island of its indigenous people. He received 100 acres of land for his work.

Fully pardoned in 1831, Jorgenson married an illiterate and alcoholic Irish convict named Norah Corbett. She was nearly half his age and, by all accounts, made his later life in Oatlands, 84 kilometres north of Hobart, mostly a misery. Jorgenson worked as a police constable and also pursued his interest in writing. He contributed articles to the Hobart press and authored several books, including his frequently unreliable memoirs. Always in debt and harried by Norah, he was regarded with some amusement as the 'Viking of Van Diemen's Land' and the 'Convict King', his story well known to convicts and settlers alike.

In 1840 the grog and neglect carried Norah away. Jorgenson died the following year from pneumonia. There was no money to bury him. After sixty-one remarkable years, his legend persists. His short reign is remembered in Iceland. Some books and a few articles have been published about his life. And his likeness can still be seen, crown and all, in crumbling stone on the Ross bridge. Norah is there too, a local tribute to their troubled relationship.

The Solicitor's Tale

On 9 November 1843, solicitor William Barber 'was then enjoying a large income, with the brightest prospects'. The following year on the same day he was standing on a beach in New South Wales with a group of transported convicts waiting for the ship to bear them to the torments of Norfolk Island.

'What a catalogue of ills I had suffered in those twelve months!,' he wrote. 'The wreck of all that I possessed in the world; the estrangement of friends, the severance from those I dearly loved, imprisonment in three different dungeons, branded with all but a capital crime, transported for life to the worst of all penal settlements.'

Barber had been found guilty of complicity in a case of fraud and forgery and transported for life. He found himself among men whose lives and customs were dramatically different to his own. Surviving dysentery and the notorious Norfolk Island prison gangs: 'Many of the most daring of the convicts have wrung a kind of respect from those over them by the terror of their vengeance, some ruffians indeed, to my knowledge, have even struck those high in command, and been suffered to go unpunished.'

But the sick and helpless could expect little consideration. To make matters worse, Barber was innocent:

> There were those in England for whose sakes, and on account of the sorrow and shame which my conviction had brought upon them, I prayed fervently to be spared for that day when I could make my innocence clear. For although with my last breath I had asserted the injustice of my sentence, in language so strong that any doubts which they might hold would have been dispelled, who was there to communicate the last words of a dying convict to his friends the other side of the globe?

Recovering from dysentery, Barber was deemed unfit for hard labour and appointed wardsman in the hospital: 'This was by far the most loathsome, perilous, and unhealthy occupation on the Island. Its duties were to preserve order in a dormitory of two hundred criminals, many of whom, as subsequent events showed, would not scruple to take the life of an individual who, like my-self, was at once their drudge and their overseer.'

The well-bred and educated lawyer now had to empty bedpans and clean the wards: 'The disgusting details of the labour thus selected for me, I will not go into.' To add to his unjust punishment, the ex-solicitor had to endure the presence of one of the fraudsters whose crimes had sent him to Norfolk Island. As this man had some previous medical training, he was appointed the doctor of the hospital and so was effectively Barber's boss.

Barber spent sixteen months in the hospital until his frequent illnesses became so bad that the chaplain had him moved to the Cascades Female Factory in Hobart, 'a more salubrious part of the Island'. He had to do the same work but conditions were better and his health improved. But he was now well enough to work and was sent to field labour in a heavy gang with a notoriously harsh overseer: 'Covered with dirt, weakened from insufficient food; sometimes drenched with rain, at others, standing up to my knees in slush, and under a broiling sun that made the mud steam around me, I continued at this horrible labour for three months.'

Barber then went to work as a clerk. After two and a half years on Norfolk Island, the penal station was closed down and the convicts transferred to Van Diemen's Land. A week later, the ex-solicitor received wonderful news. A conditional pardon was granted. He needed to get to Hobart, 90 miles away, 'through an almost untrodden region, a gum tree wilderness without for the greater part any roads, except a slight kind of sheep track'. He had to return his prison uniform to the authorities and might have been forced to make the trek naked if not for the willingness of his less fortunate companions to provide him with an assortment of ill-fitting garments and some food.

> The sun served as my compass by day, and the stars by night. My course sometimes lay along the sea-coast; but oftener deep in the woods, on emerging from which, the scenery was often extremely beautiful. After crossing mountains and fording streams, and sleeping occasionally in the shade of a tree, in three days and three nights I reached my destination. Had a stage harlequin suddenly made his appearance, he could scarcely have attracted more attention than I did, in my motley, ill-fitting suit.

From Hobart, Barber travelled to Sydney, then via Canton, Madras, Suez and Germany to Paris. Still unable to return to Britain because his pardon was only conditional, Barber made contact with the British ambassador and six months later, 'I received a free pardon, with a letter from the Secretary of State acknowledging my innocence'.

His troubles were not over yet. After his conviction Barber had been barred from the legal profession. It was some years before he was re-admitted in late 1855. He did receive compensation but there could be no real restitution for his wrongful sentence and his lost years inside the brutalities of 'the system'.

A Convict Maid

A popular British street ballad of the early nineteenth century, or even earlier, traded on the image of the fallen young woman transported to the wilds of Australia. Printed and reprinted many times, this version is prefaced with the almost certainly concocted personal story of 'Charlotte W—', giving its primarily British audience confirmation of their moral and practical fears of transportation. As was often the case with these early examples of 'fake news' about Australia produced in Britain, there is confusion about the geography of Tasmania and New South Wales:

> Charlotte W—, the subject of this narrative, is a native of London, born of honest parents, she was early taught the value and importance of honesty and virtue; but unhappily ere her attaining the age of maturity, her youthful affections were placed on a young Tradesman, and to raise money to marry her lover, she yielded to the temptation to rob her master, and his property being found in her possession, she was immediately apprehended, tried at the Old Bailey Sessions, convicted, and sentenced to seven years transportation. On her arrival at Hobart Town, she sent her mother a very affecting and pathetic letter, from which the following verses have been composed, and they are here published

by particular desire, in the confident hope that this account of her sufferings will serve as an example to deter other females from similar practices.

Ye London maids attend to me,
While I relate my misery,
Through London streets I oft have strayed,
But now I am a Convict Maid.

In innocence I once did live,
In all the joy that peace could give,
But sin my youthful heart betrayed,
And now I am a Convict Maid.

To wed my lover I did try,
To take my master's property,
So all my guilt was soon displayed,
And I became a Convict Maid.

Then I was soon to prison sent,
To wait in fear my punishment,
When at the bar I stood dismayed,
Since doomed to be a Convict Maid.

At length the Judge did me address,
Which filled with pain my aching breast,
To Botany Bay you will be conveyed,
For seven years a Convict Maid.

For seven long years oh how I sighed,
While my poor mother loudly cried,
My lover wept and thus he said,
May God be with my Convict Maid.

To you that hear my mournful tale,
I cannot half my grief reveal,

No sorrow yet has been portrayed,
Like that of the poor Convict Maid.

Far from my friends and home so dear,
My punishment is most severe,
My woe is great and I'm afraid,
That I shall die a Convict Maid.

I toil each day in grief and pain,
And sleepless through the night remain,
My constant toils are unrepaid,
And wretched is the Convict Maid.

Oh could I but once more be free,
I'd never again a captive be,
But I would seek some honest trade,
And never become a Convict Maid.

A Broken Down Gent

When John Mortlock received a sentence of twenty-one years transportation, he told the judge, 'My lord, it will save me from starvation.' Attempting to regain the family inheritance he believed to be his by right, Mortlock fired a pistol at his uncle one night in November 1842. The gun was loaded only with a blank but the charge was still attempted murder, 'shooting with intent'. Conducting his own defence the 32-year-old with a 'remarkably handsome profile' and 'easy, gentlemanly appearance' spoke movingly of his dire situation. He had no trade or profession and times were hard. He asked the jury: 'What would you have done in the same condition? With no friends to give you a penny? What would you do but starve, or commit suicide, or have fallen into the path of crime?' He said that he had lived in poverty and 'absolute destitution' for much of the last four years and been the object of derision at his humble lodgings at the Blue Boar, 'not, as many of you know, a first-rate inn'.

Mortlock's pathetic tale brought many in the court to tears and the citizens of Cambridge later petitioned on his behalf, unsuccessfully. The ex–Indian Army officer then embarked on an extraordinary experience of the transportation system, from the hulks to Norfolk Island to Van Diemen's Land. While this journey was not especially unusual, Mortlock would also experience another sentence of transportation, this time to the Swan River in Western Australia. Through it all he would persist in his claims against the family members who he was convinced had defrauded his father and himself.

Reduced to 'the condition of a galley slave', as he put it, Mortlock served over four months in irons on a Portsmouth hulk left over from the Battle of Trafalgar. His 600 companions included an elderly butler caught stealing silver, a foreign traveller and a London solicitor. These 'Knights of the Iron Chain' shared poorly ventilated and damp quarters with twenty-seven other 'degraded objects'. There was not enough food and the men were made to work at hard manual labour. Many died and it was rumoured that the head surgeon of the hospital hulk supplied bodies to doctors in Portsmouth for dissection at 6 guineas each. Flogging was restricted to no more than three dozen stripes, though the flagellator was an enthusiastic practitioner of his trade.

Mortlock was transferred from the hulk to the *Maitland* and sailed in September 1843. The voyage was a welcome relief from the hulk. Although there were no fresh vegetables available until the ship reached Cape Town, the doctor was conscientious (motivated by a 10-shilling bonus for every convict delivered alive). Floggings were few and light. Only eight died, one having fallen overboard. Four months later Mortlock arrived at Port Jackson and from there to hard labour on the dreaded Norfolk Island. It did not take long for the island to confirm its evil reputation.

The inmates were fed on a meagre diet of 'insipid hominy', salt junk 'very like old saddle' and a maize bread that tasted like sawdust. Within the first fortnight, eight of the group arriving with Mortlock were dead. Dysentery was common and treated only with boiled tree bark. 'Sea water did duty for Epsom Salts.' Each morning cross-ironed men were flogged to heavy labour beneath a scorching sun in the stone quarry or fields. Floggings of up to 300 lashes could be, and often were, inflicted. Solitary confinement, sometimes in dark holes for thirty, sixty or ninety days was feared far more. 'Such treatments, with starvation, rendered life valueless: four would cast lots—who should be murdered—who should do the deed—who should be the two witnesses—for a "spell" to Sydney, where the trial took place.'

Escapes were frequent, but success rare. Those who eluded the guards usually died of exposure, hunger and thirst. Or worse. One of the hardened 'old hands' was known as the 'man-eater'. He had escaped with another from Moreton Bay and survived by killing and eating him.

Mortlock diplomatically aimed to navigate his existence between the punishments of those in charge and the desperate violence of his fellow convicts. The daily sounds of 'the "cats" upon the naked flesh (like the crack of a cart whip) tortured my ears'. His social standing as a gentlemen shielded him to some extent from the horrors of Norfolk Island and his education provided a relatively soft job of tutoring the children of administrators and guards.

He was able to appreciate the natural beauty of the island and the seascapes around it. Whales were commonly sighted, turtles less so. Tropical fruits flourished, as did fowl and fish in the sea. A 'desecrated Paradise', Mortlock called it. In February 1846 he left the privations of Norfolk Island for those of Van Diemen's Land with sixty or seventy other convicts 'stowed away more like pigs than human beings' aboard the barque *Lady Franklin*. Nineteen days later he was landed in Hobart.

In Van Diemen's Land Mortlock was required to perform a year's hard labour before gaining a 'pass' that would allow him to work for wages. He felled trees until the following April, suffering part of the harsh winter without shoes. But even when he became free to pursue his own employment, there was little work to be had in the colony's depressed economy. Mortlock got by through odd-jobbing and short-term appointments—labouring, a constable (or 'trap') in the island force made up almost entirely of transportees, a school master, a private tutor and clerk to a road gang.

The nineteen convicts on the gang were 'housed in two wooden moveable huts resembling the cages of wild animals'. Threatened with a stint in the dreaded Port Arthur penitentiary by the corrupt officer in charge of the gang, Mortlock decided to abscond. He walked to Hobart and handed himself in, receiving a four-month sentence quarrying stone. During this time and after, he survived several misadventures while lost in the island's impenetrable bush as he sought to earn a living by whatever work was available.

In late 1852 Mortlock received a ticket-of-leave and was recommended for a conditional pardon in 1854. Effectively free, he took up the occupation of pedlar, his already extensive travels around the island giving him useful knowledge of the transport routes and the people who lived along them. Humping 70 to 80 pounds of hawkers' wares, his opossum rug, cover sheet of oiled calico, a knapsack full of supplies and, eventually, a rifle, he often stumbled for up to 20 miles to reach a hut or other human habitation clinging to the Tasmanian bush. He tramped the tracks for weeks, carrying his bundle of wares, living rough and often in peril from misadventure or bushrangers.

His efforts were rewarded. John Mortlock the pedlar became a successful colonial businessman, buying cheap and selling dear to the isolated farms and small settlements across the island. He eventually accumulated enough money to take advantage of the freedom he had now richly earned. With enough cash to fund his travels, he left the island for an extended holiday in 1855, visiting Sydney, the Turon goldfields near Bathurst and Melbourne.

The following year Van Diemen's Land was renamed Tasmania, partly to remove the taint of convictism. This made little impact on John Mortlock or any other transportees, but in 1857 what seemed a stroke of luck turned out to be the cause of further misery. An uncle left Mortlock an inheritance of 46 pounds. Not a vast sum, but a substantial amount at that time. Unfortunately, the funds tempted him to return to England to pursue the claims that had seen him transported in the first place. He was in Cambridge less than a month before being arrested. Transported convicts were forbidden to return before their original sentence had expired, regardless of their ticket-of-leave or pardoned status. The citizens of Cambridge raised a petition of 1200 signatures, but their protest was in vain.

Sporting a light moustache and a 'military and dignified' appearance, Mortlock pleaded not guilty at the dock in March 1858. The jury disagreed, but strongly recommended mercy. It was not given. The returned convict was sentenced to one year's imprisonment—followed by transportation for a further five years. The law required him to finish out the term of his original sentence.

A year in the Cambridge County Goal awaiting retransportation allowed Mortlock to draft his memoirs and pursue his inheritance claims. He was then taken in chains to London's Millbank Prison. After nine weeks in the gloomy institution, he was manacled and escorted by train to Portsmouth and once again taken aboard the convict ship *Sultana*. He arrived at Western Australia's Swan River colony in 1859. Fremantle Prison, he thought, 'by no means so repulsive as Millbank'.

Now fifty years of age and an experienced 'old hand', he was soon granted a ticket-of-leave and enjoyed a relatively congenial existence. He received a pardon in 1862, allowing him, eventually, to return to Tasmania via Sydney with 40 pounds in his pocket. From Tasmania, Mortlock took passage to Melbourne, rambled through the goldfields, wrote a letter to the *Argus* regarding the topical debate over transportation and then headed back to England where he landed in late 1864. Free.

And free to once again pursue his claims, which he did—unsuccessfully—for the rest of his life. He supported himself and his many litigations by writing, publishing and selling pamphlets, mainly telling his life story and airing his financial grievances. With only 154 pounds to his name, John Mortlock, ex-convict and likeable but deluded eccentric, died on 21 June 1882. He had suffered the hulks, two voyages of transportation, several jails and three Australian penal establishments. None of these experiences dampened his strong sense of injustice or his long determination to set things right. Whether he was right or wrong, John Mortlock's extraordinary story suggests that transportation did not necessarily lead to repentance, rehabilitation or resignation.

The Poacher's Fate

William Sykes—just 'Bill' to his mates and wife, Myra—made a very big mistake one moonlit October night in 1865. With a few accomplices he went out poaching in Silver Wood near Rotherham, as they had often done before. But this time was different. The local gamekeepers were lying in wait. Heavily armed and with a personal score or two to settle, the keepers waited until the poachers came close by their hiding place. With a yell they loosed their dogs on the poachers' beasts and attacked the surprised men. The fight that followed was savage, with no quarter given to man or beast. When it was over, the keeper Edward Lilley lay unconscious and bleeding on the cold Yorkshire ground. The poachers fled and the keepers carried their wounded companion to medical attention. He died a few days later.

The police were fairly quickly on the trail and eventually caught up with one of the poachers who they frightened into a confession and identification of his accomplices. When they came for Bill Sykes he went quietly, telling Myra and the children not to worry. But of course she did. She would worry for the next twenty-five years, her fears, troubles and hopes expressed in a series of irregular letters to Bill, transported to Western Australia. After two complicated and sensational trials, he had borne the brunt of the case against the poachers for the murder of the keeper. Eventually he was convicted only of manslaughter and paid the price of a life sentence.

Arriving at Fremantle aboard the *Norwood*, Bill Sykes went straight into Fremantle Prison for processing. Once inside he was washed, barbered and issued with uniforms, including the parti-coloured work gang uniforms that ensured the convicts stood out among the colonial population whenever they were labouring outside the prison walls. His rations were basic but adequate, including bread, meat, potatoes, salt and pepper, tea, sugar, milk and rice or oatmeal on Mondays and Fridays. He was also given regular issues of soap and soda for cleaning his clothes and body. William was sent to work on the road gangs in the Bunbury area south of Perth.

Bill Sykes the poacher was a man of few words, one of life's survivors and probably typical of the thousands of convicts transported to the Swan River between 1850 and 1868. He worked on road gangs, as an assigned servant, tried to escape, was punished for this, as well as for minor and major infractions later on, mostly associated with a weakness for the grog.

Back in Yorkshire, Myra had to provide for herself and five children. She heard no word of or from her husband for more than a year and even then only indirectly through a letter he wrote to his family. Undeterred, Myra wrote to William, asking him how his passage had been and giving news of his children:

All send their kind love to you and Edward Huttley and his wife sends their kind love also and your daughter Ann is in place and doing well and Alfread is working in [the mill] and he gets 10 pence per day.

Ann Thurza Alf William(s) sends their kind love to you but William has got long white curly hair and he was not called William for nothing for he is a little rip right.

The rough and irregular correspondence between William and Myra Sykes wound on over the next few years, mainly from Myra's hand rather than William's. Some time in 1874 she wrote: 'It harte breaks me to write like this if the prodigal son cud come Buck to his home wons more tahre woold be a rejoicing.'

A few lines further on Myra recalls her last sight of William at the Leeds Assizes: 'and you mencend about Lucking young I thort you did when I saw you at leeds my hart broke neley wenn I felt your hand bing so soft.'

On 12 January 1875, William wrote to Myra. Although this letter is lost, the gist of it is clear from Myra's reply of April 11. She begins in her usual, slightly formal manner, and, as she often did, Myra mentions the lack of letters from him. Then she tells of the terrible news she had received: 'Your relations said that you was Dead I went to Rotherham townshall and asked if they knew wheather you was dead or not one of the police sade he heard you was dead.' Poor Myra was now convinced that her William was dead, the family news casually confirmed by the authority figure of the policeman: 'I put the chealdren and my self in black for you my little Tirza went to the first place in deap black.'

After dressing herself and the children in mourning clothes, Myra is at once devastated and relieved to discover, through William's favoured sister, that she has been misinformed.

By now William and Myra's son, also named William, is old enough to write to his exiled father. A letter on 20 October 1875 begins with bad news: 'Dear father I write these few lines hopeing to find you better than it leaves us at present my mother as been very ill and me my self and I am a bit better.' Soon the letter becomes a young man's cry of pain for the father he barely knew: 'Dear father we think you have quite forgot us all my sister Ann takes it hard at you not writing oftener.' And later: 'Dear father you never name me in you letters but I can sit down and write a letter to you now.' The letter ends: 'We all send kindest and dearest love to you and God bless you and 1,000 kisses for our Dear father from your Dear son William.'

In the same envelope as young William's letter came a hasty note from Myra. The near-indecipherable handwriting indicates that she was not well in body or in mind and very worried about Ann's domestic problems. It seems that Ann was pregnant for the third time and Myra is not looking forward to having to look after her during the pregnancy: 'Dear husban I am grvd to my hart A bout my Ann I have had her Both times of her confindments and Ly shee gating on gain.' Then Myra scribbles what were possibly the last words to pass between herself and William Sykes: 'We hall [all] send our nearst and dearst Love to you with A 1000 kiss Dear Husband you must excuse writing.'

In 1877 William received his ticket-of-leave, allowing him to work for himself within the colony, and began sinking wells for a living. Later he would work for the railway department, an old ex-convict living an isolated life in the bush.

While his father was living out an exile's life, young William and the family back in Yorkshire had been busy seeking a pardon for him. With the help of the local vicar, they managed to get the bureaucracy to address their petition. A letter was sent with the official details from the Colonial Secretary's Office to the Swan River colony, suggesting that William be allowed to return to England as his age, around sixty-three years, meant he would be unlikely to offend again.

By the time the letter reached Western Australia it was too late. William was found sick in his hut shortly after Christmas 1890. He died at Toodyay hospital a few days later. His only possessions were a few pounds, an old rifle, a dog and a kangaroo-skin pouch in which were the fragile letters of Myra and William Sykes, her son. The resident magistrate at Toodyay replied to the request from the colonial secretary: 'The Superintendent of Poor Relief conveys the information that Sykes died in the hospital at Newcastle [as Toodyay was then known] on or about the 4th, or 5th, January last and that his effects are but of trifling value.'

Myra eventually remarried in 1892. She had a brief but

happy marriage but was widowed again the following year. She lived until 1894, long enough to see her children grow up and make their way in the world and have children of their own. Some of her and William's descendants now live in New Zealand and Australia.

VITA STUDIO,

HOBART.

Convict Eliza James (Mrs Joseph Small), arrived
on the Anna Maria *in 1852. This photograph*
(possibly with her daughter) would have been
taken after she had served her time and become
a free woman.

10
A Convict Stain

This most flourishing colony suffered from the stain that had
fallen upon it in its infancy . . .

Sir James Mackintosh in the House of Commons, 1828

Tom Tilley's Token

They took Tom Tilley from Stafford to the hulks at the end of
January 1786. He was bound for the unknown shores of New
South Wales with a sentence of seven years for stealing, with
force, some cloth and a bag valued at 21 shillings. Around this
time, he commissioned an engraver to inscribe a small copper
disc with a message to his loved ones, as was the custom. Tom
Tilley's handsome token read:

> Thomas Tilley TRANSPORTED 29 July 1785 for signing a note
> Sent the hulks Jan 24 1786.

On the reverse side was a beautifully drawn bird shackled to
the ground with a chain around its neck. The message to wife,
sweetheart or family was clear. It was very unlikely that Tom,
who was about forty years old, and the person or persons for
whom his keepsake was meant would ever see each other again.

Perhaps that was why he falsified his sentence from common thieving to the more sophisticated 'writing a note', or forging a document.

Accurate or not, love tokens, or 'leaden hearts' as they were often called, were frequently made for loved ones by departing convicts. Tom's was well made and expensive, though most were crude scratchings on old coins, like Charles Wilkinson's. He stole a handkerchief and was transported for life in 1824. The rough etchings on his token read:

> Your lover lives for you
> CL
> Only.
> Til death

The reverse of this token for the beloved 'CL' told the story in a few terse words:

> C Wilkinson
> Lag for Life
> Aged 17
> 1824

Convicted of murder in 1832, William Kennedy was lucky to have his sentence cut to a lifetime of labour in the colonies. He had the engraver inscribe his coin with a defiant verse:

> When this you see
> Remember me
> And bear me in your mind.
> Let all the world
> Say what they will
> Speak of me as you find

There were no such emotive sentiments for Tom Tilley, and the end of one chapter in his life was the opening of another.

The year before Tom was convicted, thirty-year-old Mary Abel (Abell) was convicted of grand larceny in Worcester. She, too, received a sentence of seven years transportation and was sent to the hulks awaiting what would be a long voyage with the First Fleet.

At some point while they were both on the hulks, Tom and Mary met and fell in love. Around August 1786 they conceived a child. William was born aboard the female transport *Lady Penrhyn* in April 1787. Tom sailed for the same destination aboard the *Alexander*.

William was baptised on 20 April 1787 aboard the *Lady Penrhyn* by the Reverend Richard Johnson and has the distinction of being the first entry in the New South Wales register of births, deaths and marriages.

The family arrived with the rest of the First Fleet in January 1788 and on 4 May they were married. Ten days later, young William died. Two months later, Mary was dead. Two years later, Tom married again. His new wife also came to the colony aboard the *Lady Penrhyn*. Oddly, her name was Elizabeth Tilley (also spelled Tully and no relation).

What happened to Tom and Elizabeth Tilley? Thomas is registered on a list of grants and leases of lands in the colony in 1794. Possibly they returned to England. Or perhaps they stayed on in the colony like most transports. Research to date has not revealed their fates. But through the accidents of history, Tom Tilley's copper love token survived. In 1987 it came into the collection of Sydney's Powerhouse Museum where it is now preserved as a rare artefact of the First Fleet and a memorial to several convict lives.

The First Australia Day

On 26 January 1788, the convict armada of the First Fleet officially announced its presence on the continent of New Holland, as Australia was known at the time: 'At Day light the English colours were displayed on shore & possession was taken for

His Majesty whose health, with the Queens, Prince of Wales & Success to the Colony was drank, a feu de joie was fired by the party of marines & ye whole gave 3 cheers which was returned by the *Supply*.'

What is now Australia's national day originated in the experiences of early colonial New South Wales, especially those who went there in chains. January 26 was being unofficially celebrated as the foundation or 'First Landing Day' of the colony of New South Wales by emancipated convicts and free settlers from at least 1808. Although not an official event, that year the festivities began at sundown on the 25th and continued well into the night with toasts, illuminated houses and bonfires. The first officer ashore in 1788, Major George Johnston, was the main toast of the evening. The next day Johnston arrested Governor Bligh, initiating the military coup that is since known as the 'Rum Rebellion'. The first recorded observation of the day was born in controversy and conflict. Its history has often continued these themes up to the present day.

An interest in commemoration suggests that those involved had cause to bless rather than curse their experiences. They were free of their debt to society and were doing well in the colony. Certainly by 1817, although still unofficial, the observance of January 26 was decidedly respectable:

On Monday the 27th ult. a dinner party met at the house of Mr. Isaac Nichols, for the purpose of celebrating the Anniversary of the Institution of this Colony under Governor Philip, which took place on 26 Jan. 1788, but this year happening upon a Sunday, the commemoration dinner was reserved for the day following. The party assembled were select, and about 40 in number. At 5 in the afternoon dinner was on the table, and a more agreeable entertainment could not have been anticipated. After dinner a number of loyal toasts were drank, and a number of festive songs given; and about 10 the company parted, well gratified with the pleasures that the meeting had afforded.

The following year, 1818, Governor Macquarie declared the day an official celebration. Government employees were given the day off and an extra pound of fresh meat. A thirty-gun salute marked the years of the colony's existence. The day was now known as 'Foundation Day' and continued to be observed as such, involving sporting traditions including sailing and horse racing.

The history of Australia Day since then has been one of increasing government involvement, some would say control, and increasing conflict over how the day should be observed or whether it should even be celebrated. In all this controversy, little mention is made of Australia Day's convict origins.

Floating Brothels

It seemed to have gone well. The *Janus* left Cork in December 1819 with a cargo of 105 women, about a third of them Irish Catholics. There were twenty-six children and some passengers, including priests Philip Connelly and John Therry. Governor Macquarie contentedly reported the arrival of the transport *Janus* in May 1820:

> This forenoon anchored in Sydney Cove the Ship Janus, Transport, Commanded by Capt. Thos. Jas. Mowatt, with 104 Female Convicts from England and Ireland, from which last Country She sailed on the 3d. of Decr. 1819, touching at Rio de Janeiro.— The Prisoners & other Passengers have arrived in good Health; but the Surgeon Supdt. Doctor Creagh—of the Royal Navy, died when the Ship had arrived off Van Diemen's Land.—The Revd. Mr. Philip Connelly and The Revd. Mr. Josiah Terry [*sic*], Roman Catholic Priests, have come out Passengers in the Janus, with the Permission of Government, for the Ministry in this Colony.

But six weeks later one of the *Janus* women, Mary Long, complained that she had been impregnated by Captain Mowatt. Lydia Esden, also of the *Janus*, had the same complaint but she blamed the chief mate, John Hedges.

Macquarie wasted no time assembling a bench of magistrates to investigate. Witnesses were called. Some said they had seen no evidence of impropriety. But Connelly and Therry stated that there had been relationships between the sailors and the female convicts from the start of the voyage. And it was not just the sailors, the women 'were as determined to communicate with the sailors as they themselves were'. In response to a complaint from the priests, new locks had been placed on the convicts' quarters when the ship reached Rio de Janeiro. But these were deemed to be ineffective in preventing continuing intercourse.

Captain Mowatt defended himself strongly, claiming that Father Connelly was trying 'to represent as blameless all those of his own persuasion'. Attention turned to the role of the surgeon, Dr Creagh, who was also implicated in the alleged wrongdoing. A part of his role was to maintain proper relations aboard the ship, which, according to Mowatt, he failed to do.

There were clearly a number of tensions aboard the *Janus* that run through the accounts given to the magistrates. But the evidence of Lydia Esden and Mary Long was convincing and the bench concluded that:

> [We] are of the opinion that Prostitution did prevail on board the said Ship throughout the Voyage from England to this Territory; that due exertions were not made on the part of the Captain and officers to prevent the same; and that the matter of Charge, as against the Captain and Officers of the said Ship individually in that respect, is true and well founded in fact.

Despite this finding, there seems to have been no consequences for the men involved. The *Janus* sailed away with Mowatt in command the following July to go whaling off New Zealand. She eventually returned to England without revisiting Sydney.

This was not the first allegation of prostitution and immoral behaviour aboard convict ships. The *Lady Juliana* was the first transport to carry female-only convicts, more than 220 of them.

She arrived as part of the Second Fleet after a voyage of more than 300 days. She had spent more than seven months in port preparing to sail, plenty of time for those aboard to get to know each other very well. According to the steward John Nicol, when the ship got to sea 'every man on board took a wife from among the convicts, they nothing loath'. Nicol also struck up a relationship with a convict woman, as did the ship's surgeon.

Some historians have subscribed to the theory that the *Lady Juliana* was 'a floating brothel', as first proposed by historian Charles Bateson. Others point out that the women were free to make whatever relationships they chose and that there is no evidence of coercion or commerce in their arrangements. Relatively few transported women had records of prostitution, despite the views of some contemporaries, most floridly expressed in officer Ralph Clark's view of the Second Fleet women as 'those damned whores'. Almost all records surviving are from the point of view of the upper classes who generally saw working-class women as morally degenerate because they often lived in de facto relationships. Not the same as prostitution, of course, but subtlety and precision were not strong qualities of Georgian and Victorian social interactions.

There were frequent similar claims made about illicit sexual relations aboard convict ships, consensual or not. These certainly took place, though were much amplified by gossip stemming from the prejudices of the time. Perceptions and misperceptions like this would continue throughout the colonial era. They became a potent element in the notion of 'the convict stain' and, despite the efforts of historians to present a more balanced view, are still strong elements of the mythology of convictism.

The Stain That Would Not Fade

In the House of Commons on 20 June 1828, Sir James Mackintosh rose to speak and argued for the establishment of trial by jury and a limited form of elected assembly in New South

Wales and Van Diemen's Land, 'except the penal settlement for offenders'. He saw no reason why:

> The inhabitants of an English colony, which had subsisted for forty years and which had grown to such magnitude, should be denied by the parent country those two great institutions of popular judicature by juries and popular legislating by their representatives, the chief boast and honour of the English race, who had preserved them under all circumstances and held them up as a model to all other nations? (Cheers).

Mackintosh went on to point out that such institutions were desirable:

> because this most flourishing colony suffered from the stain that had fallen upon it in its infancy, and which induced many persons yet to consider it as the receptacle of convicts. The only measure that could wipe out this stain was to impart the privileges of British subjects to the colonists, and put them on a footing with all other parts of the British empire, by proclaiming that they had the same rights and privileges as their countrymen in the other quarters of the world. (Cheers).

The 'convict stain' was declared. The only way to purge the Australian colonies of this dreadful blemish was to plant the institutions of English law, rewarding the hard-working 'freedman' (Macquarie liked the good old word better than 'emancipist') who had 'acquired property by his industry the power to elect a representative, and to be a juryman as a reward for his virtues'.

This point of view came from the increasing numbers of free settlers and ex-convicts, or 'emancipists' as they were known, in the colonies. The idea that the flowering new nation William Wentworth foresaw in his 1823 poem, 'Australasia—A New Britannia in another world', had its origins in something as morally, legally and now politically rancid as convicted felons was an increasing embarrassment.

This was not new. Doubts of one kind or another had been aired about the entire Australian penal enterprise even before the First Fleet sailed. But forty years later it was a central element of the fight to end transportation that came to a head in the 1840s and saw its abolition in New South Wales and later in the rebranded Van Diemen's Land, now 'Tasmania'.

Evermore lurid revelations of the horrors of the convict system, usually coded as 'unnatural crime', featured in reports, inquiries and in the pages of the lively colonial press. Many of these accounts were also published in the British newspapers and journals. People became reluctant to advertise a convict connection, whether it was their own misdemeanour or that of an ancestor. The original sin of convictism was washed away by a growing silence.

The convict stain became even more closely associated with the foundations of Australia in the term 'birth stain', an explicit slur that has echoed down the decades. Even with the current popularity of researching convict ancestors, the stain continues to influence the way we think about convictism and its role in our past. While a convict ancestor is now considered by many to be something of a social distinction, the broader story of transportation has suffered a great forgetting of the 160,000 or more women, men, children and adolescents who founded modern Australia.

The Cabbage Tree Mob

Charles Hodge, apprentice, was well liquored when he visited Mr Cherrington's place of business in Pitt Street one Sunday afternoon in 1841. With 'a cigar stuck in his mouth', Hodge became 'very insolent and pretended to be looking out for a coat to purchase'. Mr Cherrington summoned a constable and the troublesome apprentice was taken in custody and remanded until his master, Mr Bibb, could be contacted.

When Mr Bibb arrived he told the magistrate that his young charge 'had of late connected himself with what was popularly and well known as the "Cabbage Tree Mob", and since then he had become exceedingly saucy and would not demean himself as an apprentice ought to do'. He asked the magistrate to let Charles know what would be the consequences of associating with such 'disorderly characters'. The magistrate obliged, saying:

> He was sorry to hear anything said against the native youth of the Colony, because he was aware that there were many things in their favor, and many excellent traits in their character; but of late he had been frequently called upon to deal with some of them for conduct at once improper, and highly discreditable to one and all of those concerned in the disturbances, and he was determined in future to inflict the severest penalty on every one convicted before him; he also wished the prisoner distinctly to understand, that if ever his master brought him to Court for keeping irregular hours, or if he should even be apprehended in the company of those boys, he had improperly associated himself with, he would send him to the house of correction for a very long period, as it was not to be endured that the public peace was to be disturbed by any class of disorderly persons, and least of all by boys. If therefore, the prisoner consulted his own safety or respectability, he would instantly change his companions and keep good hours.

With this stern talking-to, Charles Hodge was discharged.

The 'Cabbage Tree Mob' he had taken up with was a general term of the time for troublesome bands of youth. Roaming the streets of Sydney and wearing their trademark cabbage tree hats, a colonial invention, they became increasingly difficult to control. Many of what the magistrate called 'the native youth' were the sons of convicts, also sometimes known as 'currency lads'. Their attitude to authority perhaps owed something to their ancestry and something to the restlessness that has always energised juvenile street gangs. A contemporary described them around the 1840s, when the term 'cabbage tree mob' first seems to arise:

> There are to be found round the doors of the Sydney theatre a
> sort of 'loafers', known as the Cabbage-tree mob—a class whom,
> in the spirit of the ancient tyrant, one might excusably wish had
> but one nose, in order to make it a bloody one! These are an
> unruly set of young fellows, native born generally, who, not
> being able, perhaps, to muster coin enough to enter the house,
> amuse themselves by molesting those who can afford that luxury.
> Dressed in a suit of fustian or colonial tweed, and the emblem of
> their order, the low-crowned cabbage-palm hat, the main object
> of their enmity seems to be the ordinary black headpiece worn by
> respectable persons, which is ruthlessly knocked over the eyes of
> the wearer as he passes or enters the theatre.

The children of this generation would become the larrikins
who caused so much trouble in Sydney, Melbourne and elsewhere later in the century.

Bottoms Up!

Visitors to the Cascades Female Factory in Hobart can buy
a colourful postcard showing a scene in the history of that
institution. The popular souvenir depicts a group of convict
women baring their bottoms at three dignitaries. The caption
is 'A Singular Act of Female Rebellion in Van Diemen's Land'.

The story goes that Lieutenant-Governor Sir John Franklin
and Lady Franklin were visiting the factory one Sunday to
join the colony's chaplain who was delivering a sermon to the
inmates. The visitors were positioned in front of 300 or so convict
women, all taking the word of the Lord together. At some point
in the proceedings, the convict women turned their backs to the
dignitaries before them, lifted their skirts and slapped their bare
behinds in a gesture of unmistakeable meaning.

The postcard shows this marvellous moment of class
defiance and the shock on the faces of the Franklins and the
cleric. But, sadly, it never happened. The postcard was created
in 2004 and the group mooning is just a myth, originating in

the addled spleen of a disappointed Anglican priest named Robert Crooke.

Crooke came to the colony with the aim of becoming the chaplain, a secure position. Through his own failings he was unsuccessful and left the island under a cloud in 1858. He spent the rest of his life castigating the Anglican Church in Tasmania, most especially the chaplain who, Crooke, believed, held the job that should have belonged to him. The flashing bottoms story was a piece of fantasy that Crooke confected in his ignored writings.

But two generations later, Crooke's granddaughter showed her grandfather's rantings to a biographer of Sir John Franklin who unwittingly included the bottom-baring incident as fact. Like all such believable untruths, especially a vulgar one, it went on to have a life of its own as 'history'. It still does, despite historians trying for years to debunk it. In vain do they point to the demonising of the convict women as they appear in the very popular postcard.

No matter how often the myth is busted, it just keeps rolling on. This, of course, is how we have all been encouraged to see convict women through decades of popular novels, stories, television and even some histories. The defiance of authority implicit in the story and the postcard make it even more appealing to the strong streak of anti-authoritarianism in the national identity. That is a myth, too, which just makes it even more powerful.

The Gundagai Cat

The *Golden Grove* was one of the First Fleet store ships, sometimes called 'the Noah's Ark of Australia' due to the number and variety of livestock she conveyed to Botany Bay, including: 'one bull, four cows, and one calf; one stallion, three mares, and three colts; one ram, eleven sheep, and eight lambs; one billy-goat, four nanny goats, and three kids; one boar, five sows, and a litter of 14 pigs; nine different sorts of dogs; and seven cats.'

In the 1870s it was said that one of these First Fleet cats was still living at the amazing age of 100 at the New South Wales town of Gundagai. The centenarian moggy was so aloof she would only eat pork sausages. By the 1920s, the feline was said to have reached the even more advanced age of 190 years. This assertion was published in at least one English newspaper and picked up and reprinted in the American and Australian press. While the Americans swallowed the tale whole, the factoid was properly dismissed by Gundagai locals as what in those days was called a 'mare's nest', meaning a grossly inaccurate claim, or what we might today call an urban legend or just fake news.

By then, of course, Gundagai was famous for the dog that sat on the tuckerbox in the folksong known as 'Nine Miles from Gundagai':

I'm used to punching bullock teams across the hills and plains,
I've teamed outback these forty years in blazing droughts and
    rains,
I've lived a heap of troubles down without a blooming lie,
But I can't forget what happened to me nine miles from
    Gundagai.

'Twas getting dark the team got bogged the axle snapped in two,
I lost my matches and my pipe ah what was I to do,
The rain came on twas bitter cold and hungry too was I,
And the dog sat in the tucker box nine miles from Gundagai.

Some blokes I know have stacks of luck no matter how they fall,
But there was I lord luvva duck no blessed luck at all,
I couldn't make a pot of tea nor get my trousers dry,
And the dog sat in the tucker box nine miles from Gundagai.

I can forgive the blinking team I can forgive the rain,
I can forgive the dark and cold and go through it again,
I can forgive my rotten luck but hang me till I die,
I can't forgive that blooming dog nine miles from Gundagai.

But that's all dead and past and gone I've sold the team for meat,
And where I got the bullocks bogged now there is an asphalt street,
The dog ah well he took a bait and reckoned he would die,
I buried him in that tucker box nine miles from Gundagai.

By then, the dog had become so famous for whatever it actually did in the tuckerbox that the good folk of Gundagai had erected a statue to its folkloric memory. Cat yarns, no matter how foundational, were not welcome.

Shades of the System

The transported convicts who lived and died in many parts of Australia remain with us in various ways. As well as the many heritage sites associated with jails, bridges and other public works built by convict labour, they have also bequeathed us a great many ghost stories.

George Grover was transported to Van Diemen's Land in 1825. His record shows that he was at first considered a trouble-maker and spent a lot of time in irons, the usual punishment for mild insubordination. But by 1829 he revelled in the official title of 'Flagellator at Richmond'. The famous stone bridge was undergoing renovations and Grover is said to have made himself unpopular with the convicts by riding on the hand-drawn carts of stone and whipping the convicts along like beasts.

One foggy night in March 1832, the Richmond Flagellator visited a local farm for a drinking session. According to witnesses he left the party in a well-oiled state. At two o'clock that morning a constable found Grover broken and barely alive on the rocks beneath the Richmond Bridge. Grover died and four men were accused of throwing him over the edge of the bridge, 8 metres above the rocks below. The official verdict was that Grover had accidentally fallen to his death while intoxicated, though few probably believed that to be true. Since then his ghost has been reported roaming the bridge on foggy nights, searching to revenge himself on his killers.

And he has a furry ghost friend, at least according to popular belief. A large black dog has been seen prowling the bridge from time to time. The beast appears, walks to the end of the bridge, then vanishes. Often the dog helpfully escorts people across the bridge. Although often called 'Grover's Dog', this ghostly canine does not seem to match the dog allegedly kept by Grover the Flagellator until he met his unpleasant end beneath Richmond bridge. There are various versions of the story; one claims that Grover had a vicious mongrel dog but it was black and white in colour.

Richmond is also the location of Australia's oldest surviving jail, built by convicts from 1825. Like all places of penance in the convict system, it was a place of misery, degradation and violence. For some, that dark past is etched into the stone walls. There have been reports of moaning and sighing within the buildings and one of the cells is said to terrify some people who enter it. Many do. The jail is now a popular tourist attraction where visitors can see and visit solitary confinement cells, the chain gang holding room, the cook house, the flogging yard and the privy, or toilet.

Another famous flagellator has lived on after death. In this case not a convict but one of the jailers. Captain Logan was commandant of the Moreton Bay penal settlement from 1826. He was an efficient but cruel man who was universally hated by the convicts unlucky enough to come under his control. Logan's favoured method of punishment was 'the triangle', rudely fashioned of three pieces of wood. Those sentenced to a flogging were spread-eagled across the structure, ensuring a full spread of the flogger's lash across their bodies. It is said that many did not leave the triangle alive.

Logan's dark legend lived on not only in the famous convict ballad usually known as 'Moreton Bay' or 'The Convict's Lament' but also in the supernatural. Two ghost stories are told of the captain's life and death.

Riding home alone from one of his frequent mapping explorations into the bush, Logan saw a convict on the bush track that ran through what is now South Brisbane. Suspecting the man was escaping, Logan commanded him to stop. The man did as he was ordered but then turned and came towards the captain. When he got close enough he grabbed hold of a stirrup. Logan thrashed at the man with his riding crop but to his horror the crop went right through the convict. Frightened, Logan urged his horse into a gallop. But the apparition held tightly to his stirrup until he reached the Brisbane River, then vanished.

Relieved but unsettled, Logan realised that he knew the identity of his shadowy assailant and why he had been assaulted. A month or so earlier, a convict named Stimson escaped and was recaptured and flogged on Logan's triangle where he died in agony. The place where he was recaptured was exactly the same spot where Logan encountered the spectre.

But the tale does not end there. At midday on 18 October 1830, a gang of convicts was working along the river bank when they noticed the commandant waving as he rode along the other side of the river. Assuming he was asking to be ferried across, a couple of convicts rowed the punt across the river to pick him up. When they got there, Logan had unaccountably disappeared. They later learned that the commandant had been murdered, probably by Aborigines, in the early hours of that morning and 70 kilometres away. The spot on the Brisbane River bank where the convicts had seen him riding was the same place Logan previously encountered the shade of Stimson.

There are few convict locations without some supernatural associations. Port Arthur is troubled with many unnatural sights and sounds, as is the Old Hobart Gaol. Troubling shades of convicts past are seen or felt in Sydney's Hyde Park Barracks and many colonial sites throughout New South Wales, Tasmania and Queensland. The especially grim history of Norfolk Island is rich with sad stories, and Aboriginal spirits are restless on Rottnest Island. The telling and retelling of these tales link the dark days of the convict past to our present.

Last of the Expirees

There were several reasons why a young farm worker in mid-nineteenth century Oxfordshire might set fire to a haystack. An accident. Youthful folly. Or payback for real or imagined wrongdoing by the farmer. Firing a farmer's property was often revenge for real or imagined injustices. Samuel Speed was convicted of this crime in 1863 and sent to Western Australia for seven years.

He was still there in 1938. Almost one hundred years of age, he was interviewed by a journalist from the Perth *Mirror* in the Old Men's Home, built on the site of the Mt Eliza Convict Depot. Samuel's memory was a bit foggy, but he gave a good account of his experiences as the only known survivor of Australia's convict system to that time, the last expiree.

Samuel arrived in what was then the colony of Swan River in 1866 aboard the transport *Belgravia*. 'Among those unfortunates transported, he recalls, were men in every walk of life; doctors, lawyers, shirt-soiled gentlemen and social outcasts tipped together in the pot-house of humanity that was the Swan River Colony.'

In his early to mid-twenties, Samuel was to experience a penal system from which many of the old evils had been purged: 'Vividly Sam Speed recalls the trip out on the *Belgravia*. The waiting on the hulks at Chatham was an awful time. "Whatever stories you hear", he said, "the officers were pretty good to us. We had plenty of food, and my back bears no lash marks today".'

Samuel made up his mind early to be an exemplary prisoner. 'He kept free of the trouble many of the hot-heads ran into.' He was proud of the fact that he had no black marks against his name from the time he stepped ashore at Fremantle and had never been flogged. So good was his conduct that he was made a bondsman after three years, allowing him to live and work in the colony, effectively as a free man. He worked for a number of settler families and on the building of the first wooden bridge over the Swan River at Fremantle: 'And now they're telling me it's being pulled down for a new one. Let's hope they make as good a job of it as we did in those days.'

He remembered the escape of the Irish Fenians aboard the American whaler, *Catalpa*, in 1876 and knew the escapee and bushranger Moondyne Joe: 'knew of his dramatic escape to the bush around Bunbury; knew of the fruitless hue and cry that was raised by the prison authorities. But "Moondyne Joe" got clear away.'

Despite his age, the chirpy Samuel was considered by the home's attendants to be as 'lively as a two-year-old'. They said that when his bath was ready 'he jumps in and out as nimbly as though he were getting ready to go courting again'. Asked if he ever married, Sam replied: 'Marry? Me, marry! Not on your life, not with all the girls chasing me like they used to. I was a regular "nineteen-er".' [wicked]

Samuel's sentence was up in 1871, at which time he became a completely free man, an 'expiree'. Nearly seventy years later, perhaps it was a busy love life that kept him hale and hearty. Or perhaps it was that Samuel Speed, last of the convicts and arsonist, 'never smoked in his life'.

'Gentlemen convicts at work and the convict "centiped" Port Arthur 1836.' Shows close-ranked convicts carrying a long log on their shoulders during fence construction.

Appendix

Convict locations

This is a select list of places in Australia associated with transported convicts, their incarceration, punishments and labour. Many of the larger establishments and also locations such as Fremantle and Norfolk Island have a number of significant sites associated with them. Some convict traces survive and can be visited, particularly in Tasmania.

WORLD HERITAGE AUSTRALIAN CONVICT SITES
The following eleven sites were inscribed on the UNESCO World Heritage List on 31 July 2010. They are considered to be the most significant locations associated with convict transportation to Australia:

Cockatoo Island Convict Site (New South Wales)
Great North Road (New South Wales)
Hyde Park Barracks (New South Wales)
Old Government House (New South Wales)
Kingston and Arthurs Vale Historic Area (Norfolk Island)
Brickendon and Woolmers Estates (Tasmania)
Cascades Female Factory (Tasmania)
Coal Mines Historic Site (Tasmania)
Darlington Probation Station (Tasmania)
Port Arthur (Tasmania)
Fremantle Prison (Western Australia)

SOME OTHER SITES OF SIGNIFICANCE (NOT
NECESSARILY BUILDINGS)
Admiralty House, Sydney, NSW
Albany, WA
Albany Old Gaol, WA
Apple Shed (Apiary), Campbell, ACT
Bass Strait
Bathurst, NSW
Berrima, NSW
Blue Mountains, NSW
Botany Bay, NSW
Bunbury, WA
Castlemaine, VIC
Champion Bay (Geraldton), WA
Coal River (Newcastle), NSW
D'Entrecasteaux Channel
Derwent Valley, TAS
Duntroon House, ACT
Duntroon Royal Military College Conservation Area, ACT
Dunwich Convict Causeway, Stradbroke Island, QLD
Eagle Farm Women's Prison and Factory, Brisbane, QLD
Emu Plains, NSW
Fort Gellibrand Central Battery Precinct, Morris St, William-
    stown, VIC
Fort Scratchley Above Ground Buildings, Newcastle East,
    NSW
Fremantle (city), WA
Geelong, VIC
Goat Island, NSW
Goose Island Lighthouse, TAS
Goulburn, NSW
Gundagai, NSW
Hawkesbury River, NSW
Hill End, NSW
Hive Survivor Camp, Sussex Inlet, NSW
Kangaroo Island, SA

Launceston, TAS

Macquarie Harbour, TAS

Macquarie Lighthouse cottage and lighthouse wall, Vaucluse, NSW

Manly Beach, NSW

Maria Island, TAS

Moreton Bay (Brisbane), QLD

Mudgee, NSW

Newcastle, NSW

Norfolk Island (additional to World Heritage sites), EXTERNAL TERRITORY

Oatlands, TAS

Parramatta, NSW

Paterson Barracks Commissariat Store, Launceston, TAS

Penrith, NSW

Picton, NSW

Pinchgut (Fort Denison), NSW

Pinjarra, WA

Point Puer, TAS

Port Jackson, NSW

Port Macquarie, NSW

Port Phillip, VIC

Redcliffe, QLD

Richmond, NSW

Richmond Gaol, TAS

Rose Hill, NSW

Ross Probation Station and/or female factory, TAS

Rottnest Island, WA

Sarah Island, TAS

King Island, TAS

St Albans, NSW

Swan Island Lighthouse, TAS

Swan River, WA

The Rocks, NSW

Toodjay, WA

Toongabbie, NSW

Victoria Barracks, Paddington, NSW
'Vinegar Hill' (Castle Hill), NSW
Willow Court asylum and infirmary, New Norfolk, TAS
Windmill Tower and Commissariat Store, Brisbane, QLD
Windsor, NSW
York, WA

Glossary

An explanatory list of official and unofficial terms about or related to transported convicts in Australia. Some of these descriptions might give the impression of a well-ordered and efficient set of documentary procedures, but there was considerable variation in how tickets-of-leave, pardons and assignments were applied and administered, depending on who was in charge and what was needed at a particular time and place. There was also a thriving industry in forging official documents that could further undermine 'the system'.

Assignment: The process of allotting convicts to particular jobs under the supervision of an official or a civilian 'master'. Convicts so deployed were usually called 'assigned servants' or 'assignees'.

Cant: Slang of British criminals, also spoken in Australia and influencing Australian colloquial speech.

Cat (the): Short for 'cat of nine-tails', a whip with a wooden handle to which a varying number of tough leather thongs were fitted, often knotted to cause maximum pain for the victim. A single whip might also be used for floggings, though the crueller 'cat' was generally preferred.

Certificate of Freedom: Given to convicts at the end of their sentence as proof that they were once again free citizens with full rights.

Chains: These items of restraint included neck collars, leg irons and a variety of handcuffs. Chains were also weighted, the heavier varieties being used for more severe punishments.

'Working in chains' or being on an 'iron(ed) gang' meant performing very hard labour while wearing chains.

Conditional Pardon: Freed a convict of a life sentence on condition that he or she did not return to Britain, on pain of death. Could be revoked.

Emancipist: Term used mainly in New South Wales and, to some extent, in Van Diemen's Land, for a convict who had received either a conditional pardon or a full pardon. Came to be used broadly for all ex-convicts and to denote a political faction championing the civic and political rights of ex-convicts.

Expiree: Term used mainly in Western Australia for a convict who had served out a sentence or been given a conditional or complete pardon.

Female Factory: Prison for women combining incarceration, manufacturing labour (hence the name), childcare and, in theory at least, reformation. The 'factories' at Parramatta and Hobart (at the Cascades) were the best known but not the only such institutions.

Lag: A convict, often as 'an old lag', usually meaning a re-offender. To be 'lagged' was convict slang for receiving a guilty verdict and subsequent sentence.

Muster: Roll call of convicts to verify their presence.

Pardon (also Free, Full or Absolute Pardon): A full pardon without conditions. Usually issued after ten or twelve years to those with life sentences.

Passholder (Class Probation Pass Holder): Term used in Van Diemen's Land for documentation regulating wages and conditions for assigned convicts.

Slops: Official issue of convict clothing.

Stockade: From military stricture for an enclosed, secure area. Floggings and musters were often carried out in stockades.

System, The: Unofficial but widely used term for the British imperial penal arrangements in Australia.

Ticket-of-Leave: Allowed a convict to live and work freely as long as he or she did not leave a designated area, reported regularly to the authorities and attended church on Sunday (if possible). Infractions could, and often did, mean a return to servitude.

Transport: Could refer to a convict who had been transported or to a ship used to transport convicts.

Triangle: Triangular wooden structure for flogging. Victims hands were tied together at the top and their feet tied apart at the bottom, ensuring taut skin for the maximum infliction of pain.

Turned off: Hanged.

Workhouses (also known as Poorhouses): Early form of British welfare in which the parish was funded to build and run establishments to house the poor. Inmates were required to work to defray the public costs. Workhouses were dreaded by those who had need of them as they often separated families and were generally places of profound misery and, sometimes, corruption.

Notes and Sources

PROLOGUE
Eyewitness description of an early flogging at Bathurst court house in
  Alexander Harris, *Settlers and Convicts, or Recollections of Sixteen
  Years' Labour in the Australian Backwoods*, C Cox, London, 1847
  at <http://setis.library.usyd.edu.au/ozlit/pdf/harsett.pdf>, accessed
  March 2017.

INTRODUCTION
John White, *Journal of a Voyage to New South Wales*, Debrett,
  London, 1790, entry for 29 January 1788, <http://gutenberg.net.
  au/ebooks03/0301531h.html>, accessed April 2017.

1 UNPROMISING BEGINNINGS

TROUBLE ON THE WAY
John Easty, *Memorandum of the Transactions of a Voyage from
  England to Botany Bay, 1787–1793: A First Fleet Journal*, Trustees
  of the Public Library of New South Wales, Sydney, 1965, p. 7.
Annual Register, October 1790, p. 220.
David Collins, *An Account of the English Colony in New South
  Wales*, vol. 1, T Cadell Jun. and W Davies, London, 1798, p. 294
  at <http://setis.library.usyd.edu.au/ozlit/pdf/colacc1.pdf>, accessed
  May 2017.
Old Bailey Proceedings 10 January 1787, online at <www.oldbailey
  online.org/browse.jsp?div=s17870110-1>, accessed March 2017.

THE HUNGRY LAND
John White, *Journal of a Voyage to New South Wales*, London,
  1790, entry for 2 February 1788, <http://gutenberg.net.au/
  ebooks03/0301531h.html>, accessed April 2017.

THE ORGY THAT WASN'T
Arthur Bowes Smyth (Smythe), 'A Journal of a Voyage from

Portsmouth to New South Wales and China. 22 March 1787–12 August 1789', at <http://www.nla.gov.au/apps/cdview/?pi=nla. ms-ms4568, transcript at http://acms.sl.nsw.gov.au/_ transcript/2007/D00007/a1085.html>, accessed July 2017.

See Grace Karskens, 'The Myth of Sydney's Foundational Orgy', 2011, at the Dictionary of Sydney <http://dictionaryofsydney.org/entry/ the_myth_of_sydneys_foundational_orgy>, accessed August 2016.

ENCOUNTERING OTHERS

Geoffrey C. Ingleton (ed), *True Patriots All*, Angus & Robertson, Sydney, 1952, p. 2.

If the date is correct, this may have been the first execution in the colony, though that is usually said to have occurred more than a week later. See 'A Practical Problem'.

Bowes Smyth, pp. 107ff.

Ralph Clark, *The Journal and Letters of Lt. Ralph Clark 1787–1792*, entry for 7 February 1788 at <http://setis.library.usyd.edu.au/ozlit/ pdf/clajour.pdf>, accessed November 2016.

A PRACTICAL PROBLEM

Though Bowes Smyth gives the date as 26 February, James Scott gives the 27th, see NSW Capital Convictions Database at <http:// research.forbessociety.org.au/record/1>; also John White, *Journal*, entry for 27 February 1788 at <https://ebooks.adelaide.edu.au/w/ white/john/journal/chapter2.html>, accessed May 2017.

Bowes Smyth, pp. 107ff.

John White, *Journal*, entry for 30 February 1788 at <https://ebooks. adelaide.edu.au/w/white/john/journal/chapter2.html>, accessed June 2017.

Transported Convicts to Australia, <https://sites.google.com/site/ transportedconvictstoaustralia/home/7-the-convict-hangman>, accessed March 2017.

Available at <https://gallery.records.nsw.gov.au/index.php/galleries/ 50-years-at-state-records-nsw/1-3/>, accessed February 2017.

National Museum of Australia <www.nma.gov.au/exhibitions/irish_in_ australia/exhibition_overview/arriving>, accessed March 2017. A commemorative plaque marks the spot on the corner of Essex and Harrington Streets where Barrett was hanged and probably buried.

THE LURE OF GOLD

London Chronicle, 4 June 1789, in Various, Unknown, 'Early News From a New Colony: British Museum Papers' at <http://gutenberg. net.au/ebooks13/1300291h.html>, accessed February 2017.

Charles White, *Convict Life in New South Wales and Van Diemen's Land*, Free Press Office, Bathurst, 1889, chapter 5, <http://gutenberg.net.au/ebooks12/1204081h.html>, accessed March 2017.

THIS SOLITARY WASTE OF THE CREATION
Letter from a female convict, Port Jackson, 14 November 1788 in *Public Advertiser*, 14 June 1793, *Historical Records of New South Wales* vol. 2, pp. 806–07, quoted in Hugh Anderson, *Farewell to Judges and Juries*, Red Rooster Press, North Melbourne, 2000, p. 216.

FREE BY SERVITUDE
Geoffrey C. Ingleton (ed), *True Patriots All*, Angus & Robertson, Sydney, 1952, p. 240; <www.geni.com/people/Joseph-Smith-convict-Neptune-1790/6000000010898484697>, accessed November 2016.

A MEEK AND TENDER WIFE
The proceedings of the Old Bailey: London's Central Criminal Court, 1647 to 1913, online at University of Sheffield Humanities Research Institute at <www.oldbaileyonline.org/browse.jsp?id=t18120701-10&div=t18120701-10&terms=Susannah_Lalliment#highlight>, accessed June 2017.

Vasco de Sousa, 'Then She Stole the Sailor's Heart' at <http://ptara.co.uk/2012/02/14/then-she-stole-the-sailors-heart/>, accessed April 2017, referencing the journal of Judge Jeffery Hart Bent, travelling aboard the *Broxbornebury* to take up a judicial appointment in the colony of New South Wales.

Hawkesbury on the Net: Cemetery Register at <www.hawkesbury.net.au/cemetery/walters/sawf001.html>, accessed April 2017. The cemetery is on private land.

THE LAST FIRST FLEETERS
There is another story that she was serving as a maid to the wives of these officers. The ladies were concerned at having to wade through the shallows in their dresses and so Betty was carried ashore as a demonstration that there was no danger. Reg A Watson, 'Betty King: First White Woman in Australia', *Tasmanian Times*, 27 January 2014, <http://tasmaniantimes.com/index.php/article/betty-king-...-first-white-woman-in-australia>, accessed April 2017.

Fellowship of First Fleeters, <www.fellowshipfirstfleeters.org.au/elizabeth_king.htm>, accessed November 2016.

Charles White, *Convict Life in New South Wales and Van Diemen's Land*.

2 PERILOUS VOYAGES

A SIGHT TRULY SHOCKING
The writer arrived on the *Lady Juliana* and wrote this letter in July
1790, in *Morning Chronicle*, 4 August 1791.
This and other extracts from Johnson's correspondence compiled in
George Mackaness (comp and ed), *Some Letters of Rev. Richard
Johnson, B.A. First Chaplain of New South Wales*, Part 1, vol. XX
(New Series), D. S. Ford, Printers, Sydney, 1954.

IRISH REBELS
Sydney Gazette and New South Wales Advertiser, 2 October 1803;
Historical Records of New South Wales, Vol. IV; *Historical
Records of Australia*, Series 1, Vol. II, pp. 128–31.

THE FEVER SHIPS
Redfern's report was part of the despatch between Governor Macquarie
and the Commissioners of the Transport Board, 1 October 1814,
Historical Records of Australia, Series 1, Vol. 8, pp. 274–92.

ATTACKED BY AMERICA
Charles Taylor, *The Literary Panorama and National Register*, Vol. 2,
1815, p. 487 (though Taylor seemed to think the story was a
hoax).
Sydney Gazette, 12 August 1815, p. 2.
The Caledonia Mercury, 27 February 1815, p. 2.
Nile's Weekly Register Supplement to Volume VIIIr, pp. 172–3,
<https://books.google.com.au/books?id=_ekMAAAAIAAJ&pg=
RA1-PA407&dq=vittoria+convict+ship&lr=&as_brr=1&redir_
esc=y#v=onepage&q=vittoria%20convict%20ship&f=false>,
accessed March 2017.

THE MIGHT-HAVE-BEEN MUTINY
'DREADFUL Mutiny on board the Chapman Convict ship', broadside
in Alexander Turnbull Library, Wellington, New Zealand
(Ferguson) 673a, evidence of Michael Collins, convict.
For an analysis of this case, see Susan Ballyn, 'Brutality versus
Common Sense: The "Mutiny" Ships, the Tottenham and the
Chapman' in Anna Haebich and Baden Offord (eds), *Landscapes
of Exile: Once Perilous, Now Safe*, Peter Lang, Bern, 2008.

A MELANCHOLY MYSTERY
From the *Hobart Town Courier*, 17 April 1835, p. 2 and *Hobart Town
Courier*, 24 April 1835, pp. 2–4.
Hobart Town Courier, 8 May 1835, p. 4.
Geoffrey C. Ingleton (ed), *True Patriots All*, p. 156 from a broadside
(Ferguson 1954).

See <www.mmnet.com.au/australian_landscape_photos/writer/
   Shipwreck.html>, accessed February 2017.
Monuments Australia, <http://monumentaustralia.org.au/themes/
   disaster/maritime/display/70866-%22george-iii%22>, accessed
   February 2017.

SKELETON ISLAND
The Sydney Monitor, 18 July 1835, p. 2.
Victor Malham, <http://malham-rennie.blogspot.com.au/2013/11/v-
   behaviorurldefaultvmlo.html>, accessed February 2017.
Tamara Glumac, 'Seaweed from 1835 convict shipwreck site
   transformed to remember lives lost', ABC News, <www.abc.net.
   au/news/2016-04-09/seaweed-1835-shipwreck-site-transformed-to-
   honour-lost-convicts/7312804>, accessed February 2017.
Kevin Todd, 'Locating the Neva: Art and History, *Double Dialogues*,
   Issue 13, 2010 at <www.doubledialogues.com/article/locating-the-
   neva-art-and-history/>, accessed February 2017.

3   THE CONVICT UNDERWORLD

WIFE FOR SALE
Geoffrey C. Ingleton (ed), *True Patriots All*, Angus & Robertson,
   Sydney, 1952, p. 58; Bruce Kercher, *Debt, Seduction and Other
   Disasters: The Birth of Civil law in Convict New South Wales*,
   Federation Press, Sydney, 1996 pp. 66–7; 'Wife Selling', Jacqueline
   Simpson and Steve Roud, *A Dictionary of English Folklore*,
   Oxford University Press, Oxford, 2000, p. 390.

CONVICT MAGIC
Ian Evans, 'Seeking Ritual in Strange Places: Dead Cats, Old Shoes and
   Ragged Clothing. Discovering Concealed magic in the Antipodes',
   2015, <www.marrickville.nsw.gov.au/Global/Development/
   Heritage/Absence%20of%20the%20Document%20copy%202.
   pdf>, accessed February 2017.
Ian Evans, 'Defence Against the Devil: Apotropaic Marks in Australia',
   <www.academia.edu/4148179/Defence_Against_the_Devil_
   Apotropaic_Marks_in_Australia>, accessed February 2017.

MRS GRAVY'S HUSBANDS
A broadside from *The Australian* of 1826 reproduced in Geoffrey C.
   Ingleton (ed), *True Patriots All*, p. 104.

SPECIAL TREATMENT
Sydney Gazette, 9 December 1826, p. 3.
Michaela Ann Cameron, 'Parramatta Female Factory', *Dictionary of
   Sydney*, 2015 at <http://dictionaryofsydney.org/entry/parramatta_
   female_factory>, accessed March 2017.

STITCHES IN TIME

Claire Smith, 'Doing Time: Patchwork as a tool of social rehabilitation in British prisons', *V&A Online Journal* No. 1, 2008, <www.vam.ac.uk/content/journals/research-journal/issue-01/doing-time-patchwork-as-a-tool-of-social-rehabilitation-in-british-prisons/>, accessed August 2016.

National Gallery of Victoria, 'Making the Australian Quilt 1800–1950', 2016, <www.ngv.vic.gov.au/wp>, accessed March 2017: <content/uploads/2015/12/AustralianQuilts_ArtworkLabels.pdf>.

NO COMMON CRIMINAL

Chief Justice Sir William à Beckett, quoted in Jill Eastwood, 'Suffolk, Owen Hargraves (1830–?)', *Australian Dictionary of Biography*, National Centre of Biography, Australian National University, <http://adb.anu.edu.au/biography/suffolk-owen-hargraves-4665/text7713>, published first in hardcopy 1976, accessed June 2017.

The Times, 11 August 1868, p. 9.

David Dunstan (ed), Introduction to *Owen Suffolk, Days of Crime and Years of Suffering*, Australian Scholarly Publishing, Melbourne, 2000.

Southern Argus, 3 October 1868, p. 4. Another version of the story in *The McIvor and Rodney Advertiser*, 2 October 1868, p. 4.

THE FLASH

Occurrence Book of York police lock-up, nd.

Watkin Tench, *A Complete Account of the Settlement at Port Jackson in New South Wales*, G. Nichol and J. Sewell, London, 1793.

James Hardy Vaux, *Vocabulary of the Flash Language* in or shortly before 1812 (published 1819).

Desidd, 'Use of Flash Language in Australian English: Background and Evolution', posted 23 April 2016, <https://desidd.wordpress.com/2016/04/23/use-of-flash-language-in-australian-english-background-and-evolution/>, accessed November 2016.

SKIN DEEP

Simon Barnard, *Convict Tattoos: Marked Men and Women of Australia*, Text Publishing, Melbourne, 2016, p. 6.

David Kent, 'Decorative bodies: The significance of convicts' tattoos', *Journal of Australian Studies*, Vol. 21, Issue 53, 1997; James Bradley and Hamish Maxwell-Stewart, 'Embodied explorations: Investigating convict tattoos and the transportation system' in *Representing Convicts: New Perspectives on Convict Forced Labour Migration*, Ian Duffield and James Bradley (eds), Leicester University Press, London, 1997, pp. 75–89.

THE JURY GUILTY FOUND HER

Charles Picknell, *The Kains: Female convict vessel* (Charles Picknell's journal and Thrascyles Clarke's notes), Sullivan's Cove, Adelaide, 1989. Picknell's journal kept aboard the *Kains* in 1830 includes a version of this song, though it is thought that it may have been added long after the journal was written, possibly the 1870s.

4 THE SYSTEM

THE HULKS

James Tucker, ('Giacomo Rosenberg'), *The Adventures of Ralph Rashleigh: A Penal Exile in Australia, 1825–1844*. First published in 1929, though thought to have been written in the 1840s.

A *Complete Exposure of the Convict System. Horrors, Hardships, and Severities, Including an Account of the Dreadful Sufferings of the Unhappy Captives. Containing an Extract from a Letter from the Hulks at Woolwich, written by Edward Lilburn, Pipe-Maker, late of Lincoln*, from a broadside in the Mitchell Library (Ferguson 3238).

Henry Mayhew, John Binny and Benno Loewy, *The Criminal Prisons of London, and Scenes of Prison Life*, Griffin Bohn, London, 1862, p. 200.

THE DOGLINE

Launceston Examiner, 19 April 1859, p. 2.

Although often told, documentary verification of this tale has not yet turned up.

Martin Cash (edited by James Lester Burke), *The Adventures of Martin Cash: comprising a faithful account of his exploits, while a bushranger under arms in Tasmania, in company with Kavanagh and Jones in the year 1843*. Mercury Steam Press Office, Hobart, 1870, pp 66-7.

CANARIES AND MAGPIES

Major George Druitt's evidence to Commissioner Bigge, 1819 in *Report of the Commissioner of Inquiry into the State of the Colony of New South Wales*, The House of Commons, 19 June 1822, chapter V at <http://gutenberg.net.au/ebooks13/1300181h. html#ch-02>, accessed June 2017.

W. Gates, *Recollections of Life in Van Diemen's Land*, Lockport, New York, 1850, pp. 62–3.

Female Convict Research Centre, <www.femaleconvicts.org.au/index. php/convict-institutions/convict-clothing>, accessed February 2017.

OBTAINING A WIFE

J.C. Byrne, *Twelve Years' Wanderings in the British Colonies, from 1835 to 1847*, Richard Bentley, London, 1848.

James Mudie, *The Felonry of New South Wales*, self-published, London, 1837.

THE CONVICT'S LAMENT

Geoffrey C. Ingleton (ed), *True Patriots All*, Angus & Robertson, Sydney, 1952, p. 121.

This version of the song is from a manuscript collected in Queensland in 1916. See also J. Meredith & R. Whalan, *Frank the Poet*, Red Rooster Press, North Melbourne, 1979, pp. 31–8 and R. Reece, 'Frank the Poet' in Gwenda Davy & Graham Seal (eds), *The Oxford Companion to Australian Folklore*, OUP, Melbourne, 1993.

THE IRONED GANG

John Hirst, *Freedom on the Fatal Shore: Australia's First Colony*, Black Inc., Melbourne, 2008, pp. 27ff.

Woomera (edited by K. Delaforce), *The Life and Experiences of an Ex-Convict in Port Macquarie*, K. Delaforce, Sydney, 1984, p. 35 (first published 1900).

Geoffrey C. Ingleton (ed), *True Patriots All*, p. 160. This account was presented as propaganda in favour of ending transportation, but the details are accurate.

THE INNOCENCE OF THOMAS DREWERY

Dorothy Small, 'An Innocent Pentonvillain: Thomas Drewery, Chemist and Exile 1821–1859', *The Journal of Public Record Office Victoria*, issue no. 14, 2015, <http://prov.vic.gov.au/publications/provenance/provenance2015/an-innocent-pentonvillain>, accessed February 2017.

'THE MOST ABSURD, PRODIGAL, AND IMPRACTICABLE VISION'

The Bee, October 1791 at <http://gutenberg.net.au/ebooks13/1300291h.html>, accessed March 2017.

Dublin Chronicle, 1 December 1791 at <http://gutenberg.net.au/ebooks13/1300291h.html>, accessed March 2017.

The Sydney Morning Herald, 12 June, p. 2, and 19 June 1849, p. 2.

J. Syme, *Nine Years in Van Diemen's Land: comprising an account of its discovery, possession, settlement, progress, population, value of land, herds, flocks etc.; an essay on prison discipline; and the results of the working of the probation system; with anecdotes of bushrangers*, self-published, Dundee, 1848.

5 PAIN AND SUFFERING

HANGED THREE TIMES
Sydney Gazette, 2 October 1803, p. 2 giving the name as Samuels, though some sources give Samuel. See also Geoffrey C. Ingleton (ed), *True Patriots All*, pp. 27–8; 261. Some sources give different weights for the rope testing.

THE LASH
George Barrington, *A Sequel to Barrington's Voyage to New South Wales*, C. Lowndes, London, 1801 at <http://setis.library.usyd.edu.au/ozlit/pdf/barsequ.pdf>, accessed July 2017.

THE TREADMILL
Sydney Gazette, 21 July 1825 in Max Howell and Lingyu Xie, *Convicts and the Arts*, Palmer Higgs, Vic., 2013, np.
Similar, if cruder, devices had been in use since the sixteenth century, see J. Thorsten Sellin, *Slavery and the Penal System*, Quid Pro Books, New Orleans, 2016, p. 82.
Hyacinthe de Bougainville, *The Governor's noble guest: Hyacinthe de Bougainville's account of Port Jackson, 1825*, translated and edited by Marc Serge Riviere, Melbourne University Press, Carlton, 1999.
John Briscoe, *A letter on the nature and effect of the tread-wheel, as an instrument of prison labour and punishment, addressed to the Right Hon. Robert Peel with an appendix of notes and cases*, Hatchard & Son, London, 1824.
The Australian, 13 January 1825, p. 3 at <www.jenwilletts.com/convict_ship_minerva_1824.htm>, accessed June 2017; the same incident reported in the *Sydney Gazette and New South Wales Advertiser*, 13 January 1825, p. 2.

THE IRON COLLAR
The Sydney Monitor, 26 January 1833, p. 2, 'Ordered to be Printed by the House of Commons'.

WHIPPING BOY
The Sydney Monitor, 9 October 1830, p. 3.
Charles White, *Convict Life in New South Wales and Van Diemen's Land*, Free Press Office, Bathurst, 1889, chapter 21 at <http://gutenberg.net.au/ebooks12/1204081h.html>, accessed March 2017.

THE HANGED BOY
The Perth Gazette and Western Australian Journal, 6 April 1844, p. 3; *Inquirer* (Perth), 10 April 1844, p. 2.

ONE HUNDRED LASHES
Excerpt from Marcus Clarke, *For the Term of His Natural Life*,
     chapter fifteen. First published in serial form between 1870–72.

TO PLOUGH VAN DIEMEN'S LAND
This version was collected by folklorist Lucy Broadwood in England
     around the early twentieth century, though there are many printed
     broadside versions from at least the 1830s. One appeared in
     The Launceston Advertiser, 21 November 1839. See also Hugh
     Anderson, *Farewell to Old England: A Broadside History of Early
     Australia*, Rigby, Adelaide, 1964, p. 82.

6 TROUBLEMAKERS

BOTANY BAY HERO
Stephan Williams (ed), *A soldier's punishments, or, autobiography of
     a Botany Bay hero by Michael Keane & two other tales of 1826*,
     Popinjay Publications, Woden ACT, 1994. Keane's *Autobiography
     of a Botany Bay Hero*, was first published in *The Australian*,
     11 November 1826, p. 4.

THROWN UNPITIED AND FRIENDLESS UPON THE WORLD
George Loveless was separated from the group and later sent to Van
     Diemen's Land.
James Loveless, James Brine, John Standfield (a Dorsetshire Labourer.),
     Thomas Standfield, *A Narrative of the sufferings of J. Loveless,
     J. Brine, and T. & J. Standfield, four of the Dorchester Labourers;
     displaying the horrors of transportation, written by themselves*,
     John Cleave, London, 1838.

THE BEAST OF GOAT ISLAND
From *Meliora*, vol. IV, 1862 at <https://archive.org/stream/
     meliora04lond/meliora04lond_djvu.txt>, accessed January 2017.
     This account is based partly on Anderson's own testimony.
     Today, visitors to Goat Island can see the scooped-out rock where
     Anderson is said to have been chained.

NYMPHS OF THE PAVE
Based on T.C. Creaney, *The Huddersfield Four*, Female Convicts
     Research Centre, 2015 at <www.femaleconvicts.org.au/docs/
     convicts/TheHuddersfieldFour.pdf>, accessed February 2017.

FLASH MOB AT THE CASCADES
The Colonial Times, 10 March 1840, p. 4.
Cascades Female Factory, <http://femalefactory.org.au>, accessed
     February 2017.

Phillip Tardif, *Notorious Strumpets and Dangerous Girls: Convict Women in Van Diemen's Land, 1803–1829*, Angus & Robertson, Sydney, 1990, pp. 1062–6; 1424–9; 1684–9.

THE PATRIOTS
Except four who were convicted of civil crimes, they went to Van Diemen's Land with the Americans.
Quoted in Gregory Blaxell, 'A Slice of Canada in Australia', *Afloat*, 2007 at <www.afloat.com.au/afloat-magazine/archive/2007_December2007_AsliceofCanadainSydneybyGregoryBlaxell.htm#.WNi6RTtBVds>, accessed March 2017.
Cassandra Pybus (ed), *The Exile's Return: Narrative of Samuel Snow Who was Banished to Van Diemen's Land, for Participating in the Patriot War in Upper Canada in 1838* (Cleveland, 1846) at <http://iccs.arts.utas.edu.au/narratives/snow3.html>, accessed June 2017.

THE OLD LAGS' HERO
Geoffrey C. Ingleton (ed), *True Patriots All*, p. 242.
William Moy Thomas, 'Transported for Life', *Household Words*, Vol. V, No. 124, 7 August 1852, pp. 482–9, being the account of William Barber who was on Norfolk at the time of the events described.

THE GHOST POET
Kilkenny Journal, 18 January 1832, see Bob Reece, 'Frank the Poet' in Gwenda Davey and Graham Seal (eds), *The Oxford Companion to Australian Folklore*, Oxford University Press, Melbourne, 1993, p. 187.
Mark Gregory, <https://frankthepoet.blogspot.com.au/2011/01/for-company-underground.html>, accessed December 2016; R.H.W. Reece, 'MacNamara, Francis (1810–1861)', *Australian Dictionary of Biography*, National Centre of Biography, Australian National University, <http://adb.anu.edu.au/biography/macnamara-francis-13073/text23647>, published first in hardcopy 2005>, accessed December 2016.
Bathurst Free Press and Mining Journal, 18 June 1862, p. 2.
Mark Gregory, 'Frank the Poet: Francis MacNamara, 1811–1861', <https://frankthepoet.blogspot.com.au>, accessed February 2017, has links to most of the main sources of Frank the Poet's life and legend.

7   PLACES OF CONDEMNATION

PLUTO'S LAND
From reports and other papers relating to a visit to the Australian colonies and South Africa, 1832–1840 by J. Backhouse & G.W. Walker. MLB706.

THE RATS' NEST
The Perth Gazette and Western Australian Journal, 1 September 1838, pp. 138–9.

Peter Gifford, 'Murder and the Execution of the Law on the Nullarbor', *Aboriginal History Journal,* vol. 18, no. 2, 1994, p. 114.

Katherine Roscoe, 'Rottnest Island: A Prison for the Indigenous Australian Convicts', Convict Voyages at <http://convictvoyages.org/wp-content/uploads/2017/02/Rottnest-Island.pdf>, accessed June 2017.

Rottnest Island Authority—Our History, <www.rottnestisland.com/the-island/about-the-island/our-history>, accessed February 2017.

COAL RIVER
Commercial Journal and Advertiser, 17 August 1840, p. 2.

THE NORFOLK ISLAND SUFFERING OF THOMAS COOK
Thomas Cook exiles [*sic*] lamentations; or biographical sketch, 1841, State Library of NSW, A 1711; Kay Walsh and Joy Hooton, *Australian Autobiographical Narratives,* Vol. 1: to 1850, National Library of Australia, 1993, p. 39.

ON THE SQUARE, EVER
William Moy Thomas, 'Transported for Life', *Household Words,* Vol. V, No. 124, 7 August 1852, pp. 482–9.

Price Warung, 'The Liberation of the First Three', 1891; Marcus Clarke, *For the Term of His Natural Life,* first published in serial form between 1870–72.

THE WATER RATS
Diary of Joshua Hamlet Gregory, 1842, Norfolk Island Museum, transcribed by Don Brien. This research in Don and Sue Brien, 'Were the Water Rats on Norfolk Island Australia's First Surf Life Savers?', unpublished paper, 2017, used with permission.

A RUNNING FIRE OF CURTSEYS
Godfrey Charles Mundy, *Our Antipodes: or, Residence and Rambles in the Australasian Colonies, with a Glimpse of the Gold Fields.* First edition, Richard Bentley, London, 1852.

A CONVICT'S DREAM
The Critic (Hobart), 8 May 1914, p. 3.

NOT A BAD MAN AT HEART
Empire (Sydney), 16 October 1867, p. 6. While this sounds almost too bad to be true, the details of T's life appear authentic, even if perhaps given some journalistic spice and polish by the *Empire* staff.

8 DESPERATE ESCAPES

A HEROIC STRUGGLE FOR LIBERTY

Frederick A. Pottle, *Boswell and the Girl from Botany Bay*, Viking Press, New York, 1937. See also Watkin Tench, *A Complete Account of the Settlement at Port Jackson*, self-published, London, 1793 at <http://adc.library.usyd.edu.au/data-2/p00044.pdf>, p. 147, accessed April 2017.

Tim Causer (ed), *Memorandoms of James Martin*, The Bentham Project, University College, London, 2014 at <http://discovery.ucl. ac.uk/1558725/1/Memorandoms-by-James-Martin.pdf>, accessed June 2017.

THE VAGABOND OF THE WOODS

Charles White, *Convict Life in New South Wales and Van Diemen's Land*, Bathurst, 1889, chapter 6 at <http://gutenberg.net.au/ ebooks12/1204081h.html>, accessed March 2017; A H Chisholm, 'Wilson, John (?–1800)', *Australian Dictionary of Biography*, National Centre of Biography, Australian National University, <http://adb.anu.edu.au/biography/wilson-john-2803/text4001>, published first in hardcopy 1967, accessed online 14 November 2016; David Collins, *An Account of the English Colony in New South Wales*, vol. 2 (London, 1802).

CHARLOTTE THE PIRATE

V. Blomer, 'The Fate of the Brig Venus Seized in 1806', *Convict Connections Chronicle*, Convict Connections 2013 at <www. convictconnections.org.au/newsletter_articles.html>, accessed March 2017; Mary Louise Ormsby, 'Badger, Charlotte', *Dictionary of New Zealand Biography. Te Ara—the Encyclopedia of New Zealand*, <www.TeAra.govt.nz/en/biographies/1b1/badger-charlotte>, accessed 7 March 2017. Charlotte's enigmatic story has been the subject of plays and books.

A TASTE FOR FLESH

Reverend Robert Knopwood, *Narrative of the escape of eight convicts from Macquarie Harbour, c. 1824*, Dixson Library, State Library of New South Wales.

Hobart Town Gazette, 28 January 1826, given in broadside form in Geoffrey C. Ingleton (ed), *True Patriots All*, p. 107.

The Awful Confession and Execution of Edward Broughton and Mathew Maccavoy, &c., broadside in the Mitchell Library, in Geoffrey C. Ingleton (ed), *True Patriots All*, pp. 125–6. Original spelling of names.

FROM HELL'S GATE TO CHILE

James Porter autobiography, Mitchell Library, State Library of New
  South Wales, DLMSQ 604, composed between 1840 and 1844.
H. Maxwell-Stewart, 'Seven Tales for a Man with Seven Sides', in
  L. Frost and H. Maxwell-Stewart (eds), *Chain Letters: Narrating
  Convict Lives* (Melbourne University Press, Melbourne, 2001),
  pp. 64–76.

THE GREAT ESCAPER

The Perth Gazette and West Australian Times, 15 March 1867, p. 2.
I. Elliot, *Moondyne Joe: The Man and the Myth*, University of Western
  Australia Press, Perth, 1979, second edition, Hesperian Press, Perth,
  1998; Graham Seal, *The Outlaw Legend: A cultural tradition
  in Britain, America and Australia*, Cambridge University Press,
  Cambridge, 1996, p. 144; M. Tamblyn, 'Johns, Joseph Bolitho
  (1827–1900)', *Australian Dictionary of Biography*, National Centre
  of Biography, Australian National University, <http://adb.anu.edu.
  au/biography/johns-joseph-bolitho-3859/text6139>, published first
  in hardcopy 1972, accessed online 20 December 2016.

REBEL HEROES

A.G. Evans, *Fanatic Heart: A life of John Boyle O'Reilly 1844–1890*,
  University of Western Australia Press, Perth, 1997, p. 98. See
  also C.W. Sullivan, III., *Fenian Diary: Denis B Cashman aboard
  the Hougoumont, 1867–1868*, Wolfhound Press, Dublin, 2001;
  'Correspondence Entry Books of Letters from Secretary of State.
  Despatches 1856–73', CO 397/28 (part 2); J. O'Reilly, *Moondyne*,
  published in Boston in 1879, in Australia the following year
  and frequently reprinted since; Alexandra Hasluck, *Unwilling
  Emigrants*, OUP, Oxford, 1959, p. 75.
The correspondence files of the Colonial Office include a considerable
  amount of correspondence relating to O'Reilly's case, see
  'Correspondence Entry Books of Letters from Secretary of State.
  Despatches 1856–73', CO 397/28 (part 2).

9 THE FELONRY

Though he may well not have composed it.

THE MAN WHO INVENTED AUSTRALIA'S BEER

G.P. Walsh, 'Squire, James (1755–1822)', *Australian Dictionary of
  Biography*, National Centre of Biography, Australian National
  University, <http://adb.anu.edu.au/biography/squire-james-2688/
  text3759>, published first in hardcopy 1967, accessed March 2017.

THE REAL ARTFUL DODGER
Heather Shore, 'Transportation, Penal Ideology and the Experience
    of Juvenile Offenders in England and Australia in the Early
    Nineteenth Century', *Crime, Histoire & Sociétés / Crime, History
    & Societies* [En ligne], Vol. 6, n°2 | 2002, mis en ligne le 25 février
    2009, <https://chs.revues.org/416>, accessed June 2017.

THE BOTANY BAY ROTHSCHILD
'A.L.F.'—late of New South Wales, *The History of Samuel Terry in
    Botany Bay, &c.*, London, 1838; Gwyneth Dow, 'Terry, Samuel
    (1776–1838)', *Australian Dictionary of Biography*, National
    Centre of Biography, Australian National University, <http://adb.
    anu.edu.au/biography/terry-samuel-2721/text3833>, published first
    in hardcopy 1967, accessed online 30 December 2016.
Thomas Atkins, *Reminiscences of twelve years' residence in Tasmania
    and New South Wales, Norfolk Island, and Moreton Bay, Calcutta,
    Madras, and Cape Town, the United States of America, and the
    Canadas*, Malvern Advertiser, 1869.

THE LEGEND OF MARGARET CATCHPOLE
Richard Cobbold, *The History of Margaret Catchpole* (1845), Oxford
    University Press classics edition, London, 1907, p. xiii.
Carol Birch, *Scapegallows*, Virago, London, 2007.
Margaret Catchpole's letters are available through the State Library
    of New South Wales at <www2.sl.nsw.gov.au/archive/discover_
    collections/history_nation/justice/convict/MargaretCatchpole/
    catchpole.html>; Joan Lynravn, 'Catchpole, Margaret (1762–
    1819)', *Australian Dictionary of Biography*, National Centre of
    Biography, Australian National University, <http://adb.anu.edu.au/
    biography/catchpole-margaret-1886/text2219>, published first in
    hardcopy 1966, accessed online 24 January 2017.

THE CONVICT KING
Jorgen Jorgenson, *The Convict King: Being the Life and Adventures
    of Jorgen Jorgenson, Monarch of Iceland, Naval Captain,
    Revolutionist, British Diplomatic Agent, Author, Dramatist,
    Preacher, Political Prisoner, Gambler, Hospital Dispenser,
    Continental Traveller, Explorer, Editor, Expatriated Exile, and
    Colonial Constable.* Retold by James Francis Hogan, Ward
    & Downey, London, 1891, p. 157. (Jorgenson's surname was
    Jorgensonsen, he changed it to Jorgensonson in 1817.)

THE SOLICITOR'S TALE
William Moy Thomas, 'Transported for Life', *Household Words*,
    Vol. V, No. 124, 7 August 1852, pp. 482–9.
The Australian Star (Sydney), 5 December 1896, p. 7.

A CONVICT MAID

Philipp Butterss & Elizabeth Webby (eds), *The Penguin Book of Australian Ballads*, Penguin Books, Vic., 1993, with the note: 'From a broadside in the Mitchell Library. Printed by Birt, 39 Great St. Andrew Street, Seven Dials.'

A BROKEN DOWN GENT

The number may have been fewer, but in any case around a dozen of the *Maitland's* human cargo died or were murdered within eighteen months of their arrival on Norfolk Island. See G.A. Wilkes and A.G. Mitchell (eds), *Experiences of a Convict Transported for Twenty-One Years*, Sydney University Press, Sydney, 1965, p. 65.

J.F. Mortlock, *Experiences of a Convict, Transported for Twenty-One Years* (edited by G.A. Wilkes and A.G. Mitchell). Sydney University Press, Sydney, 1965 (first published London, 1864–5).

THE POACHER'S FATE

Graham Seal, *These Few Lines: The Lost Lives of Myra and William Sykes*, ABC Books, Sydney, 2006 contains the full surviving correspondence of Myra and William.

10   A CONVICT STAIN

TOM TILLEY'S TOKEN

Colonial Secretary's Office (Fiche 3267; 9/2731 p. 18).

Powerhouse Museum, <https://ma.as/73510>, accessed February 2017. See also <www.rootschat.com/forum/index.php?topic=734380.0>, accessed February 2017.

THE FIRST AUSTRALIA DAY

Philip Gidley King, Private journal, in two volumes, Vol. 1 titled: 'Remarks & Journal kept on the Expedition to form a Colony in His Majestys [*sic*] Territory of New South Wales', entry for 26 January 1788 (mistakenly given as 27 January by King), State Library of New South Wales.

Sydney Gazette, 1 February 1817, pp. 2–3.

Australia Day Council, <www.australiaday.org.au/australia-day/history/1938-the-sesquicentenary-and-the-day-of-mourning/>, accessed June 2017.

FLOATING BROTHELS

Charles Bateson, *The Convict Ships, 1787–1868*, Brown, Son & Ferguson, Glasgow, 1969; Siân Rees, *The Floating Brothel: the extraordinary story of an eighteenth-century ship and its cargo of female convicts bound for Botany Bay*, Hodder Headline Australia, Sydney, 2001; Robert Hughes, *The Fatal Shore: A History of the Transportation of Convicts to Australia, 1787–1868*, Collins Harvill, p. 279, London, 1987.

Michael Flynn, *The Second Fleet: Britain's grim convict armada of 1790*, Library of Australian History, Sydney, 2001; Joy Damousi, *Depraved and Disorderly: Female Convicts and Gender in Colonial Australia*, Cambridge University Press, Cambridge, 1997; Anne Summers, *Damned Whores and God's Police*, (1975), NewSouth Books, Sydney, 2016.

THE STAIN THAT WOULD NOT FADE

Reported in the *Hobart Town Courier*, 15 November 1828, p. 2.

Babette Smith, *Australia's Birthstain: The startling legacy of the convict era*, Allen & Unwin, Sydney, 2008.

THE CABBAGE TREE MOB

The Sydney Herald, 4 May 1841, p. 2.

Godfrey Charles Mundy, *Our Antipodes: or, Residence and Rambles in the Australasian Colonies, with a Glimpse of the Gold Fields*, Richard Bentley, London, 1852, three volumes, <http://adc.library. usyd.edu.au/data-2/munoura.pdf>, accessed February 2017.

The Cabbage Tree Mob is also mentioned in an 1843 play set in Sydney, Richard Fotheringham and Angela Turner, *Australian Plays for the Colonial Stage*, UQP, Brisbane, 2006, pp. 61ff.

BOTTOMS UP!

Michael Connor, 'Fabricated Feminist Flashers', *Quadrant Online*, 1 May 2010 at <https://quadrant.org.au/magazine/2010/05/ fabricated-feminist-flashers/>, accessed February 2017. In 2004 a Hobart publisher, Michael Tatlow, commissioned the bare bottoms artwork and postcard from artist Peter Gouldthorpe.

Lucy Frost, 'The Flash Mob, and the Flashing Bottoms: Sorting out a popular confusion', Female Convicts Research Centre, 2013 at <www.femaleconvicts.org.au/index.php/convict-institutions/flash-mob>, accessed February 2017.

THE GUNDAGAI CAT

The Mercury (Hobart), 17 June 1876, p. 3.

The Gundagai Independent and Pastoral, Agricultural and Mining Advocate, 2 May 1927, p. 2.

'Nine Miles From Gundagai' at <http://folkstream.com/064.html>, accessed July 2017.

SHADES OF THE SYSTEM

For more Tasmanian ghosts see Will Mooney, 'Ghost Stories',
    The Companion to Tasmanian History, Centre for Tasmanian
    Historical Studies, University of Tasmania, 2006, <www.utas.edu.
    au/library/companion_to_tasmanian_history/G/Ghost%20stories.
    htm>, accessed November 2016.
Richard Davis, *The Ghost Guide to Australia*, Bantam, Sydney, 1998,
    p. 223.

LAST OF THE EXPIREES

Mirror (Perth), 27 August 1938, p. 22; Register of Heritage
    Places—Sunset Hospital Assessment Documentation
    02/09/1997, p. 2 at <http://inherit.stateheritage.wa.gov.au/
    Public/Content/PdfLoader.aspx?id=1ec6a19a-74a7-4b72-ad36-
    d56c5ad5e357&type=assessment>, accessed August 2016. Samuel
    Speed died in 1938.

Further Reading

Australia's transported convicts have been studied by many writers. Some have been academics, some family and local historians, some by authors writing for a broad readership. Writers have differed in their interpretations of the convict era and its ongoing consequences. This lively debate shows no signs of ending, suggesting the topic still matters. Here is a selective list of such books. A few have already been mentioned in the 'Notes and Sources' to each chapter, but most have not.

Alexander, Alison, *Tasmania's Convict: How Felons Built a Free Society*, Sydney: Allen & Unwin, 2010.

Atkinson, Alan, *The Europeans in Australia, a History*, Volume One. South Melbourne: Oxford University Press, 1997.

——*The Europeans in Australia, a History*, Volume Two. South Melbourne: Oxford University Press, 2004.

Barnard, Simon, *Convict Tattoos: Marked Men and Women of Australia*, Melbourne: Text Publishing, 2016.

Cowley, Trudy and Snowden, Dianne, *Patchwork Prisoners: The Rajah Quilt and the Women Who Made It*, Hobart: Research Tasmania, 2013.

Daniels, Kay, *Convict Women*, Sydney: Allen & Unwin, 1998.

Frost, Lucy and Maxwell-Stewart, Hamish, eds., *Chain Letters: Narrating Convict Lives,* Carlton South: Melbourne University Press, 2001.

Hughes, Robert, *The Fatal Shore,* London: Collins Harvill, 1987.

Keneally, Thomas, *The Commonwealth of Thieves,* Sydney: Random House, 2005.

Levell, David, *Tour to Hell: Convict Australia's Great Escape Myths,* St Lucia: University of Queensland Press, 2008.

Macklin, Robert, *Dark Paradise: Norfolk Island—Isolation, savagery, mystery and murder,* London: Hachette, 2013.

Nicholas, Stephen, ed., *Convict Worker: Reinterpreting Australia's Past,* Cambridge: Cambridge University Press, 1988.

Oxley, Deborah, *Convict Maids: The Forced Migration of Women to Australia,* Cambridge: Cambridge University Press, 1996.

Rees, Siân, *The Floating Brothel: The Extraordinary Story of an eighteenth-century ship and its cargo of female convicts bound for Botany Bay,* Sydney: Hodder, 2000.

Smith, Babette, *A Cargo of Women: Susannah Watson and the Convicts of the Princess Royal,* Sydney: UNSW Press, 1998; Rosenberg, 2005.

—— *Australia's Birthstain: The Startling Legacy of the Convict Era,* Sydney: Allen & Unwin, 2008.

——*The Luck of the Irish: How a Shipload of Convicts Survived the Wreck of the Hive to Make a New Life in Australia,* Sydney: Allen & Unwin, 2014.

Swiss, Deborah, *The Tin Ticket: The Heroic Journey of Australia's Convict Women,* New York: Berkeley Books, 2010.

Acknowledgements

Many thanks to those who helped make this book: Maureen Seal, Rob Willis, Mark Gregory, the Convict Women's Research Centre and T.C. Creaney, Don and Sue Brien, Kylie Seal Pollard, Elizabeth Weiss, Genevieve Buzo, Susan Chow and Julia Cain at Allen & Unwin.

Photo Credits

Page xiv 'Landing of Convicts at Botany Bay', from Captain Watkin Tench's *A Narrative of the Expedition to Botany Bay*, first published in 1789.

Page xx Convicts embarking for Botany Bay, pen and wash by Thomas Rowlandson, 1756–1827. Courtesy of the National Library of Australia, Bib ID: 1738410.

Page 26 Convict uprising at Castle Hill, Sydney, watercolour, 1804, also known as the 'Battle of Vinegar Hill'.

Page 52 'A Government Jail Gang, Sydney, N.S. Wales'. Inscription beneath says, 'London, published August 10th 1830, by J. Cross, Holborn, opposite Furnivals Inn' [*sic*]. Plate No. 3 of part 2 of 'Views in New South Wales and Van Diemens Land'.

Page 74 Flogging prisoners, Tasmania. Pencil drawing from c. 1850s by James Reid Scott, 1839–77.

Page 100 'Relics of Convict Discipline'. Convict disciplinary articles: leg-irons, a ball and chain, handcuffs, whips (one of them a cat-o'-nine-tails), rifles and a sword. Photograph possibly by Australian photographer E.W. Searle while working for J.W. Beattie in Hobart during 1911–15.

Page 126 'Female Factory, Cascades' in Hobart, Tasmania, from glass plate negatives and photographs collected by E.R. Pretyman over 1870–1930.

Page 156 'Bloodhounds on Eaglehawk Neck to prevent the escape of convicts', Tasmania. Part of the collection of photographs compiled by Australian photographer E.W. Searle while working for J.W. Beattie in Hobart during 1911–1915. Courtesy of the National Library of Australia, Bib ID 4556400.

Page 180 Moondyne Joe, (Joseph Bolitho Johns, 1830–1900). This is the only known photograph of him. He stands holding a tomahawk and wearing a kangaroo skin cape. The original photograph was taken by Alfred Chopin and first published in the *Sunday Times* on 27 May 1924, illustrating an article on Moondyne Joe by Charles William Ferguson.

Page 204 'Hobart Town Chain Gang'. Photographic record of a black and white print, part of J.W. Beattie's collection, 'Beattie's snapshots, Tasmania', ca. 1900s.

Page 232 Eliza James (Mrs Joseph Small), convict on the *Anna Maria*, which arrived in Tasmania 26th January, 1852. This photograph is part of a miscellaneous collection of photographs from 1860–1992.

Page 252 'Gentlemen convicts at work and the convict "centiped" Port Arthur 1836. Beattie: Hobart 5918'. Shows close-ranked convicts carrying a long log on their shoulders during fence construction. This is a photograph of an original artwork from the J.W. Beattie collection, 'Albums of photographs of Tasmania, 1820–1860'.